HERITAGE TRANSFORMED

HERITAGE TRANSFORMED

by

Ian Baxter

Oxbow Books

Oxford and Oakville

Published by
Oxbow Books, Oxford, UK

ISBN 978-1-84217-457-9

This book is available direct from

Oxbow Books, Oxford, UK
(Phone: 01865-241249 Fax: 01865-794449)

and

The David Brown Book Company
PO Box 511, Oakville, CT 06779, USA
(Phone: 860-945-9329 Fax: 860-945-9468)

or from our website

www.oxbowbooks.co.uk

A CIP record for this book is available from The British Library

Library of Congress Cataloging-in-Publication Data

Baxter, Ian.
Heritage transformed / by Ian Baxter.
    p. cm.
  Includes bibliographical references.
  ISBN 978-1-84217-457-9
  1. Cultural property--Great Britain--Management. 2. Strategic planning--Great Britain. I. Title.
  CC135.B39 2011
  363.6'90941--dc23
                2011041335

Cover: Illustration by Whistler, from "The Last of Uptake"

Printed in Great Britain by
Hobbs the Printers, Totton, Hampshire

Contents

Acknowledgements vi

List of Figures vii

Abbreviations used in the text ix

Research Summary x

Preface xi

Chapter 1   Introduction: an intangible heritage 1

Chapter 2   The transformation of heritage 5

Chapter 3   Management: the tool for transformation 11

Chapter 4   The transformation of heritage into English Heritage 21

Chapter 5   The transformation of heritage into archaeology and vice-versa:
              The Monuments Protection Programme 45

Chapter 6   From fire to fake? Uppark and The National Trust 63

Chapter 7   Brodsworth Hall: a brand new time capsule 79

Chapter 8   Constructing the glass case: transformation within the Museum of London
              and Cambridge University Museum of Archaeology and Anthropology 96

Chapter 9   Conclusion: heritage transformed 106

Bibliography 109

Acknowledgements

Life was not easy as a heritage researcher in the early 1990s – both archaeologists and management scientists were wary, the subject matter was difficult to get a firm grasp of, and funding agencies at the time appeared to just be confused. That being said I would like to thank Sidney Sussex College and Margaret Baxter for providing me with fieldwork grants and support and the Department of Archaeology, University of Cambridge, for its administrative backup when the initial research was undertaken. At The National Trust and English Heritage, thanks are given to both headquarters and property staff at Brodsworth Hall and Uppark for making me most welcome during case study fieldwork, and putting up with me lurking behind them with a clipboard. Graham Fairclough must be thanked for providing support for my exploration of the Monuments Protection Programme, and for snatched exchanges at numerous conferences. Nick Merriman also provided valued support for my initial exploration of the Museum of London.

The case studies would not have come to fruition at all without the enthusiasm of John Hinchliffe, former Director of Corporate Affairs at English Heritage, and I thank him most heartily for fascinating conversations, exploration of ideas, and providing huge amounts of paperwork and documents. I would also like to thank Robin Boast for advising me on research ideas, and always forcing me to make my own mind up having provided diametrically opposed ideas to my supervisor. To Kate Pretty, former Pro-Vice Chancellor at the University of Cambridge, I would like to extend gratefulness and thanks, for fitting me in to her schedule somewhat unannounced, rejuvenating my interest when I lost momentum, and being an incredibly efficient and cheerful mentor, both during this project and since in my academic career. Equally, in the intervening years between completion of the research and its appearance, Ben Cowell has provided a great source of inspiration and enthusiasm for chewing over the more esoteric aspects of heritage management in which we have a common interest.

Finally, I would like to thank my wife Mary – for all her support and ideas, and giving me the opportunity to explain to somebody the minutiae of heritage management, whether she liked it or not.

List of Figures

2.1   The model of transformation 5

2.2   Examples and effects of transformation from concept to object and vice-versa 6

3.1   Basic functions of management 12

3.2   Weber's characteristics of bureaucracy 14

3.3   Five processes in strategic management 15

3.4   Identifying the strategic position 15

3.5   Strategic planning model 15

3.6   The duality of strategic management – the Spock/Kirk metaphor 15

3.7   Types of environment 16

3.8   The socio-cultural environment 17

3.9   Strategic choice 18

3.10 The Manning-Haas sequential hierarchy of demand 19

3.11 Organisational culture 20

4.1   Examples of public institutions whose remit includes funding, policy and co-operative management with other service level organisations in the heritage sector 21

4.2   The three essential elements of the corporate purpose 24

4.3   National Heritage Act 1983: section establishing English Heritage as an institution . . 24

4.4   English Heritage and Department of National Heritage Funding Agreement 1996/97 . . . . . . 25/26

4.5   The Department of National Heritage's aims 27

4.6   English Heritage Corporate Plan 1989–93 Central Statement 28

4.7   English Heritage Corporate Objectives: 1990, 1991 & 1992 29

4.8   English Heritage Corporate Objectives 1993–1997 29

4.9   English Heritage Corporate Objectives 1994–1998 30

4.10 English Heritage Corporate Objectives 1995–1999 30

4.11 English Heritage Mission Statement 1988 31

4.12 English Heritage Mission Statement 1992 31

4.13 Historic Scotland Framework Document 32

4.14 The cultural recipe 33

4.15 English Heritage values and behaviours 34

4.16 English Heritage Summary Statement 1996–2000 38

4.17 English Heritage programme delivery 1996 42

4.18 Extract from Review of Results 1995/96 44

5.1   Hadrian's Wall illustration from cover of guidebook 45

5.2   Western section of Hadrian's Wall Management Plan Summary 46

5.3   Schedule Plan for Baconsthorpe Castle 47

5.4   Entry for Baconsthorpe Castle in English Heritage member's handbook 48

5.5   Schedule Plan for St Mary's Abbey 49

5.6   Monument Class Description 54

5.7   Three-way tension of scale 55

6.1   Uppark house following restoration 64

6.2   The owners of Uppark 65

6.3   The fire at Uppark in 1989 during the first restoration programme 65

6.4   Regional National Trust publicity leaflet 67

6.5   Orientation leaflet 67

6.6   Ground floor plan of the house 68

6.7   The Manning-Haas sequential hierarchy of demand 69

6.8   ASEB Grid Analysis and cell identifiers 69

6.9   Illustration by Whistler, from "The Last of Uptake" 76

7.1   Property publicity leaflet 80

7.2   Brodsworth – Original architectural plan, hall today & artist's interpretation 81

7.3   Brodsworth – Artist's interpretation 81

7.4   Orientation leaflet – site plan 82

7.5   House plan 83

7.6   Main hallway 84

7.7   Drawing room 84

7.8   Boat bedroom, conserved as found 84

7.9   Billiard room 85

7.10 Kitchen 85

7.11 Brodsworth details produced for tour operators 90

7.12 Brodsworth details produced for tour operators (Continued) 91

8.1 CUMAA Anthropology gallery 96

8.2 Museum of London in 2000 97

8.3 Museum of London Act (1965) relevant sections . 99

8.4 Extract from 'Statutes & Ordinances of the University of Cambridge' 99

8.5 Extract from the Ordinances of the University of Cambridge, establishing the Museum of Archaeology and Anthropology 99

Abbreviations used in text

AONB	Area of outstanding natural beauty
ARM	Archaeological Resource Management
ASEB	Activities, Settings, Experiences and Benefits
CBA	Council for British Archaeology
COI	Central Office of Information
CPD	Continuing Professional Development
CPI	Corporate Performance Indicator
CPRE	Council for the Protection of Rural England
CRM	Cultural Resource Management
CUMAA	Cambridge University Museum of Archaeology & Anthropology
DCMS	Department for Culture, Media & Sport
DETR	Department of the Environment, Transport and the Regions
DNH	Department of National Heritage
DoE	Department of the Environment
EH	English Heritage
FMPR	Financial Management and Policy Review
GDP	Gross Domestic Product
GIS	Geographical Information Systems
HBMCE	Historic Buildings & Monuments Commission for England (English Heritage)
HEFCE	Higher Education Funding Council for England
HLF	Heritage Lottery Fund
HMG	Her Majesty's Government
HMSO	Her Majesty's Stationery Office
HPR	Historic Properties Restoration
ICOM	International Council of Museums
LB	Listed Building
MARS	Monuments at Risk Survey
MoL	Museum of London
MPP	Monuments Protection Programme
NHMF	National Heritage Memorial Fund
NT	The National Trust
PPG16	Planning Policy Guidance Note 16
RCHME	Royal Commission on the Historic Monuments of England
SAM	Scheduled Ancient Monument
SMR	Sites and Monuments Record
SWOT	Strengths, Weaknesses, Opportunities and Threats
UK	United Kingdom
UNESCO	United Nations Environmental, Scientific and Cultural Organisation
WWW	World Wide Web

Research Summary

This research was originally undertaken as a doctoral thesis at Cambridge University between 1995–98. It considers how 'heritage' is objectified within public institutions and becomes representative of a national past. A model is proposed for this objectification process within the sphere of public institutions, and subsequently five case studies explore the variety in the transformation of heritage. The model proposes that heritage is transformed from concept to object and the agency of change is 'management'. Exploration is made of management using strategic management analysis to understand the relationship between public institutions, heritage objects and their use. The analysis shows a development from administration to strategic management as a way of effecting change in public institutions over time producing new heritage objects and markets for them.

The case studies examine: English Heritage's corporate management structure, promoting a 'national heritage'; the Monuments Protection Programme, identifying and protecting specific historic and archaeological sites of national importance; Uppark House, where The National Trust displays a restored country house following a fire; Brodsworth Hall where English Heritage has 'conserved as found' a decaying country house; and comparison between the Museum of London and Cambridge University Museum of Archaeology and Anthropology, where institutions with similar aims take different approaches to managing themselves. The model demonstrates the need for public institutions to be aware of the way in which the adoption of management strategies creates 'new' heritage as a cultural resource.

Preface: Historic research in heritage management

It is very important to note that this book is very late in appearing due to a series of unfortunate events with publishers along the way. The delay of a decade has, however, had a curious side-effect. Normally, it would render such research thoroughly out of date, but, in fact, appearing as it does at the end of 2011, it would seem that some of the ideas and understandings of management contained within the book are back in vogue: we have come full circle, and the work can be usefully placed into the wider historical context for the development of management of the historic environment in Britain during the late 1990s. The book should therefore be seen as one of the pieces in the jigsaw charting the development of heritage management: specifically management thinking about heritage.

The underlying aim driving the research was to explore the role of management, and in particular strategic management, as a set of tools and techniques, as it could be applied to the work of heritage professionals and organisations in their everyday activities. The research was designed to add to the emergent thinking of the time within cultural resource management (CRM, now more readily known as historic environment management). The research was therefore one of the first detailed explorations of the context and role of corporate management techniques within the heritage sector, deriving and applying a model to a range of CRM scenarios and business environments to understand how heritage was being created. This appreciation of different management techniques, and the emphasis on the need to understand the applicability of them within heritage conservation organisations, helped pave the way for a re-examination of the role of these institutions and also the role of heritage in modern society.

This, of course, culminated just after the timeframe of this research in the publication in the UK of *Power of Place* (2000), and the subsequent *Force for the Future* (2001), highlighting the value of heritage to a number of areas of government interest, including regeneration, social inclusion, education, and tourism. In terms of organisational development, the turn of the century also saw large-scale reorganisation of both English Heritage and The National Trust, and changes to a number of other heritage organisations and societies. Indeed, an agenda of devolution and regionalisation saw the first decade of the 21st-century spawn a range of new heritage organisations and co-ordination fora established, reorganised, and indeed some now disbanded. Regardless of the vagaries of change in organisational structure over the years, the need for appreciation of the role of internal corporate management and strategy has continued and developed to ensure organisations are both fit for purpose and able to serve both the sector and its stakeholders, customers, participants, and audiences effectively and efficiently.

Themes highlighted in the case studies within the research, considering the process of conservation through the Monuments Protection Plan, and also site operations at

an individual level, have since been reflected in the review of protection arrangements by the English Government aiming to establish a single Heritage designation prescribed in legal terms which recognises sites monuments and buildings together as places within a wider historic environment (DCMS 2004). Reflections of the case studies are also seen at the site level where, whilst philosophical and methodological developments have moved on, subject specialisms and the techniques of engaging audiences have continued to contextualise sites in an environment, foster greater and alternative forms of understanding the historic environment, and at the level of tourism service, striven to explore the role of the visitor, their motivation and their experiences.

As for the model of transformation, itself at the centre of the research, it is of its time, and may now be considered too simplistic, given the sophistication of internal planning techniques and strategies which are now being adopted within the sector's larger organisations. This simplicity does, however, continue to flag up the necessity of understanding the very role of the institution and its business and managerial context, however large that institution is. (It is worth remembering that the majority of heritage organisations are small scale and rely on volunteer efforts: a diffusing of the myths that strategic management is complex or unnecessary, as purported in the research still has clear validity for many.)

Indeed, this remains one of the only studies which explicitly links an understanding of what management *does* and how strategic management theory relates to the heritage sector. Heritage management texts and reports of late have rather responded to a Government-driven agenda of analysing methodologies to establish the value of heritage in different contexts (social, economic, etc.), ignoring the still-needed holistic exploration of heritage management (EFTEC 2005; HEREC & English Heritage 2005; Carman 2004). The redefinition of heritage as the historic environment sector has presented new management challenges, not least trying to establish what the sector is, does and how to effect strategic planning within it. This requires use and understanding of management information (and not least sources of information to supply such decision-making). The implicit challenge set within this book for the sector to engage with management theory therefore still stands. However, programmes such as heritage auditing and Heritage Counts and Heritage at Risk can clearly be seen to represent a managerial desire to organise data for particular purposes (strategic thinking), and we are now at the stage of building the foundations for an effective and management information system for the sector and its constituent organisations in the next decade. It is vital for the historic environment to address this next stage of using management information strategically as, in an increasingly competitive world for public support and public resources, the political will is re-examining the notion of value and its applicability to the heritage with a critical eye given global economic pressures and reformation of our very notions of the public sector.

Valuation techniques, returns on investment (economic and social) and performance indicators will delve ever deeper into the historic environment and our management of it – and we as heritage professionals must therefore understand the changes to the business environment in which we are now operating. It is therefore hoped that the publication of this book will not only be of use to future historians of heritage management in the UK and researchers interested in the political and organisational context of a key part of the cultural sector in the country during the late 1990s but also those currently who would heed the call to conceptually analyse (and at a more basic level understand) the role of management within the historic environment. It is hoped that the explorations within its pages are one more rivet in the bridge between the science and philosophy of managing a resource and the historic resource itself.

Ian Baxter
University of Cambridge, Institute of Continuing Education
September 2011

1   Introduction: an intangible heritage

This study considers how heritage is created as an object within public institutions and becomes representative of the national past. This occurs through a theoretical process, which I label 'objectification'. It considers both the tangible and the intangible nature of heritage and the inter-relationship between those two states through consideration of the objectification process, the agency of change and the implications of such change.

Heritage in its intangible state has an ineffable quality, where an idea of 'past-ness' is understood. Heritage as such cannot be objectified – you cannot pick up a heritage in a shop or visit a physical heritage. The objectified state of heritage exists as a range of cultural resources: archaeology, historic buildings and monuments, crafts, museums, literature and artforms, amongst many other physical manifestations. These physical forms, which I consider as 'objectified heritage' can be visited, touched, bought and experienced. However, each of these encounters with the objectified heritage adds to our overall response and understanding of the intangible nature of heritage – the understanding of past time which exists conceptually, and which is more difficult to articulate and identify than specific historical events, though recognised as existing by all.

Heritage exists both intangibly and tangibly in varied spheres and scales. It exists within and affects the political, social, economic, public and private spheres, and many actions undertaken by communities in the modern world may well be dictated by their heritage – human action in the past and interaction with the contextual 'physical' world around them. Heritage is intimately linked therefore to identity, most clearly debated within the political sphere, which is ultimately representative of a range of communities with different traditions and origins. Nation-states clearly distinguish their heritages – and this can be a cause of both inclusion and exclusion within communities. The range of uses for heritage is both broad and enlightening, telling much about our surroundings and the communities in which we live. For example, within the former Yugoslavia, maintenance of ethnic identities has led to war, whilst in the United Kingdom more peaceful debate considered the character of the country at the end of the twentieth century

– torn between visions of cricket and warm beer, and a 'cool Britannia' image of vibrant multi-cultural artistic and cultural pursuits.

Such political uses of heritage have clear consequences for the economic sphere in which the phenomenon also exists. Heritage has both no economic value (due to its intangible nature), and very clear economic value, where market forces and prices fluctuate daily in both the auction rooms and shops in the high-street. Heritage is big business, by virtue of its links to the political and social sphere, and inclusion in the 'tourism' business. Museums and heritage sites are huge attractions around the world, where the historical nature and culture of the country that is represented warrant major economic and political consideration. Furthermore, the establishment of heritage as of importance in the political sphere has created economic markets for the disciplines of which it is comprised. For example, archaeology in the United Kingdom is now a key consideration in the planning process, and archaeological investigation in advance of development is a clearly defined business following the building boom of the 1980s. Archaeological work is undertaken within specific business units operated by many local authorities.

The social sphere of heritage perhaps gives rise to its political and economic use. Heritage is ultimately a social creation, deriving from communities existing in particular geographic locations, undertaking certain actions through time to create their own physical environment of sites with different uses, buildings, and physical 'communities', and their own 'history' charting such action and development. Heritage has come to comprise all of this – viewing the world around us in the present-day with an eye on its historical connotations or development, and articulating such history through identification of historic structures, environments and activities – understanding them through disciplines such as archaeology, art, literature, architecture and so on. The objectified heritage does not exist in the past anymore – it exists in the present as we encounter it today, yet it provokes the intangible recognition of the past, which we now conceptualise as heritage.

The scales at which heritage exists are equally varied, though they correspond more to clearly defined physical entities and boundaries with links to the social sphere in which individuals and communities operate. In both its intangible and tangible nature, heritage can exist personally, within the family or community context, and at local, regional, national and international scales. An object considered to be part of the heritage, one which holds historical value, may be an item owned by one person such as a piece of jewellery, or a building owned by a family, objects representative of, or unique to, a community or nation, and icons or comparative cultural resources evaluated on an international scale such as World Heritage Sites and certain museum collections.

I argue in this book that certain public institutions have been established to mediate between these spheres and scales of heritage, and that although they may operate at a community-wide or national scale, their effects are seen across the entire range of 'heritages', because they produce a heritage which we may or may not accept as a public heritage. This notion of an identified public heritage, representative of other spheres, and at different scales, forms the central exploration of this thesis.

I explore this public heritage by looking at what certain public institutions concerned with archaeology and the built environment are expected to do, and the way in which they do it. This is based upon a principal model which proposes that the intangible heritage, which I have considered briefly above, is transformed into an objectified heritage that we can easily recognise and fit back into our own perception and understanding of an intangible phenomenon. The transformation is therefore continual – from concept to object and object to concept, constantly adding to an understanding of and use for heritage within the community.

I do not consider psychological and philosophical analysis of heritage here, as I wish to concentrate on the particular instance of exploring how heritage is articulated in the public sphere in the United Kingdom. I consider how 'public' bodies such as government, being set up to represent the views, aims and culture of the country in which we live and which governs its constituent communities, transforms the concept of heritage into an objectified state for its particular uses.

The management sciences approach transformation and change using simile and metaphor, in exploration of how people and organisations interact in economic, social and political spheres. Thus management science has begun to articulate change and transformation with an eye on future development and direction within the specialism of strategic management. This uses explorative methods to assess the position of an individual or organisation within an 'environment'. I suggest that management's articulation of change and transformation is applicable to this study of the transformation of heritage, and the methods employed within the management sciences are therefore used in this thesis to explore a variety of examples of objectification of a 'public heritage'.

The book is organised into nine chapters, with five separate case studies exploring the objectification process in differing circumstances in the heritage field. The perspectives utilised explore management action achieving the transformation in three of the case studies. In the other two case studies the view of the end users or consumers explores the effects of management action on the transformation of heritage. A jump is therefore made from analysis of choice in making policy (effecting the transformation), to the implications of that policy in the encounter with the objectified heritage at a historic site where the policy of the manager is not explicitly articulated.

Chapter 2 considers the model of transformation, the way in which the intangible heritage must be objectified in order to understand it, and the institutional context in which public heritage becomes objectified. Chapter 3 explains the various themes utilised within strategic management, the relevance of exploring management of the heritage, and the historical development from an administrative viewpoint to a strategic perspective on the historic environment.

Chapters 4 to 8 comprise individual case studies, and explore institutional management of public heritage resources at different scales. It is established within Chapter 4 that the highest level of effective analysis of heritage management is with national non-governmental heritage organisations, as their remit is unaffected on a day-to-day basis by the political process. The corporate structure of English Heritage is examined, charting the historical development of its management structure during the 1980s and early 1990s, and the way in which this public institution 'creates' a national public heritage for England. Exploration of the institution's environmental context shows the different stakeholders in the organisation and its work, and the objectification processes undertaken in order to identify and protect the country's heritage.

Chapter 5 explores part of the objectified heritage created by English Heritage in one of its major management programmes. The Monuments Protection Programme aims to identify and protect archaeological and historic sites of national importance. Thus its operation comprises objectification of heritage as specific sites and monuments, and then further selection within those sites for dedicated legal protection. A very particular public heritage is created in this way, using policy decisions of managers concerned with the protection of the historic environment in their own professional terms, rather than for a particular end user within the general public.

Chapters 6 and 7 consider two country houses from point of view of the tourist. Here the public face of heritage is explored, using management analysis of the encounter between an audience and a heritage object. The clear distinction between management's intent in objectification, and the effect of the encounter by the public with the public heritage is seen. Chapter 6 looks at Uppark in West Sussex, owned by The National Trust, which reopened in 1995 after extensive restoration following a major fire. Chapter 7 explores Brodsworth Hall in South Yorkshire, acquired by English Heritage which adopted a 'conserve as found' philosophy towards a country house in serious decline, and opened to the public for the first time in 1995 as a 'new' heritage attraction.

The final case study, in Chapter 8, compares differences in institutional management of two separate museums, the Museum of London and Cambridge University Museum of Archaeology and Anthropology. Here analysis reveals how institutions, identically labelled as 'museums' and with the same remit of preserving a collection of historic objects, operate very differently with regard to both their internal aims, relationship with external users as a result of their own institutional context and expectations placed on them.

Concluding comments in Chapter 9 are very brief, drawing together common themes addressed in the illustrative case studies, assessing the concept of transformation of the heritage, and the manager's role in heritage, as having more than purely business and economic responsibilities. The use of the model proposed at the start of the thesis and the methods used for exploration are also reflected on.

2   The transformation of Heritage

Creating the model: transformation from concept to object

The concept of heritage is an intangible *entity* characterised by instantaneous psychological awareness of the past and passage of time (Tilley 1994). Recognition of heritage helps form an identity and sense of place in the world for an individual or collection of individuals (such as a nation-state) and ownership of an environment to inhabit (Rowlands 1994; Wright 1985 and Jones 1996). Somebody can 'own' their heritage. The 'becoming' of heritage or its transformation from the intangible concept to the tangible object is achieved and able to be effected by use of the systems and processes collectively termed 'management'. Heritage exists in many different contexts: I am interested in the application of the model where management acts as the agent of change, in *public* organisations such as English Heritage (Chapter 4). Management as the agent of change in the public heritage will be considered in the next chapter (Chapter 3). Thus I am not dealing with the creation of heritage by individuals within society, such as autobiography or social history.

Two stages form the complete model of transformation (Figure 2.1), and it is further illustrated by example in the next section. The first stage of the model transforms an intangible sense of place into the tangible past in the form of objects, physically identified in time and space. These objects are subsequently transformed again in the second stage through interpretation or presentation as heritage, into secondary intangible concepts, reinforcing the intangible state. The first stage of this circular model is problematic as it is here that the tensions of the tangible and intangible are resolved, though it is exactly this stage that is overlooked by many practitioners in the area. Exploration of the first stage in this process of transformation can resolve problems in where and how the concept of heritage is created and sustained. Through exploration of public heritage organisations and objects, I will show that *management*, providing assessment and action with intention, is the agent of change, providing both context and ability for such change. Management as an agency and its actuality of mechanism, system and process uses a variety of tools to effect the transformation from concept to object. I explore some of these, such as SWOT (Strengths, Weaknesses, Opportunities and Threats) analysis and Environmental Assessment in the following chapters.

Figure 2.1 *The model of transformation*

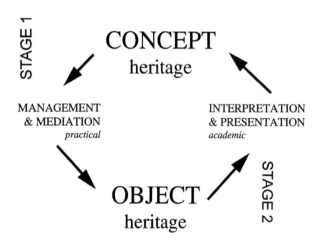

Certain assumptions from phenomenology, utilised within archaeology and heritage, may be inappropriate in the light of this model when applied to the public heritage (Ingold 1993; Tilley 1994). The belief that significance is carried within the 'self' can only be drawn upon if the viewer or audience of an object is grounded in a particular disciplinary viewpoint (Shanks 1992), and can therefore 'speak the language' of the object or objects in question. This is often seen as a problem in museum and gallery education (Hodge and D'Souza 1994). I argue that the use of objectification is explicit in the creation of heritage, and this therefore suggests that something else is needed as a translator or modifier. Internal awareness of a past or heritage is not enough for a person to identify and interpret everything that heritage includes. That translator is provided by management as it 'normalises' the concept of heritage through interaction with objects publicly identified as heritage (the actuality of the transformation). Management normalises or standardises the heritage in transformation from concept to object, by subjecting physical objects to tests and evaluations. The end result, standardised as the public heritage, therefore becomes an inclusive entity, allowing non-specialist audiences to participate in and understand the interpretation of such a heritage. The later case studies demonstrate the point at which transformation occurs, enabled by the processes of management. These will show not so much the minutiae of how heritage objects are created, but the variability of contexts for the way in which heritage becomes an actuality, each using the under-explored first stage of management action.

Example of the Model in action

The model is formed by two stages, concept and object. As a circular process however, the transformation can be assessed at three points: primary concept, object, and secondary concept. The primary and secondary concepts are the same, in the sense that the secondary concept is a reinforcement of the first, though the transformation has altered our perception of and knowledge about the public heritage through the use of management. This can be seen in the worked example below (Figure 2.2), which considers two different objects identified as public heritage within the organisations considered in the later case studies. Stage 1 is a conceptual understanding of the literal physical existence of the object before the viewer. Stage 2 sees transformation from the concept into an identifiable physical object through choice, involving labels and identities. This occurs as a result of specific action within an institutional context (public heritage management agency). Once identified, the conceptual understanding of the viewer is reconfigured through interpretation or presentation of the physical object: thus the structure is a particular building existing (as heritage) within a variety of spheres or contexts. In the example below it can be seen that St Mary's Abbey in Norfolk is all of the things noted, and exists at all times in one physical form, but is understood as a public heritage object only through the transformation explored here. The objectification is therefore necessary in order to understand exactly what the concept of the public heritage is.

Heritage Management Agencies

England has no central 'antiquities' service as seen in other countries such as India (Thapar 1984), though as other authors have charted (Saunders 1983; Chippindale 1983), England has a long history of protective measures and management for ancient monuments, latterly extended to historic buildings (McGill 1995). This is mirrored in the rest of the United Kingdom (papers in Hunter and Ralston 1993). Such historical development is not considered here, though it is acknowledged that a complex variety of historical events, coupled with an equivalent 'contextual history' of archaeology (Carman 1996, 90) has produced the modern situation of law and institutional management in this country. The full range of organisations and groups that can be labelled as 'archaeological managers', implying that they have some concern with acting on or manipulating the 'resource' (Darvill 1987) is huge – not least since the acceptance that the term 'management' is relevant to archaeology as a discipline in the most abstract sense. The size of the CBA's 'British Archaeological Yearbook' (CBA 1996 a) gives credence to this. In its widest sense, anybody acting in a discrete group with aims considered to be wider than the individual, and working within some kind of planning framework, can claim to be a manager of the resource: this includes societies (either researching or excavating and therefore managing knowledge); professional units acting in a business environment; or larger management organisations such as a County Council 'heritage' sections.

A problematic heritage

The problem, which I resolve using the model in the case studies, is to identify exactly what the agent of change is and does in the creation of public heritage, and to explore the tension points at the point of 'becoming' or change. The nature of the past and its relation to heritage has produced regularly highlighted 'pegs' on which to hang arguments or critique in heritage management. This is seen in the writings of Hewison (1987), Lowenthal (1985 & 1996), Fowler (1992) and comment in newspapers such as the Guardian. Used as 'core texts' in heritage studies, these authors still fail to engage with the realities of system and process in the public heritage – the transformation itself. Concentration remains focused on the interpretation of the heritage, the second stage of the model outlined. Reaction to the different forms of heritage is typically given as opposition of the concept of

Figure 2.2 *Examples and effects of transformation from concept to object and vice-versa.*

Stage 1: Concept (primary)	Stage 2: Object	Stage 1: Concept (secondary)
The raw materials of heritage	*Heritage created and reinforced*	*Heritage reconceptualised*
Man-made landscape feature	Ruin – in the form of monastery	Wider spheres: spiritual, moral, religious, economic
	Identified and given name: St Mary's Abbey	Given socio-cultural value
	Premonstratensian religious foundation	Scheduled Ancient Monument
Man-made object	Characterised as: tool (handaxe)	Culture, cognition, time
	location & date	Given socio-cultural value
	Technological character: Acheulean	Museum collection

heritage and the objects labelled as heritage, without due consideration for how those objects came into being in the first place. Furthermore, there is frequent mixing of public and private heritage creations without clear distinction. The targets have often been historic 'objects': interpreted in a particular way such objects have caused controversy and many publicly conducted arguments. The restoration and presentation of Uppark is an excellent example of this and is considered as a case study later (Chapter 6). Such objects are used in everyday life as the building blocks for interpretation of the past: post-modern theory argues a multiplicity of pasts, and thus relies on a suite of different objects and interpretations relevant to different audiences (Merriman 1991). Whilst these 'heritages' may also be problematic, this is of academic concern and not considered here.

The greater problem has arisen from the preceding transformation: there is no critical understanding of how the objects are chosen in the first place, and the need for objectivity (literally) to create something which can subsequently be manipulated through differing presentation or interpretation. Management is the agency: it changes things. Yet this remains unconsidered when the more obvious differences in heritage object can be contrasted in polemic. Vagaries in the history of development of heritage management as a discipline are not considered further in this thesis: 'historical' CRM texts now abound (Hunter 1996; Harrison 1994; Cleere 1989; Chippindale 1983).

I have suggested that the transformation of heritage creates heritage objects (though such heritage objects are not always firstly created within the public sphere as considered here). Secondly what management does as an agent of change is allow choice rather than creation per se, though such choice of what does and does not become heritage 'creates' the public heritage as the outcome. Though heritage is normalised or standardised in the transformation process, public institutions as the agents of change represent a variety of different heritages, both public and private. There is interaction between creation and choice therefore: where choice cannot operate, objects may well be physically created. Selectivity is a further process relating to specific choices that can be made, and itself is different from choice.

The selectivity and specificity of transformations

The change from concept to object does not occur in a random fashion as heritage is created in the modern world. There are various contexts and structures in which the transformation is achieved. Most important and least understood is the public heritage, where public is taken as that which is provided as a service by bodies such as government or public agencies and charities. There are two forms of selectivity in the transformation to be noted. The first is the selectivity imposed on the form of and way in which heritage may be created in the public domain; and secondly, the selectivity that management utilises in its operation within that domain. For the purposes of illustrating the model in this thesis the specific kind of

heritage explored is that which is created by dedicated public institutions within Great Britain. One of the case studies considers the central player in England, English Heritage. It is suggested that the organisation's position as the governmental body responsible for management of the country's heritage makes it central to any understanding of other kinds of heritage created within different spheres, both public and private. This is due to its 'official' nature recognised in and governed by statute. Application of the model of transformation suggests that at the point of 'becoming', or change from one existence of heritage to another, specific selections and choices must be made within a clearly defined context. There is thus the need at this point for the building of a structure such as an institution or process within it, to provide the context that enables change. This structure enabling change can be identified as a 'container' existing in a particular context, the institution or agency. Within this agency transformation is further enacted through the operation of a collection of systems and processes labelled as management. Each of these operations works within a particular environment, and the model of transformation is best explored from the point of view of the management process, which itself explores the environmental context providing the ability to operate (Johnson and Scholes 1989). Already it can be seen that we are dealing with a complex situation containing many variables: tension is inevitable as constant change is required (CPRE 1994; Veal 1994). Tensions are exacerbated by the variability that confronts management. The processes of management act as the balance for this change, and the different case studies highlight the fact that though tension, variability and change is constant, all operate within the first stage of the model created in this thesis (Figure 2.1). An admission must be made however, that although management attempts to identify the raw materials of heritage, these themselves may already have been 'processed'. The problems inherent within the raw materials of heritage, resulting from the fact the agents do not work in a vacuum, are a further part of the management system and process. Referring back to Figure 2.2, the raw materials of heritage are the either the stone built ruin (understood conceptually as St Mary's Abbey), or the modified flint (understood as a Palaeolithic hand-axe). However, it can be seen that these raw materials of heritage are not raw geological material. This geological material, be it granite or flint, has been processed in order to make the tool or the stone, the basic construction of the heritage object. This will be further explored in Chapter 5, where the Monuments Protection Programme's aim of identifying the archaeological resource has to assess what the 'raw materials' of archaeological sites are. The transformation process therefore necessitates management selectivity in identification of the raw materials of heritage objects. As noted, this is a further complication.

Variables

The variability within the transformation of heritage, mediated by management, is worth further consideration in terms of spheres, scales and language. The object is a physically definable entity and can be subjected to management, and yet that object is signified as being part of a concept (heritage), which cannot. This is seen in the worked example (Figure 2.2), where tangible objects also exist within and as intangible concepts. Application of the model also identifies structural oppositions based in the logic of Aristotle, Levi-Strauss or Douglas such as public/private; old/new; important/not important; identified/unidentified. This identification achieved through management, reflects increased professionalisation within the subject, and thus provides the basis for the case studies exploring the management of sites such as Uppark and Brodsworth, or institutions like English Heritage. Structural oppositions identified within the heritage reinforce the essence of becoming and change in the subject matter and its operational or physical existence in the world. At any time, and within either stage of the model, there may be mediation between these and other oppositions: the intricacies of system and process deal with them in turn, and signify them within the spheres and scales further considered.

It has already been noted that the effects of change do not merely adjust heritage as if in a vacuum. Though the relation of a heritage object to a person, people or place is a direct function of the second stage of the model, interpretation, management mediates the object's physical existence. This existence occurs within several spheres and scales. An object may be personal, local, national or global: such variability may be seen in the items curated in the Museum of London, an archaeological site identified and assessed through the Monuments Protection Programme worthy of national legal protection, or a place designated on a comparative cultural scale, like Hadrian's Wall, of world heritage value. The objects may be of more relevance to one audience than another, and though, as noted, such considerations may be played out in the interpretative schemes applied to the objectified past, the selectivity of sphere and scale has already been implicitly chosen by that process of objectification. Some 'things' become the objectified heritage, others do not: those, which are not objectified, remain 'conceptual' and more difficult to interpret in physical terms. Whilst the scales of change are largely identified in terms of scale and geography (individual, local, national etc.), the spheres are identified as sociological, political or economic. Motivations for utility of the created heritage tend to fall within these spheres. Thus in the Museum of London, exhibitions policy since the early 1900s has reflected the trend in museums' exhibition practice of focusing upon 'cultural mix' (e.g. 'Peopling of London' and Capital Concerns programme); whilst at Brodsworth there are demands for some return on the investment in conservation of the house and its contents, by promoting tourist facilities such as the shop, restaurant and special events. Such trends are considered in detail in the case studies.

Both spheres and scales, and the identification of change have in common the use of labels. It is important to note that the use of language or etymology, through specific words on labels, is a further concern. It is not entered into in any depth in this thesis, and it is sufficient to note that the variable use of labels in identifying objects, concept, spheres and scales, can become highly contentious, provoking emotional response. Management, positively or negatively, increases the use of labels due to its normative approach: objects and processes are identified and labelled more often than not for functional reasons to aid understanding (Ambrose and Runyard 1991). Such a seemingly simple procedure can, however, cause its own controversy by the very fact that labels are often of an 'indefinite' nature – i.e. language is used in descriptive terms at the point of change, before the model continues through to the interpretative stage. Objects may thus be reacted for or against before the intended point for reaction once they have been 'managed' and are subsequently being 'presented' (Watkins 1995). The use of labelling in the exploration of management is thus temporary, but allows for the normative to become the emotive, however unintentional. Semiotics considers the value-laden aspects of labels and signs further, but I wish here to treat labels objectively as an aide-memoire in the management process (Giddens 1993; Jensen 1995).

System and process

Up to this point I have used the generic term of 'management'. The basic instructions for using such a tool are now considered. The objectified heritage, whilst created from 'raw materials', already exists in the world in its final 'physical' form as seen in the example (Figure 2.2): what management actually does is use a variety of systems and processes within them, to collate and manipulate information – a reconfiguration of conceptual understanding to create a public heritage within a public agency. This establishes the context and environment, which may allow a certain kind of object to be identified, and therefore 'become' a physical entity recognised as public heritage. Management therefore uses systems to give an already existing physical form signification as representative of heritage. Actual physical change usually occurs also, (the ruin may be conserved and the hand-axe may be put into a museum collection), but the system of identifying the heritage is the first task of management. To do this objects are decontextualised in order to be identified and later recontextualised through interpretation as heritage. Full decontextualisation, recontextualisation and filtering out of subjectivity to identify archaeology's raw materials is practically impossible, though management techniques have the ability to do the best possible job. Thus the Monuments Protection Programme, acting within statutory regulations identifies and quantifies the physical reality of archaeological remains, before assessing them within certain parameters of value. Decontextualised archaeology (as near a raw material as the discipline will allow) is recontextualised instilling geographic landforms and constructions with cultural significance: this is before the explicit process of interpreting this new heritage object within the second stage of the model.

An immediate reaction to the exploration of such a model of transformation could be that it reduces heritage to nothing more than a set of functional responses, and a step-by-step process with pre-ordained outcome. Such an accusation can be countered by saying that the move from administration to management (differences which will be explored further in the following chapter) takes a necessarily pragmatic approach. The sum of its parts, identifying the human and physical environment that may create heritage objects, is far from functionalist, and is grounded in awareness of human interaction with the world. Development within the science of strategic management from the 1960s to the 1990s also reflects this (Leavy 1996). The processes of decontextualisation and recontextualisation reconcile tension by identifying the human action and reaction to the world around us. There is thus constant mediation of action, context and information to achieve this: necessarily this produces many systems and sub-processes to be worked through – for that reason the intricacies of day-to-day management are not considered, as they form individual components of a larger tool. I am focusing on the operation of that tool itself.

The institutional context for transformation

A little more may be said about the specific sphere in which the model of transformation is primarily applied. The context for change using management can usually be expected to be institutional. As far as this thesis is concerned, those institutions are affected by law and government in a procedural fashion. That is to say that there is interaction between institutions, but certain contextual arrangements entail some agencies having greater effect on others. For example, the National Trust as an institution is affected more by English Heritage than vice versa because it is a private charitable organisation, and the central government Department for Culture, Media and Sport (formerly National Heritage), affects English Heritage more than vice versa, because English Heritage is officially a quango. The basis for these institutional arrangements exist in the statutory responsibilities laid down by law. These have two effects relevant to the transformation: firstly they create the public institutions responsible for heritage, and place certain tasks on them through statutory and added non-statutory responsibilities; and they provide the legal context in which certain aspects of the heritage may be created and managed – for example scheduled monuments and listed buildings. Any public institution cannot undertake every task associated with the context in which it operates, nor would it want to for varying reasons. Its closeness to the basic statutory framework for the existence of a public heritage, however, usually provides for some role, if only regulatory, in most aspects of that public heritage. Law within the model therefore has the dual function of enabling, and the ability to be relied on if necessary for mediation of the public heritage. Law enables and expects certain actions to be undertaken, and furthermore when necessary can be leaned upon as justification of certain courses of action. This is seen in the context of the corporate activities of English Heritage in Chapter 4 and is equally applicable to the National Trust

and Museums considered here. Within that remit, due to the carefully constructed nature of law, there remains wide scope for the variability, selection and representation of a public heritage, however constrained the form may seem.

Containers of change and the framework for the model

The intention to act, presupposed by the creation of such public institutions in law creates certain structures of behaviour. This framework in which an institution can be constructed is imposed from without and within. The reason for the framework's existence at all however, lies beyond the remit of law, and in the case of heritage can be attributed historically to the theory of market failure. This theoretical structure provides the need for heritage (up until now) to be managed in a certain way within the public domain created by government. Market failure suggests a viable economic market may not be sustainable for all objects within society, usually those which do not produce obvious and immediate personal return: such as environmental conservation, certain medical research, or historic object preservation as dealt with here. More often than not the onus falls on government to act for the greater good of a community and provide management and economic support for the perceived societal need. Thus, for example, the government has undertaken to protect archaeology since the passing of the first Ancient Monuments Act in 1882.

The social context for administration of the public heritage in the past has been considered by others (Garnham 1983), and has been considered as largely an accident of government intervention (Carman 1996). Such action in the past combined with the theory of market failure allows the model to be developed, as the recent shift has been made from administration of the heritage to management of the heritage. This change in the field of management science will be considered in the next chapter. Previously the public heritage has been administered under law and taken for granted, due to the theory that there was no economic market for the past as a concept. Preservation of historic objects is considered to be a social necessity, but not necessarily one which identified consumers are willing to pay for – a market for the past cannot be sustained – hence market failure and government intervention. Changes in management have brought about a shift from functional administration to humanist strategic management, where environmental analysis in a management sense is pre-eminent (see Chapter 3). As a result of this markets can now be identified, and the transformation from concept to object becomes more complex, with the accompanying need for equally complex managerial systems. I would suggest that the changing framework of heritage has only recently focused on the need for an understanding of how heritage objects are created. The model provides a self-reflexive opportunity for analysis, and such an approach is taken through the case studies, which deliver the variety of transformations. It must be acknowledged that transformation has existed at all times in creation of the public heritage, but the means of delivery has changed, providing new justification for a certain form of public management of the heritage.

Existing in time: other kinds of change

Three other themes, which are concerned with time, are summarised below, but not considered further in this thesis. They should however be recognised as relevant to the context of the transformation from concept to object, with both management action and heritage objectified as being intimately bound to the concept of time.

In examination of the transformation, the model allows comparison between a changing heritage or past to other kinds of change and their existence in the present. Furthermore, it can be seen how things affect the agent rather than the model itself at any point in time. Time itself further affects the agent. The philosophical stance of Saint Augustine (Augustine 400) states that we only exist in the present, though there are three kinds of present – past present, present present and future present. Each of these is mediated through perception – and management. We continue to exist in the present only, but must be mindful of the passage of time allowing us to identify change and transformation with a historical perspective (Gosden 1994). Just as the heritage is altered and constantly reconfigures itself through objectification and subsequent conceptualisation by interpretation, so other changes occur in spheres interconnected with heritage having consequential effects.

For instance, value is a theme that only recently came to be looked at within archaeology, in the complementary works of Darvill (1993) and Carman (1996), approaching the general and particular respectively. American research has been concerned with the similar term, 'significance' (Bruier and Mathers 1996). Direct comparison may be made in the development of the discipline of archaeology as a subject, and the change of emphasis between theory and practice. Archaeology as a discipline constantly undergoes transformation from an objective scientific subject to a subjective arts subject, depending on the experience of the viewer or practitioner. General trends in society can be viewed from a sociological perspective, with emphasis changing from arts to sciences, and greater sophistication of techniques of exploration in both. Such is the case of general human development, awareness and participation in maintaining a civilised society, charted by authors such as Gifford (1990). These trends in society have consequential effects on the agency and the way in which objects are treated.

In focusing on the questions of how transformation happens, using the objective and positive analytical strands of the management sciences, the various layers of subjective and objective action and observation may be identified and themselves valued: thus the model, and its exploration through case studies, shows how change and balance is maintained, in the particular instance of the public heritage. The consideration of the past as a 'resource' is called into question here. Most recently archaeology has been determined by some (Darvill 1993; Carver 1996) to be a finite resource. The combination of this argument with the continual transformation of heritage would suggest that there will be a saturation point of the object, a saturation point of heritage. Utilisation of this model for understanding changes in heritage would suggest the opposite however – variability is so great that, combined with the passage of time and change in other thematic areas, 'new' heritage will constantly be created by virtue of our existence in the present. This therefore suggests archaeology is sustainable as a physical resource, by virtue of its place as heritage (Sola 1994). The fact that wartime remains and council house architecture are now considered as important constituents of the heritage where they were not five years ago proves the point. The techniques of management employed to sustain the heritage as part of the wider human environment will insure against total loss of particular object features of the historic environment, by the ability of those objects to be valued as important or a rare example.

Perception transformed

A positive conclusion about the human environment can be drawn from utilisation of this model as a means of exploring aspects of the public heritage. Analysis of the variability in transformations involved at a point in time (being the present) may show that the normalising influences seen in management of the public heritage equates with the suggestion that culture comprises encounter with the 'ordinary' (Williams 1958; Jencks 1995). It further suggests that future challenges may lie not in the identification of the heritage but in the wherewithal to utilise skills in manipulating the large amounts of information generated with the object heritage: such is the sophistication of management systems. This alone necessitates understanding of the transformation of heritage (the agency), and the model takes the first tentative steps in accomplishing such a goal.

3　Management: the tool for transformation

What is management?

This chapter explores the concept and systems of management where it is applicable to the transformation of the public heritage and offers a brief outline of management technique, exploring the tool most relevant for use in heritage management. It leads from an overview of what management is, to more specific considerations of management's relevance to heritage and archaeology, and finally to the techniques used for analysis.

The term 'management' has been used in the model as a label for the agent of change used within the transformation from concept to object. I wish to begin by defining the terms of management as applied in this thesis but will not enter the debate on whether management is a discipline or a technique. A simple explanation suffices in the context of this thesis: I am defining 'management' here as *an organised ability to effect and cope with change*. The use of management as a developing discipline in its own right enables tasks to be brought to fruition successfully where 'change', internally and externally, has increased in speed and occurrence. The increasing rate of change within the business world demands an understanding of change (Hannan & Freeman 1989, 23). Management is used as a tool to cope with and itself enable change, and also understand it: as just such a concept, it is integral to understanding the transformation. Management is about understanding what goes on in a variety of contexts. Such a view of what management is seems to correlate well with more detailed research both within the management sciences and from other disciplines, which have considered similar problems. Handy suggests that,

> 'diagnosis lies at the heart of management [but at the same time] diagnosis brings dilemmas. It is seldom possible to optimise on all the variables. There is no theory that unlocks those dilemmas. Diagnosis clarifies but seldom solves. The quest of judgement is the ultimate justification of the managerial role.' (1985, 17)

Transformation of any kind (apart from the model here) does not just happen by itself however, and the area of research known as organisational ecology considers the environments in which change occurs.

'Most sociological theories emphasise the actions of individuals, interest groups, social classes and institutions. Yet almost all modern collective action takes place in organisational contexts; and organisations are the main vehicles for action in modern society.' (Hannan & Freeman 1989, 3)

Within other disciplines the application of management models has been found useful as a disciplinary tool – integration seems to have been particularly successful in environmental disciplines and planning (Adams 1996; Dillon & Jones 1996; McGill 1995).

Historical development of management thought

Before considering public administration, central to the analysis of this thesis, a brief summary of the development of management as a discipline is given. Literature on the subject matter is extensive, and merely an overview of trends is presented. Heritage management is specifically considered in the concluding sections of this chapter.

Modern management thinking started by analysing what came to be called the Classical School coupled with Fayol and Taylor's 'Scientific Management' (Fayol 1949). This 'saw the discussion and development of bureaucratic organisations as rational entities, with the principles of planning, organisation, command, co-ordination and control given high importance' (Cooper 1993, 347). Time and motion studies were central to these ideas, with a focus on the system and process of delivering end products in manufacture. Criticism of this methodology pointed out that the human element was missing, and that 'scientific management' treated people like machines. Out of this there developed studies, which formed the 'Human Relations School', concentrating on the motivation to work, and the human environment in which work was carried out. Mayo's 'The Social Problems of an Industrial Civilisation' was a central study in this school (Mayo 1949) and linked Maslow's analysis from a psychological viewpoint (Maslow 1970) with similar work later by Herzberg et al (1959). From this came the 'contingency theorists' focusing on three main areas and the links between them and the output from manufacturing industry – technology, innovation and uncertainty (Proctor 1982, 17). This was the first point at which there is an obvious eye kept on the wider world in which an organisation exists, and can be said therefore to be the early precursor to strategic thinking. The 'Systems approach' was to follow that, with explicit focus on the methodology of decision making and carrying out action following decisions. The initial 'decision-making approach' led on the more developed 'total systems approach' (Proctor 1982), again with its eye on the wider world.

Recent development in management thought has been the establishment of corporate strategy as part of a strategic management outlook. 'The emphasis has moved away from the operational function of management to its strategic function, i.e. away from how best to perform a job towards the setting of goals and deciding what an organisation ought to be doing' (*ibid.* 35). The strategic outlook will be returned to later, since it provides the dominant influence for this thesis.

Market Failure

I am not analysing a traditional organisation or manufacturing process in an exploration of public heritage management. Essentially I am examining the production of historic culture (a variant of cultural production) (Jencks 1995) in the form of objects, and more particularly the purpose and aim of such production. This is approached by examining the context in which heritage is managed: this context is known as the 'environment' in management terms. A particular aspect of this environment is that the notion of market failure, already mentioned in Chapter 2, is applied to it. The idea of market failure has been relied on traditionally as a reason for maintaining public sector involvement in certain aspects of management. And though, as Hughes (1994, 104) points out, market failure should not be used as the sole rationale for 'producing a definitive role for government', in many areas this situation has arisen. The basic functions of government are reproduced in Figure 3.1: it does not follow that government is willing to pay for all of these from the public purse, but equally there are certain functions which have fallen to government where the inhabitants of a country are unwilling to pay directly for them. Damage to the natural environment (and in this we may include cultural resources also) has always been the 'textbook example of externality and market failure.' (*ibid.* 105)

Therefore cultural resources, the heritage in general, have been left for government to look after and regulate historically, even though the original intentions of the government officials involved may have been more privately oriented, as discussed in Carman's (1996) social context for heritage law (see also Champion 1996). Furthermore once bound up as a duty of public administration, heritage management has been subject to the development of such administration, with all its complicating factors – political, legal and economic (Hughes 1994; Ross 1991). Archaeology

has therefore historically become bound up with the environment, and the environment subsequently with social policy. Dillon and Jones (1996) argue from this that the waters have been muddied for studying the environment properly, as so many 'context dependent notions' (*ibid.* 116) are relied upon.

Challenging Market Failure

The discipline of management science has critically examined market failure and tested such examination, and in certain cases has found it to be a flawed argument in the case of both the natural environment and heritage. Examples include the willingness of people to pay extra for 'environmentally-friendly' products, and the rise in demand for 'historic properties' for office accommodation (English Heritage 1993 b). The case studies within this thesis, charting the change in use of management as a tool, supports the view that the principles of market failure cannot be applied as a blanket term to 'the environment' any longer, and this includes the 'historic environment', which I am concerned with here. This has only recently come under scrutiny in the establishment of evaluation methodologies by the Heritage Lottery Fund.

This reassessment of market failure has prompted government (which has traditionally 'propped up' such 'causes') to examine its own role and management, and it is now supporting new market creation. This change reflects development in the ethos of public administration, and this is considered with a historical perspective. Though a somewhat complicated picture emerges, Jordan argues that 'the research for an understanding of the organisation of British government is best made by seeking historical explanations of particular arrangements, then for a set of principles that underpin the complexity' (1994, 44). History here provides useful explanation for the modern situation. This development provides further contextual exploration (or environmental analysis) for the model, justifying its current adoption as an explanation for heritage production. As far as market failure as a justifying idea goes times have indeed changed, and it is the adoption of new management tools in the public sector, where understanding and information becomes paramount, which have suggested that market failure can no longer be used to justify total public management of the heritage.

Figure 3.1 *Basic functions of government. (from Hughes 1994, 104)*

1	Providing economic infrastructure
2	Provision of various collective goods and services
3	The resolution and adjustment of group conflicts
4	The maintenance of competition
5	Protection of natural resources
6	Provision of minimum access by individuals to the goods and services of the economy
7	Stabilisation of the economy

The further influence of social policy analysis and tourism studies has assisted in the re-examination (Davies 1995). An example of this change is reported by the National Trust for Scotland where social valuation of the organisation is supported economically. 'The ethos behind voluntary charitable organisations [which we may deem public in this thesis] is a special aspect of life in the UK, and the commitment of individuals to the success of the national movement to protect the heritage will be seen later as contributing in no small measure to its financial and operating efficiency.' (Borley 1994, 23) Even when under 'economic pressure' (*ibid.* 25) financial support is given to organisations, such as the National Trust for Scotland, whose value is perceived publicly. Taking such support to be a wider part of leisure activity, sociological analysis has suggested that, 'leisure is no longer to be understood as the trivial use of 'spare time'. Instead it is becoming a key element of meaning in people's lives and in providing the context in which new social groupings may develop and be sustained.' (CPRE 1994, 31) Such 'value', including protection of the natural and built heritage, has previously been argued within the varying disciplines as benefiting from market failure.

Public and Private; Profit and Not-for-profit – discussion of convergence in management ethos

Within the British administrative system (i.e. government and civil service) confusion exists, as Jordan (1994) notes that there is 'doubt' (1994, 169) over exactly what government is. He quotes Norton Lang's comments from 1954 stating that 'however attractive [the idea of] an administration receiving its values from political policy-makers may be, it has one fatal flaw. It does not accord with the facts of administrative life' (*ibid.* 5). After discussing the divide in some detail, Jordan concludes that the simple public/private divide (a convenient one), is a 'blunt and ideological division that has petrified thought on the actual relations between the two categories' (1994, 188). This convenient divide perpetuated in government and elsewhere to the detriment of developing heritage management until relatively recently: government departments have now begun to address this divide however.

Within the next sections, I will show that in fact a market *is* now created through administrative rules and institutional establishment (in this case English Heritage and comparative organisations), and those institutions act on a not-for-profit basis (market failure). As will be shown in the individual case studies, through developing such institutions along modern management lines of thought (strategic management involving corporate planning) both in the present day and the future, as a result of the wider political process, real markets may be established. This lessens the need for not-for-profit remits, though still supporting the 'cause' of heritage protection and development.

Simply put, through detailed self-analysis of an organisation, coupled with the recent 'New Right' political environment

for public sector management (Flynn 1990), products and profits can now be produced where previously there were none. The 'New Labour' approach to public sector management, adopted since the change of British government in May 1997 would not seem to be any different. Indeed, twelve 'guiding principles for market testing and contracting out', have been published, underlining the 'Government's commitment to work with the private sector in modernising public services.' The aim is to provide 'better value...better quality services at the best price for taxpayers.' (Cabinet Office 1997, 114)

It should be restated for clarity, that the change in public sector management technique has been brought about through a combination of developing public administrative theory and more general management theory. The most recent developments have, however, been brought about more through the political will to contain public expenditure (Flynn 1990), and therefore rely more on the management theory of profit-making organisations than the traditional not-for-profit administrative theory. This has been most obvious in the realms of 'social policy', where the 'trade-off between quality and cost is explicit' (*ibid.* 113), though difficult to resolve. Texts on such developments in public sector management or administration have tended in this respect to focus on such case studies as the National Health Service, or welfare provision (*ibid*; Jordan 1994; Hughes 1994).

Whilst the divide between the goals and operations of non-profit and profit-making organisations is becoming smaller, brief comment can be made on those differences that are perpetually cited: such views are increasingly difficult to justify when applied wholescale to public administration. Argenti (1989), in building his own 'system' (*ibid.* 409) of corporate planning summarises these differences. In setting 'objectives for non-profit-making organisations', he puts forward the opinion that 'they cannot determine their corporate objectives to the same standard as companies can' (*ibid.* 87). This is still the case in an overall survey of public organisations though, as will be seen from the case studies here, as the process of strategic management takes hold of an organisation and examines the roles and functions that organisation performs, the process can identify specific areas within the organisation, which can act to the same standard as companies. At the 'corporate objective' level, which Argenti is keen to distinguish from strategic and operational objectives, this difficulty is still acknowledged through reference back to the concept of heritage being one area which can be labelled as a market failure.

The statement that, 'profit is not only not the aim, but is often wholly incompatible with it,' (*ibid.* 87) has its origins in the traditional view of public management as administration. Public or governmental administration was seen essentially as a bureaucracy, and under the original assumption that Weber's traditional model of bureaucracy was the best way of delivering public services (Andreski 1983). Consigned more now to sociological histories such as Giddens (1993) than of relevance to management theorists in the wider world, the concept is still widely identified immediately with public sector management and thought.

The development of public administration

For the purposes of an area in which market failure and government intervention is necessary it would seem that the bureaucratic model proposed by Weber is perfect. Its characteristics are outlined in Figure 3.2. In short however, as Hughes (1994) summarises, 'there are several rationales for the replacement of traditional public administration: the realisation that public service functions are more managerial than administrative; responses to the attacks on the scale and scope of government; changes in economic theory; and parallel changes in the private sector.' (*ibid.* 21)

Figure 3.2 *Weber's characteristics of bureaucracy (after Weber: Runciman 1978, 956-63).*

1   There is a clear-cut hierarchy of authority.
2   Written rules govern the conduct of officials.
3   Officials are full-time and salaried.
4   There is a separation between the tasks of the official within the organisation and life outside.
5   No member or members of the organisation own the material resources with which they operate.

Weber argued that 'modern bureaucracy is a highly effective mode of organising large numbers of people' (Giddens 1993, 288); the civil service was seen as the prime example. Woodrow Wilson had identified the advantages of such a model in 1886, saying that 'administration lies outside the proper sphere of politics...the evils of the spoils system [in America] resulted from the linking of administrative questions with political ones.' (quoted from Hughes 1994, 33) A combination of economic, social and political factors associated with the 'New Right' as argued by Flynn (1990) and others, forced theorists and administrators to look again at the operation of public service and the machinery of government and bring about an 'era of change' (Hughes 1994, 21). The upshot of this is that the bureaucratic model has 'now been discredited both theoretically and practically.' (*ibid.* 22) It is beyond the scope of this thesis to consider these changes in any detail, or the full reasons for them: here it is wished merely to set the scene for an analysis of a public sector organisation in case studies (English Heritage) in the context of changing values and management styles across the whole of the public service.

Public service has been subject to the changing styles of management over the years, though in rearguard action as a result of one of the main critical points about public service organisations: that they are slow to respond. 'New Public Management', the starting point for change in the public sector, was driven by the 'virtuous three Es': economy, efficiency and effectiveness (Politt 1990, 59). Relevant changes in government as a result of applying management thought include the creation of the giant Department of the Environment in the 1970s and since then, as a result of changes in thought, movement of that

Department's responsibilities into smaller executive bodies, and even the creation of a new Department (of National Heritage, now Culture, Media & Sport) out of some of its wide environmental and planning functions. The newer strategic management marries well therefore with this and the overriding political concerns of a government with capitalist ideals. The identification of the four available instruments of government: provision, subsidy, production and regulation (Hughes 1994), implicitly highlight planning as a necessary concern. Hence, a paradigm shift away from administration as being the prime delivery of government services, to management of services and product provision for a customer, the general public.

The creation of markets in the public sector has been through a 'set of administrative rules, [and therefore] the determinants of market structure differ from those of real markets which are shaped by technology, knowledge and relative economic power.' (Flynn 1990, 97) From the exploration already made of the 'heritage phenomenon', it can surely be said that any creation of markets and introduction of competition in a field dominated by an intangible concept will have very different characteristics, and this makes the analysis of the 'new' management of the heritage all the more interesting and necessary. Flynn gives a warning to be borne in mind through the analysis, suggesting that even though the management techniques of the profit sector are being increasingly applied to the non-profit sector as similarities are identified,

'...managing services requires a different approach from managing manufacture, mainly because the service organisation has to recreate the relationship between itself and its users. The relationship has to be defined within users' perception of the service. Then the whole organisation has to focus its efforts on ensuring the service occurs according to the design.' (*Ibid.* 151)

In the field of heritage management the 'users' are of course integral, as we are dealing with the human environment. No single line of management analysis is therefore suitable, again emphasising the variabilities inherent in the transformation from concept to object. Three management themes are drawn upon within this analysis: strategy as a way of thinking, environmental analysis as a tool, and consideration of the 'human element' for dealing with internal and external organisational relations. Each is considered in turn.

Strategy and strategic thinking: its use

I have considered strategic management in different ways here to establish change over time in management style, and change effected within organisational remit. The process of corporate or strategic planning is considered for example, where applicable in the analysis of English Heritage in Chapter 4. Jones summarises the aims of this planning process by suggesting that any organisation has to ask three questions of itself: 'Where are we now? Where do we want to go? How are we going to get there?' (1996, 11).

The strategic planning outlook is one applicable to an entire organisation, and is reproduced at the smaller scale through the hierarchy of an object's or organisation's management. This can be seen clearly in the case study concerned with English Heritage's management, and its effects will be seen at a smaller scale on the site-based studies. The object's or organisation's environment is assessed where this supports the aims of the five processes in strategic management that Jones identifies, presented in Figure 3.3.

Figure 3.3 *Five processes in strategic management. (Jones 1996, 11)*

Phase 1:   Defining the business and establishing strategic aims
Phase 2:   Setting objectives and performance targets linked to these aims
Phase 3:   Formulating strategy to achieve target objectives
Phase 4:   Implementing and executing the plan
Phase 5:   Evaluating performance & reformulating the strategic plan and/or implementation of plan

Johnson and Scholes (1989) who are largely followed in the analyses here, present the models behind the exploration of corporate strategy in a graphical form, making the understanding of links and processes somewhat easier (Figures 3.4 & 3.5). They argue that 'strategy and the management of strategy can be thought of in at least two rather different ways. First it can be seen as a matter of essentially economic analysis and planning, and second it can be seen as a matter of organisational decision making within a social, political and cultural process.' (*ibid.* xvii) The ultimate advantage of strategic management over previous schools of thought therefore is the way in which it answers the three questions posed earlier by Jones (1996): coupled to this is the expectation within the school of strategic management thought that it can reconcile scientific management 'with an understanding of the human and social side of management.' (*ibid.* xix)

It should be noted that within strategy as a management outlook there has been change and development, and the effects of this can be seen in the case studies. 'Since the early 1980s there has been growing disillusionment with the capacity of strategic planning to deliver on those promises and growing disenchantment with the very notion of formalised strategic planning itself.' (Leavy 1996, 9) Transformation within strategic thought has shifted the emphasis 'from preoccupation with growth and

Figure 3.4 *Identifying the strategic position (Johnson & Scholes: Fig. 1.2).*

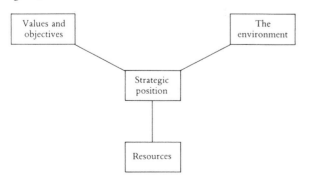

Figure 3.5 *Strategic Planning model (Johnson & Scholes, Fig 1.4)*

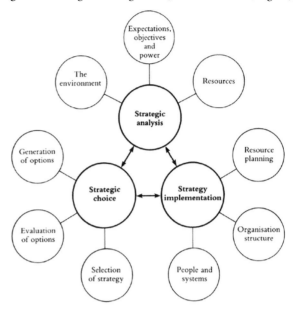

diversification to reassessment of core....Driven primarily by the emergence of the new economy, the processes of transformation and renewal have since become among the most central concerns of the strategy field.' (*ibid.* 84) These essential changes are further reproduced in Figure 3.6, using a Star Trek metaphor, and furthermore proposing dualities changing through time.

Figure 3.6 *The duality of strategic management – the Spock/Kirk metaphor. (from Leavy 1996, 105, Fig. 2)*

Mr Spock (1960s/70s)	Captain Kirk (1980s/90s)
(rational-instrumental)	(romantic-interpretative)
managing	leading
scientist/technologist	humanist/philosopher
generic	idiosyncratic
commanding/controlling	inspiring/empowering
securing conformity	harnessing diversity
adaptive	inventive
objectives/instrumental	purpose/institutional
structure/systems	culture/processes
decision-making/positioning	learning/leveraging
strategy as problem solving	strategy as potential fulfilling
strategy as planning	strategy as crafting
strategy as prose	strategy as poetry
(typified by Ansoff)	(typified by Mintzberg)

This is gratifying for the model in this thesis, as consideration of the various environments of heritage and the human element are themselves necessary. The kind of analysis undertaken in the case studies therefore is supported within current management thought (Kirk-like, future-oriented). In my exploration of the model through the various case studies, I am thus approaching heritage management from a strategic perspective: this is most appropriate as it concerns the task of preserving the past for the future.

CPI, Environmental Analysis and SWOT

These are the fundamental tools of analysis used in modern strategic management. They are used to understand the function and place of the organisation or object in the wider world. Further techniques are utilised, though these are not considered in this thesis as they are concerned with more day-to-day operation of management functions. Though I have previously reflected on the heritage being considered generally as a non-profit-making resource suffering from traditional market failure, the model and case studies show clearly that adoption of strategic management tools challenge these assumptions.

Whilst the general characteristics of strategic decisions can be readily translated across from profit-making organisations to non-profit-organisations, there are obviously unique circumstances in dealing with the heritage sector. Firstly, as Argenti (1989) points out, 'the planning team in non-profit-organisations have a much harder task. Unless they have been highly rigorous in their definition of the corporate objective they will find it is difficult, or even impossible, to quantify it. They would have to return to this definition and sharpen it up so it could be translated into figures.' (*ibid.* 153) This is the problem of finding a suitable Corporate Performance Indicator (CPI). In business this is easy – it is a matter of whether the organisation is making a profit or not. In non-profit-organisations, such an equivalent CPI may not be so easy to establish, as 'money is the only universal measure of value we have yet invented so it is no use protesting that it is irrelevant [in the case of] non-profit-organisations.' (*ibid.* 151) Targets and performance indicators can be considered in the light of the overall argument in the thesis that archaeology and the heritage are being increasingly commodified/objectified to serve as resources that can be measured in numeric terms, either monetary value or by other means. This is not suitable for every situation, however, and use of adapted methods of environmental analysis such as those of the tourist industry (Prentice 1993 and 1995) allow some degree of assessment of other sociological benefits, according to a CPI.

Other complicating factors include internal and external pressure (political and economic). An organisation must question whom it is serving: a customer and a paymaster may not be one and the same, particularly where government involvement is concerned. This is also seen in Chapter 8 in the exploration of Cambridge University Museum of Archaeology & Anthropology. This is further qualified by Johnson and Scholes (1989):

'The likelihood is that funding bodies may be diverse and, quite likely, not direct beneficiaries of the services offered. Moreover, they may well provide funds in advance of the services being offered in the form of grants for example. The implications here are several. The influence from the funding bodies is likely to be high in terms of the formulation of organisational strategies; indeed the organisations may well develop strategies as much to do with and influenced by the funding bodies as by their clients. Moreover, since they are heavily dependent on funds, which emanate not from clients but from sponsors, a danger is that the organisation becomes more concerned with resource efficiency than service effectiveness. It is also likely that there will be multiple sources of funding and this, linked to the different objectives and expectations of the funding bodies, might lead to a high incidence of political lobbying, difficulties in strategic planning, and a requirement to hold decision making and responsibility at the centre where it is answerable to external influences rather than delegate it within the organisation.' (*ibid.* 19)

The strategic position of discrete units in the heritage sector (comprising organisations and heritage objects for our purposes) may be assessed through identification of the organisation's environment and resources. Johnson and Scholes (1989) identify five steps that must be followed to assess the 'strategic position' (*ibid.* 53) of any organisation. These are as follows: 'audit of environmental influences; assessment of the nature of the environment; identification of environmental forces through structural analysis; identification of competitive positions; and identification of key opportunities and threats' (*ibid.* 54). This analysis is, of course, aimed specifically at profit-making organisations, so some of the steps are less relevant than others, such as the identification of a competitive position. However, the principles of the analysis are useful, and will be followed for this thesis' purpose. Figure 3.7, outlines the various factors for identification of the environment, from Proctor (1982), and consideration of the case studies's environments will utilise this and the general principles of Johnson and Scholes (1989). I cannot emphasise enough the importance in understanding the different types of environment within which heritage exists (and therefore has to be managed), and this will be returned to again and again in the case studies.

Figure 3.7 *Types of environment. (from Proctor 1982)*

1. The Proximate Environment
   '... A business organisation can be regarded as a resource conversion system.. The proximate environment is concerned with how and where to obtain the various resources which are employed in conversion processes and whence and how the system's output should be distributed.' (*ibid.*)

   a: sources of labour supply
   b: sources of finance
   c: sources of materials
   d: customers and middlemen

   '... there are also proximate bodies which have a direct influence on management activities.' (*ibid.*) (Essentially this may comprise the recipe for the organisation.)

   a: trade unions
   b: competitors
   c: local communities

2. The general environment (constraints)
   a: economic
   b: legal
   c: political
   d: socio-cultural [see below]
   e: technological

Most of the headings in Figure 3.7 are self-explanatory. Proctor does, however, break down the general environmental constraints further. For the purpose here of analysing the heritage sector the socio-cultural environment is the most important, due to the fact that organisations are dealing with the 'unknown quantity' that is the 'heritage'. As a thematic and abstract concept, with relation to personal and national identity, and its explicit link with the process of history, the greatest sphere that a heritage management institution such as English Heritage or a museum can have, is in the socio-cultural environment. Proctor (*ibid.*) considers this sector of the general environment to include various categories presented in Figure 3.8 below.

Figure 3.8 *The Socio-Cultural Environment. (from Proctor 1982)*

a: social
    (structure, family patterns and occupational structure)

b: cultural
    (ideologies, beliefs, values and norms)

c: demographic
    (age, sex and geographic structure of the population)

d: educational

Each of the environmental factors outlined in Figures 3.7 and 3.8 will be considered in the case studies in order to establish their strategic position in the present. Beginning with the proximate environs of the organisations, the sources of labour supply have changed as a result of development in management as a social science and also as a result of the wider development of archaeology and heritage management as a discipline. Certain tasks have become specialised jobs in their own right, whilst new labour forces or specialities are being drawn upon due to the increasing overlap of archaeology and the business community. This is particularly as a result of PPG16, and the effect of archaeology becoming a statutory consideration in the planning process, and also the impact of lottery money available for development in the areas of museums and tourism.

In taking, 'an initial view of the nature of [an] organisation's environment' (Johnson and Scholes 1989, 53), the stability of the environment is assessed, along with the likelihood of change. For the heritage this is relatively straightforward. The nature of the environment is relatively static in terms of management institutions (i.e. there are unlikely to be large public bodies established, similar to English Heritage or the Museum of London); but the subject matter, or more general environment that determines what heritage is (comprising socio-cultural factors described previously) does show signs of change – society is constantly developing and values placed on anything such as heritage constantly fluctuate. The subject matter is an intangible abstract concept, and thus organic in development.

Johnson and Scholes (*ibid.*) conclude, that 'if the environment is in a dynamic state or shows signs of becoming so, then a more future-orientated perspective is more sensible.'

Heritage management operates in just such an environment, and in terms of strategic management, this future-orientated perspective is just what English Heritage, the National Trust and museums attempt to take through their research and tourist development programmes – end products of the entire corporate planning process.

Within these considerations, SWOT analysis is undertaken. A classic strategic management tool, SWOT analysis looks at the Strengths, Weaknesses, Opportunities and Threats, as a part of or facing the organisation, its resources and environment. SWOT analysis proves difficult to undertake because of the hybrid nature of heritage management organisations, though worthwhile in further analysis of the heritage 'environment'. Strengths and weaknesses relate to the nature of the internal management and resources of an organisation. Identification of opportunities and threats must look at both the internal functions of the organisation as well as its environmental position in the 'outside world'. Thus an organisation may identify a weakness or threat from the statutory position of the organisation, but internally through 'honestly' assessing functions, such weakness may stem from an internal problem, where the organisation cannot address its statutory position in the best way. Clear analysis results in assessing factors that the organisation has to 'cope' with and cannot do anything about, and those factors where the organisation can alter its activities to improve its situation. Within the public sector, such processes are open to increasing scrutiny by the public and other government departments such as the Treasury which provides public bodies with funds: SWOT analysis has resulted here in 'market-testing' across many public bodies, producing its own opportunities and threats.

The combination of all the above assessments of the various environmental influences, issues facing an organisation, and the social responsibility instilled by the nature of the establishment of the organisation provide for the final stage of major assessment: strategic choice. Johnson and Scholes conclude that, 'objectives and, indeed, strategies are better thought of as the product of a complex interplay between: the expectations of individuals and groups; the values of society; organised groups and the dominant culture of the organisation.' (*ibid.* 140) The strategic options available are those possible actions that support the corporate objectives of an organisation. The reliance in English Heritage, for example, is on the expert nature of the organisation enabling it to identify and protect heritage in England. The specific environment in which any choice must be taken is dominated by that of the legal framework, the public sector ethos, targets set, historic decisions made by the organisation and the finances available for implementation of a choice. The final action, i.e. choice made and acted upon, will of course have resulted from the entire analysis made above, creating a management structure which is able to internally deliver choices which can be assessed. Figure 3.9 below shows the framework for evaluating strategic choice or possible strategies in a decision process model, and each is screened through modelling and assessment enabling choice of the best way forward. The strategic eye on the future has this monitoring built in, and it is formalised in the organisation as an audit department, coupled with strategy review, once any choice has been made and particular strategy implemented. Certain strategies of the organisation (especially those where it is acting within a statutory duty) mean that there is only one choice for that strategy and delivery, such as giving grants outlined by listed building legislation or curatorial responsibilities; other strategies may have multiple choices, such as possible developments for historic properties to increase visitor numbers. Again, here, mini-versions of the whole process may be employed to turn high-level corporate objectives into decisions about exactly how to proceed and what any one person's tasks are at any time.

Middleton (1994) has assessed current planning initiatives in the heritage sector and suggests that heritage organisations are increasingly operating as an industry and, from a management viewpoint, those organisations have therefore to be treated as a business. However, he notes that it cannot be restated enough that 'management is not an end in itself' (*ibid.* 11), and techniques cannot be taken off the shelf and employed wholesale in an organisation without an understanding of the purpose of them. I agree with this completely.

Adapting the manager's tools

Studies within the tourism sector have adapted the traditional management science tools of SWOT for their own purposes: these developments will be considered in the light of the site-based case studies, where tourism is a prime motivation for management. Developed by Beeho and Prentice (1996), 'ASEB (Activities, Settings, Experiences, Benefits) Grid analysis is based on conventional SWOT analysis and the Manning-Haas Demand Hierarchy (Manning 1986), and is applied to aid consumer-led product development and promotion at museums. As a management tool, it will become invaluable as museums seek to become more visitor-orientated, focusing on the needs and motivations of the visitors so that they will enjoy their visit and come again...' (Beeho & Prentice 1996, 232) Such a technique supplements typical socio-demographic analysis.

The Manning-Haas hierarchy, itself a sociological tool, and presented in Figure 3.10, emphasises the consumer rather

Figure 3.9 *Strategic choice. (Johnson & Scholes Fig. 2.3)*

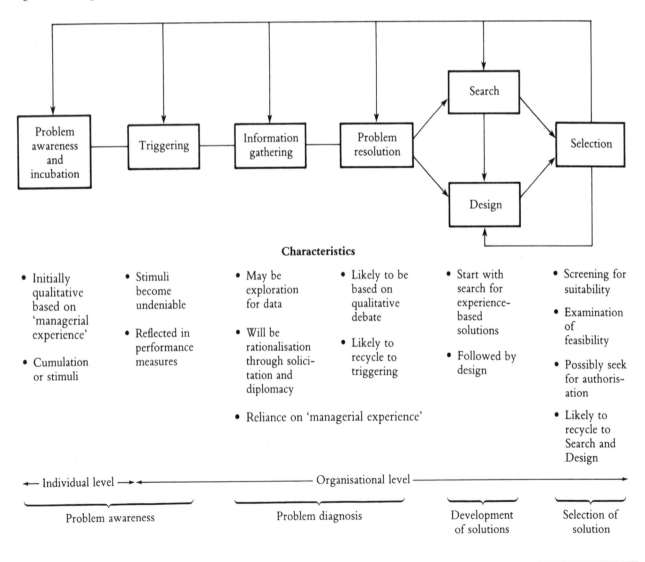

than the provider in such SWOT analysis. Essentially this is a behavioural approach proposing people undertake certain activities to fulfil their needs or attain certain goals. It is similar in certain respects to the more generalised hierarchy of needs proposed by Maslow (1970). Its socio-cultural bias accords with the 'Kirk-like' development of strategic management used here.

Figure 3.10 *The Manning-Haas sequential hierarchy of demand. (from Beeho & Prentice 1996, 233, Table 1)*

Level of Manning-Haas hierarchy of demand	Example
Level 1:	
Activities	Wilderness hiking
Level 2:	
Settings	
A. Environmental	Rugged terrain
B. Social	Few people
C. Managerial	No restrictions
Level 3:	
Experiences	Risk taking
	Challenge
	Physical exercise
Level 4:	
Benefits	
A. Personal	Enhanced self-esteem
B. Societal	Increased commitment to conservation
Human relations: the culture of cultural managers.	

The mechanics of every decision made by an organisation cannot always follow a fixed recipe due to the variables identified in the high-level analysis. Thus there is no minute step-by-step process: the generalised steps followed in principle for strategic management of the organisation are scaled down and manipulated to suit each situation. The intangible nature of the heritage means that the final transformative mechanism that turns a strategy into a specific task, part of a programme that delivers that strategy, depends on expert individuals that make up the organisation. Personal expertise and knowledge is therefore essential in an organisation, and it should be recognised generally that any exploration of management emphasises the necessity for each individual to have an understanding of the entire background to the management process that their work and organisation operates in. (In reality however, this is rather wishful thinking.) Internal recognition is made of this expert nature through greater staff development and training, and encouragement to participate in external heritage forums. Within any heritage organisation working in a 'public' capacity as a result of market failure, recognition must be made of why and how principles of management are followed: this relies on individual involvement and expertise. Heritage management produces a very special kind of product, and its nature can only be understood by looking at the principles of the manufacturing process

– the management of the organisation itself rather than management simply as a means to achieve something.

Little has been said about the forms of organisations, in terms of organising staff in groups to achieve tasks supporting its objectives. It is beyond the scope of this study to go into the full background of organising a workforce, and reference should be made to Handy (1985) amongst others, for discussion of organisational culture. Strategic management, as it devolves strategy objectives down through the organisation, and delivery and operational decisions accumulate upwards, means that combinations of organisational form become the norm, rather than a strict hierarchical or functional organisation design. The strategic management process, through its delivery of high-level objectives and reproduction at lower levels through to job plans and delivery of those objectives, means that an organisation becomes more focused on supporting an overall aim and understanding of that aim: different strategies identified will most probably therefore reflect different jobs and groups of tasks, allowing the organisation to be restructured accordingly. Both English Heritage and the Museum of London, for example, have undergone a great deal of restructuring, and the process is not necessarily complete. The strategic management process with its inbuilt monitoring and weighing of choices, means that such organisational change is necessary for the organisation to achieve those corporate objectives. The process does not therefore advocate change for change's sake: restructuring processes are clearly aimed at constantly adapting the organisation to its environment.

The development seen previously within strategic management over the last 20 years has focused attention once again on the real machinery of management – people (as noted earlier in Figure 3.6). However, more important has been the recognition that those people who make up the organisation are not literally machines. The combination of this internal pressure with the external pressures of a society increasingly driven by consumer demand necessitates careful consideration of management of any kind of heritage, and most importantly the context of delivery: a people's heritage. Social processes of any kind thus influence the 'organisational culture' (Johnson and Scholes 1989, 37 and Figure 3.11), in turn enabling a reflection of processes within wider society, itself the ultimate intention presumably of heritage management. We therefore see that as heritage management reflects people and culture, the organisational 'recipe' (*ibid*) reflects this equally in governance; decision-making; information production and retrieval; technology; and both consumer and producer demands. The latter is recognised through 'industry standards' such as the Investors in People (IIP) scheme and the Citizens Charter 'Charter Mark' awards. Further consideration of the organisational culture is made in the analysis of the organisation of English Heritage and the Museums. These changes of course represent allegiance to the style of strategic management, with its change from Spock-like to Kirk-like attitudes (Figure 3.6).

Figure 3.11 *Organisational culture. (Johnson & Scholes Fig. 2.5)*

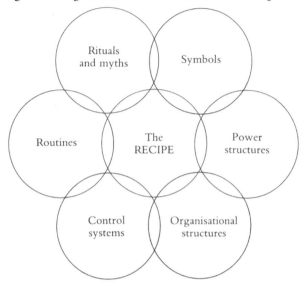

The use of Management in Heritage Management

Heritage management has been underdeveloped as a subject due to continual concentration on specific tasks within wider management structures. Collected examples of this are seen in heritage management 'handbooks' such as Hunter & Ralston (1993), Harrison (1994), and Berry & Brown (1995). Particular tasks such as ancient monument scheduling procedure, site marketing, database creation, or impact assessment are treated as self-contained units rather than establishing a corpus of heritage management, and an understanding of broad themes of management and change in the resource and its application in both practical and academic fields.

Very little recognition has been given to the development of the management discipline and its relevance to archaeology and heritage – probably because it is largely a historical exercise that has been covered widely in other subject areas. Ideas have been transferred to archaeology without much further thought as a result of this. Cooper (1993), writing for the Institute of Field Archaeologists and later in a dedicated volume on management and archaeology (1995), stands alone as an archaeologist considering the history of management. Perhaps due to the fact that the idea of management is taken for granted, as in 'reality there are elements of management in every archaeological task (Cooper 1995, 86) or, on a day-to-day basis, such issues cannot be thought over fully due to lack of time, the ideas are not followed up. In many respects, Cooper therefore paves the way for a study such as this, using the historical approach to 'give us the confidence both to develop our own explicit approaches and techniques... and to teach and publish our discussions for the benefit of the discipline as a whole.' (*ibid.*) But – he is alone, and he himself falls into the trap of stating how useful this 'new' tool is without applying it in its entirety to any case studies (Cooper 1993). Management has been previously seen by many to be an 'off-the-shelf' solution, its procedures used on a limited basis, or for more complex situations a literal solution has been brought in from outside in the form of a consultant (Kawashima 1998). I use the model of transformation to approach heritage management in a new way, utilising the management science's own techniques to engage with the concept of change and the theme of management itself.

Links can be made to the sociological aspects of the construction of heritage and identity and interaction with the world around us. Tourism studies have already started to look at this area using the term 'consumption' (Urry 1995). Analytical work has been undertaken by Prentice (1993), Ravenscroft, (1994) and Veal (1994) from political or economic perspectives, and Dillon & Jones (1996) have considered what must be understood in order to teach in the subject area of 'environmental consumerism' (*ibid.* 107) which can be said to include the heritage.

The application of the approach: strategic management of the heritage – transformations in action

Within this thesis I am going to draw on both traditional and adapted management techniques such as those of Middleton (1994), Johnson and Scholes (1989), or Beeho and Prentice (1996). I regard environmental analysis as of key importance in the case studies where illustration is made not only of the variability in management technique and purpose, but also the applicability of the central model proposed in the thesis. This further stands as a reflection of the more general trends in heritage management in the present. Transformation is seen in the heritage itself (from concept to object and vice versa), and management itself as a continuous process adapting to its environment. This approach has three key elements. Firstly, it is fundamentally positive, looking to the future with the intention of protecting the heritage as best as possible. Secondly, it is clearly identifying the manufacture or modification of heritage objects. Thirdly, it is clearly identifying the link between heritage and people: exploring the relationship between a resource and an audience or consumer.

4 The transformation of heritage into English Heritage

Introduction

The transformation from concept to object is best seen at a lesser level than that of a central government department or national organisation such as English Heritage, though such a corporate whole determines the nature of the transformation elsewhere. This chapter therefore says more about the tools of transformation, rather than the transformation itself, as played out through a particular style of management. Analysis of English Heritage, 'the Government's principal expert advisor on the historic environment' (DNH 1996 a, 97) from a managerial viewpoint shows the key shift which turns an unmodified object into an identified and presented, modified, consumable product. These products exist within the contextual environment labelled as heritage.

By concentrating on the style of corporate governance within English Heritage within a defined period, I am also able to illustrate how changes in such management have affected and now effect the overall transformation of heritage, which is explored in this thesis. Direct comparison between management of heritage resources now and twenty years ago illustrates the change. Heritage management as undertaken by the Department of the Environment or Ministry of Works in the 1970s compared to English Heritage in 1998, has seen a shift from an administered historic estate where curation was the only consideration, to a managed past, with emphasis on inclusion of communities in this historic environment and use of it as a resource. This shift also reflects changes in the socio-cultural, political and economic environment.

I have analysed management development within English Heritage from its creation in 1984 until the 1997 internal corporate planning period. Specific development since 1997 has not been analysed, though development and change is a continual 'organic' process. For example, since the General Election in 1997 the Department of National Heritage has been reorganised into the Department for Culture, Media and Sport (DCMS), and English Heritage moved towards the creation of regional teams to match with the established central government English regions (Alexander 1998). This regionalisation process (reflecting

Figure 4.1 *Examples of Public institutions whose remit includes funding, policy and co-operative management with other service level organisations in the heritage sector. (adapted from DNH 1996 a) Current names of organisations (reflecting organisational change since 1998) are noted in italics.*

Museums & Galleries Commission *(Museums, Libraries & Archives Council/MLA)*
The Museums and Galleries Commission provides advice and support for the development of, and co-operation between, museums and galleries.

Royal Commission on Historical Manuscripts *(The National Archives)*
The RCM aims to locate and record manuscripts, records and archives (apart from public records), to advise on their preservation and storage and to assist those wishing to use them.

Libraries and Information Commission *(Museums, Libraries & Archives Council/MLA)*
The L&IC was set up in 1995 to provide advice to Government on library issues and on international library and information matters and to devise a national research strategy for library and information research.

Arts Council of England *(Arts Council England)*
The Arts Council of England exists to develop and improve the knowledge, understanding and practice of the arts; and to increase the accessibility of the arts to the public in England. The Arts Council is also responsible for the distribution in England of the arts share of the proceeds of the national lottery.

Crafts Council
The Crafts Council advances and encourages the creation of contemporary craft and promotes the interest of the public in the works of crafts people and the accessibility of these works.

National Heritage Memorial Fund
The NHMF gives financial assistance towards acquiring, maintaining and preserving land, buildings, works of art and other objects of outstanding interest and importance to the national heritage, and providing facilities for their better display. The Fund is also responsible for the distribution of the heritage share of the proceeds from the National Lottery.

Royal Commission on the Historical Monuments of England *(English Heritage)*
The RCHME compiles and makes available the national record of England's ancient monuments and historic buildings for use by individuals and bodies concerned with understanding, interpreting and managing the historic environment.

Royal Fine Art Commission *(Commission for Architecture and the Built Environment/CABE)*
The RFAC advises public or other bodies on the quality of any project or development likely to affect amenities of a national or public character.

British Tourist Authority *(Visit Britain)*

English Tourist Board *(Visit Britain)*

a separate corporate governmental strategy for delivery of services) is not considered in this case study. These very recent management changes, which may yet have to be finalised, are not considered in this case study. It is argued here that an organisation such as English Heritage is as far up the hierarchy of institutional management of the country's heritage as can be reached and analysed effectively, before other forces come into play that unduly influence any proper explorative study. This is the main reason for choosing English Heritage for the most detailed case study.

Background

English Heritage is the largest institution that manages according to the processes explored in Chapter 3. The next level up the scale is the Department for Culture, Media & Sport and, though as a civil service department it is non-political, its direction is overtly political, making it not useful for exploration here. Over 50 government departments can be identified as having some kind of 'heritage' management responsibility (Cabinet Office 1996), and these are spread across the range of government responsibility. There are 10 institutions that are equivalent to English Heritage under DCMS responsibility, sharing heritage responsibilities between them: they are listed in Figure 4.1. Since 1998 rationalisation has reduced this number to seven. As explained in Chapter 3, concerned with exploration of the transformation through management, organisations will be referred to as institutions or with the generic term 'agency', implying that they act as an organisation, in management terms, with a remit to produce an end product through action of a certain kind.

Strategic management and corporate planning analysis techniques show the management of English Heritage for what it is – system and process; what it does – transformation from concept to object; and how it does it – the strategic and operational planning process by scrutinising the institution's context for providing the ability to effect such transformation. The thesis addresses the arguments for institutional analysis noted in such recent publications as Cooper et al (1995); the English Heritage Annual Report 1995/6 (1997 a); personal communication from the then Head of Corporate Affairs (John Hinchliffe, pers. com.); Davies (1995); and the Department of National Heritage's own operations, including consultation documents as precursors to new, or alteration of, heritage legislation (1996 a, b & c; DNH & Welsh Office 1996) and 'systematic scrutiny' (DNH 1996 a, 52) which review both its own remit and undertaking a Financial Management and Policy Review (FMPR) for English Heritage.

English Heritage's environmental context is thus considered in the light of the historical development of management considered in the previous chapter. The organisation's establishment, relationship to government, corporate objectives, current environmental context, and organisation as an institution are explored in sequence. Thus English Heritage's current position as an agency effecting change from concept to object can be assessed.

Heritage Management Agencies

The scale of management that English Heritage falls into is determined by its means of establishment, remit and funding arrangements. The scale comprises institutions explicitly governed or established by statute law, which have a national remit, and are funded by central government. The variety of Government sponsored bodies with a remit for different aspects of 'heritage management' has been seen in Figure 4.1. These institutions produce different kinds of transformation into heritage 'objects', such as support for a craft activity, creation of an archive of information or art forms. The case studies here, however, consider the particular transformation of heritage in the historic environment (including archaeology) and allied to this displays of historic environment object collections in museums.

As will be seen from later case studies, whilst supporting and acting within these high-level aims, more immediate delivery of limited aims are undertaken as the scale of management institutions reduces. Each, however, adheres to the model of transformation from concept to object.

Some similar agencies that can be considered for comparison are briefly described below. This is in order to give some sense of the environment in which English Heritage is operating rather than for substantive comparative purposes, which are not undertaken in this study. Greater relevance is given to this where the corporate planning process is explored later in this chapter, and the wider environment in which English Heritage operates is examined.

The unique nature of transformation within English Heritage as a public organisation is outlined in the Chief Executive's statement (English Heritage 1997, 9). The ultimate aims of English Heritage are described as including, 'Managing and presenting our historic properties'; 'Surveying, identifying and protecting the heritage'; 'Advising the Government'; 'Supporting the heritage through grants and expenditure'; 'Seeking more revenue'; 'Educating about the heritage'; and 'Giving value for money'. These high-level aims fall within the remit and ultimate goal of the top level of management in the Department of National Heritage, which seeks to 'Safeguard existing creative achievements and promote understanding of the past... by providing protection to our historic environment and our cultural inheritance; issuing advice on best practice; and providing funding to sponsored bodies that achieve these aims.' (DNH 1996 a, v; Sharman 1997)

Corporate Objectives: transforming heritage into English Heritage

Though definition of corporate objectives would appear to be relatively straightforward, even when following Argenti's (1989) analysis of how to establish them, the situation of English Heritage, being a quasi-autonomous-non-governmental-organisation (quango), clouds further the already murky waters of analysing public service/non-profit-making organisations. English Heritage is not a central government agency or department: it is independent of it, though largely financed via the Department for Culture, Media and Sport's vote and grant-in-aid. Much discussion was held between 1981 and 1984, instigated by the government, about possible reorganisation 'in the operation of the legislation which covers ancient monuments and historic buildings in England.' (DoE 1981, 1) This initial consultation exercise was followed in 1982 with a summary of the findings to date, setting out '...ideas for changes in the way in which work and responsibilities for ancient monuments and historic buildings are organised.' (DoE 1982, 1) The document also discussed the various responsibilities such an organisation would have, establishing that Government no longer wished to carry out certain functions directly.

A study of the consultations before the establishment of English Heritage in 1984 makes clear that at no point were the corporate objectives for such an organisation considered. As Argenti points out there are 'three types of decision that any corporate body can take.' (1989, 56). These are: 'deciding the corporate objective – i.e. describing what is its purpose or raison d'être; defining its corporate conduct – i.e. describing how it proposes to behave while achieving its objective or purpose; determining its corporate strategies – i.e. resolving how it is going to achieve its objective while adhering to its code of conduct.' (*ibid.* 56)

In the preliminary stages of establishing this body, it is difficult to perceive exactly what the corporate objective was. This can probably be attributed to the nature of the machinery of government. Strategic management was only just beginning to establish itself during this period, and public administration, as already noted, was concerned with administration rather than management. The rather more obvious corporate objective for English Heritage that exists now was not articulated at this juncture because of such an 'administrative' outlook.

Administration was carried out as a result of duties placed on the government through a variety of Acts. The variety of these and their relevance to archaeology and the wider 'heritage' is not an issue for consideration here; other volumes such as Hunter and Ralston (1993) have coverage of the legislation. Carman (1996) covers the legal nature of defining ancient monuments through the Ancient Monuments and Archaeological Areas Act 1979, and the law's creation of value for defined objects; his study also looks closely at the 'contextual history' (*ibid.*) behind the creation of such legislation (HMG 1979). However, these texts do not consider the wider responsibilities of government as a result of these Acts, in the form of distinguishing between management and administration. The legal framework established for the heritage (most notably through Scheduled Ancient Monuments, Listed Buildings and Conservation Areas) are essentially administrative duties placed upon a responsible government department. They do not set the framework for management and defining corporate objectives in the strategic sense that is explored here.

It can be suggested that such legislation, in the form of administrative duty, defines the corporate conduct and certain corporate strategies (to use Argenti's terms) of organisations, but not the full purpose – the transformation from concept to object itself, for which an assessment of the wider environment (both social and political) must be incorporated. It can be argued that it is not the main duty of legislation to consider this wider environment: however, when heritage legislation is considered it is difficult to determine the exact ultimate purpose or corporate objective due to the intangible nature of the heritage, and its administration by a politically-driven central government machine. For the purposes of this study, concerned primarily with the events of the 1990s, this is most pertinent, especially following shifts in emphasis for cultural concern by a new Government after the 1997 General Election.

Within the National Heritage Act 1983 it is possible to begin to see the subtle shift to a strategic management framework rather than an administrative one (HMG 1983). This (inevitably) is due to the removal of the administrative functions for the heritage from central government (and its unclear objectives) (Hughes 1994) to a new organisation separate from it. The Act was not, however, written in the terms of strategic management, and focuses mostly, (in the relevant sections for English Heritage), on administrative functions placed on it, resulting from the previous corpus of administrative heritage law. The coupling of assumptions about law relating to the heritage, the language used within the National Heritage Act (HMG 1983) and the management ethos within the public sector at that time, mean that subsequent management development and analysis can, and possibly have, overlooked fundamentally important points written into English Heritage's establishment. That is not to say that either the government department responsible (in 1983 the Department of National Heritage, now the Department of Culture, Media and Sport), or English Heritage have in any way ignored what has been written in the National Heritage Act: what has been overlooked is in strategic management terms, suggesting that in fact the Act is an underrated source of information (both within government and English Heritage) as it contains hidden corporate objectives for English Heritage. The establishing Act operates as an enabling procedure (as referred to in Chapter 2), upon which subsequent strategic management development could be based.

It is the most recent changes at the political level, through the creation in 1992 of the Department of National Heritage, economic constraints placed on that Department and its sponsored bodies (including English Heritage) since then, and increasing scrutiny by the likes of the National Audit Office (NAO 1992), the National Heritage Select Committee (HMG 1994 & 1996 a) and the Cabinet Office Efficiency Unit (Cabinet Office 1996 b), that have caused strategic management to be embraced, and prompted the establishing Act to be re-examined here as illustrative of the primary framework for an institutional transformation of heritage into heritage management.

Argenti lists three essential 'elements of the corporate purpose' (1989, 60). These elements are presented in Figure 4.2. Reinterpretation of the complex linguistic format of the National Heritage Act 1983 allows all of these elements to be identified in the 'duty' (HMG 1983, 19) placed on the organisation. In strategic management terms this allows the Act to be given renewed importance, which until now have been overshadowed by the political corporate objectives imposed from the sponsoring body above. The Act allows English Heritage to constantly affirm a non-political stance through its legislative establishment already outlining its corporate objectives and establishing its unique nature as a public institution. This is no doubt useful when considering the motivation behind many of the heritage debates of the 1990s in the public forum (Conservative Research Department 1996; Liberal Democrats 1996; Wright 1993 and Lowenthal 1996), and often politically or emotionally charged.

Figure 4.2 *The three essential elements of the corporate purpose. (from Argenti 1989, 60, Fig. 3.4)*

– The intended beneficiaries: i.e. the people for whom the organisation exists.
– The intended benefit: i.e. what the organisation is to do for them.
– The corporate performance: i.e. what level of benefit is satisfactory.

English Heritage's corporate objectives are established in Section 32 and 33 of the Act (sub-section (1)), 'Establishment of Commission' and 'The Commission's general functions' (*ibid.* 19). Carman's (1996) emphasis on linguistic format becomes important here: the word 'function' and 'duty' implies actions that must be carried out, i.e. administration. Sub-sections (2), (3) and (4) referred to at the end of sub-section (1), and which are also presented below, would seem therefore to blur the distinctions between the aims and processes of management, and this is how strategic management could come to overlook this piece of legislation. The relevant sections of the Act are presented below (Figure 4.3).

Sub-section (8) establishes that the Commission is not limited in the definition of heritage objects or sites in the same way that the Secretary of State is through the criteria of his duties in the Ancient Monuments and Archaeological Areas Act 1979 for scheduling sites, or the Historic Buildings and Ancient Monuments Act 1953 for listing buildings; nor the criteria established by the Secretary of State for exercising those functions (DoE 1990 a, Annex 4). Distinction from government and direct political influence by the relevant Secretary of State is therefore reinforced.

If we overcome the difficulty in the wording, and use of 'function' and 'duty', it can be seen that the three essential elements of establishing a corporate objective have been covered. The heritage has become objectified (ancient monument, historic building, conservation area), as has the organisation responsible for it (English Heritage). The 'intended beneficiaries' (Argenti 1989, 60) are the 'public' 'in England' as identified in subsection (1)(c) of the Act

Figure 4.3 *National Heritage Act 1983: section establishing English Heritage as an institution. (HMG 1982, 19 & 20)*

'33.-(1) It shall be the duty of the Commission (so far as is practicable)-
(a) to secure the preservation of ancient monuments and historic buildings situated in England,
(b) to promote the preservation and enhancement of the character and appearance of conservation areas situated in England, and
(c) to promote the public's enjoyment of, and advance their knowledge of ancient monuments and historic buildings situated in England and their preservation, in exercising the functions conferred on them by virtue of sub-sections (2) to (4) and section 34; but in the event of a conflict between those functions and that duty those functions shall prevail.' (*ibid.*)

'(2) The Commission-
(a) shall (so far as is practicable) provide educational facilities and services, instruction and information to the public in relation to ancient monuments and historic buildings, with particular reference to those in England, and in relation to conservation areas situated in England;
(b) may give advice to any person in relation to ancient monuments, historic buildings and conservation areas situated in England, whether or not they have been consulted;
(c) may, for the purpose of exercising their functions, carry out, or defray or contribute towards the cost of, research in relation to ancient monuments, historic buildings and conservation areas situated in England;
(d) may, for the purpose of exercising their functions, make and maintain records in relation to ancient monuments and historic buildings situated in England.

(3) Schedule 4 shall have effect to amend the enactment there mentioned-
(a) for the purpose of conferring functions on the Commission in relation to England (including functions of making grants in relation to historic buildings and conservation areas, acquiring historic buildings, acquiring or becoming guardian of ancient monuments, providing information and other services to the public in connection with affording them access to ancient monuments, and undertaking archaeological investigation and publishing the results), and
(b) for connected purposes (which include allowing the Secretary of State to approve lists of historic buildings compiled by the Commission, and imposing requirements for him to consult with the Commission before he includes a monument in the schedule of monuments or grants scheduled monument consent or designates an area of archaeological importance).

(4) Without prejudice to the generality of subsection (2)(b), the Commission may advise the Secretary of State with regard to the exercise of functions exercisable by him in relation to England under the Historic Buildings and Ancient Monuments Act 1953 and the Ancient Monuments and Archaeological Areas Act 1979, whether or not they have been consulted.' (*ibid.*)

'(8) In subsections (1) and (2)-
'ancient monument' means any structure, work, site, garden or area which in the Commission's opinion is of historic, architectural, traditional, artistic or archaeological interest;
'conservation area' means an area designated as a conservation area under section 277 of the Town and Country Planning Act 1971;
'historic building' means any building which in the Commission's opinion is of historic or architectural interest.' (*ibid.* 21)

Figure 4.4 *English Heritage and Department of National Heritage Funding Agreement 1996/97. (English Heritage 1996 a, 31)*

SECTION E: 1996/97 FUNDING AGREEMENT

ENGLISH HERITAGE FUNDING AGREEMENT 1996/97

1. This Funding Agreement between the Department of National Heritage (DNH) and English Heritage is set in the context of DNH's overall aims and the specific aims of DNH's Heritage Division. It sets out how English Heritage's objectives and performance contribute to these wider departmental aims. The Agreement, which has been drawn up following discussions between DNH and English Heritage , represents the agreed basis for the preparation of English Heritage's Business Plan for 1996/97 and Four Year Plan for 1996-2000.

GRANT-IN-AID

DNH has agreed to make available to English Heritage £104.992m during 1996/97 from resources voted for the purpose by Parliament. For planning purposes only, grant-in-aid of £101.092m for 1997/98 and £101.092m for 1998-99 have been indicated to EH. Grant-in-aid is paid monthly in line with the provisions set out in EH's Financial Memorandum.

English Heritage's grant-in-aid for 1996/97 includes ring-fenced provisions of £2m for the Albert Memorial and £400,000 for the Architectural Heritage Fund. English Heritage will ensure that the targeted level of expenditure is met.

DNH's AIMS

The overall objective of DNH's financial provision for English Heritage is to contribute to DNH's aims for the built heritage. DNH's overall aims are:

- to encourage high quality and diversity in current creative activities;

- to safeguard existing creative achievements and promote understanding of the past;

- to extend opportunities to enjoy and appreciate rewarding leisure activities;

- to promote the contribution all DNH's sectors make to national prosperity and prestige;

- to carry out these activities with proper stewardship of the resources available.

DNH's heritage aims are:

- so far as practicable, to secure the preservation and protection of the heritage, maximise the private sector contribution; and secure economic benefits where compatible with long-term conservation

- to promote access to and enjoyment of historic buildings and places;

- to ensure the effective direction and performance of heritage sponsored bodies.

ENGLISH HERITAGE AIMS AND OUTPUTS

English Heritage contributes to DNH's aims and has set the strategic objectives which are listed below (in bold) along with outputs which English Heritage has agreed to deliver. These are supported by various other targets and measures in the Business and Four Year Plans.

1. **Secure the heritage through the targeted and creative funding of repair and restoration**

By: giving conservation grants and undertaking building rescue projects;

a. Increase the number of conservation area partnerships with local authorities from 127 to 200 by March 1997 (from 1995/96 bidding round).

2. **Secure the heritage through the innovative management of English Heritage's properties**

By: bringing EH's historic properties and their contents into a good state of repair and maintaining them in good condition thereafter.

a. Clear more than one fifth of the remaining backlog repair programme (to be completed by 2001).

b. Enter into a further 30 local management agreements.

3. **Secure the heritage through influence and strategic advice**

By: identifying the buildings and monuments which merit statutory protection and providing advice on their management and conservation to Government, local authorities, owners and Lottery distributors, including the exercise of statutory controls.

a. Continue revision of the ancient monument schedules and make 1,800 new or revised recommendations, subject to agreeing with DNH a simplification of the current procedures.

b. Reach agreement with RCHME on the respective roles of EH and RCHME in survey work and finalise with DNH and RCHME arrangements for the management and operation of the computerised heritage database.

Figure 4.4 *English Heritage and Department of National Heritage Funding Agreement 1996/97. (English Heritage 1996 a, 31)* *(Continued)*

4. Increase understanding, enjoyment and pride in the heritage

By: developing the presentation and interpretation of EH's historic properties, promoting their use in education and mounting special events and concerts to enhance the enjoyment of visitors.

a. Achieve an average visitor satisfaction rating above the 1995/96 level of 8.7.

b. Increase visitor numbers to staffed sites from 5.3 million to 5.4 million.

5. Be the national focus in advancing knowledge, standards and skills in archaeology and building conservation

By: commissioning and undertaking projects to advance the understanding of England's archaeological and architectural heritage and the means of securing its preservation, and by sharing this knowledge with others.

a. Complete data-gathering for the Monuments at Risk project, for publication in 1997.

6. Increase English Heritage's influence and win support

By: increasing the awareness and influence of EH, promoting the heritage and providing membership services.

a. Increase membership by 6% (from 330k to 350k).

7. Maximise funding for the heritage

By: improving productivity, increasing earned income and diversifying sources of funding, including sponsorship and Lottery funding.

a. Ensure that any increases in payroll and running costs are offset by efficiency savings, other economies or are self-financing.

b. Increase earned income from £17.6 million to £19.0 million.

c. Secure agreement with the NHMF on the respective grant funding roles of EH and the Heritage Lottery Fund, with due regard to the requirements of additionality.

8. Deliver a professional, flexible and customer-friendly service

By: investing in the development of staff in order to achieve quality standards.

a. Turn round 75% of applications for church and secular historic building grants within 6 months.

b. Turn round 75% of scheduled monument consent applications within 3 months.

c. Turn round 70% of listed building consent notifications within 28 calendar days.

PERFORMANCE MEASUREMENT AND MONITORING

English Heritage's performance will be assessed against the outputs detailed above across the full period of this Agreement. Performance against these measures will be taken into account when looking at the Funding Agreement for next year. English Heritage has agreed to provide DNH with quarterly returns outlining their performance against the outputs set out in this Agreement and indicating the projected outturn for the whole year. Officials from DNH and English Heritage will meet each quarter to discuss performance against the targets set out in this Agreement. If at any time during the period of this Agreement it becomes apparent to either party that there are significant problems in adhering to its terms, there should be immediate discussion between EH and DNH on possible ways forward.

Conservation work at Brodsworth Hall

(HMG 1983). The 'intended benefit' (*ibid.*) is to 'secure' and 'promote the preservation and enhancement' of ancient monuments, historic buildings and conservation areas, and to 'promote the public's enjoyment, and advance their knowledge of' them, as identified in subsection (1)(b) and (c). The 'corporate performance' (*ibid.*) is implicit within subsection (1) through measurement, determined ultimately by the Commission directly and its beneficiaries indirectly.

The organisation therefore finds itself at an advantage as, due to its position, it can operate through non-political action (determined by the various Acts that it must operate within), and yet has the ability to act politically through lobbying and advice to the Secretary of State. The law, with regard to English Heritage, therefore acts as both an enabling and constraining activity. Arguments both for and against 'quangos' as frequently seen in political texts are however also given plenty of room for manoeuvre.

Corporate Objectives: checks and balances

A new initiative originally begun by the DNH is revising the way in which the strategic planning process is carried out in government-sponsored bodies. Due to the Department's large number of sponsored bodies (quangos, agencies and advisory boards, numbering approximately 50) (DCMS 1998), systematic scrutiny has become paramount due to the wider economic pressures placed on all the Departments, in terms of the three 'Es'. As the Department's annual report states, it 'is responsible for the stewardship of around £1 billion of public money. It is conscious of the need to ensure that the money is spent wisely and that all sponsored bodies are fully accountable.' (DNH 1996 a, 52) The four ways in which bodies are subject to such scrutiny are: fundamental expenditure review; funding agreements; financial management and policy reviews; and economic appraisal. One particular process is of greatest relevance to the planning procedures employed by English Heritage. This is the 'Funding Agreement' made between the DCMS and English Heritage.

Where the Department funds bodies directly, it has introduced 'Funding Agreements' between it and each of its sponsored bodies. 'The aim is to make transparent the key elements of the work that the bodies are funded to do and the outputs that will be used to measure that work. In this way it is hoped to focus on the progress being made in encouraging the participation and development of audiences, enabling innovation to blossom and excellence to prevail, and in ensuring that Departmental funding enhances competitiveness and performance of the national economy' (DNH 1996 a, 52).

> 'The Department has no wish to interfere with individual funding decisions. They will continue to be for the bodies themselves. But Funding Agreements will focus on the important work that the Department is enabling to take place and the benefits that work is delivering. Funding

Agreements will help get the most from the Department's money and improve accountability to the taxpayer whose money is being spent.' (*ibid.*)

At this point of analysis it is not proposed to comment on the implications, (political or otherwise), in the motivations behind the establishment of funding agreements. These funding agreements are considered here to be administrative tools for assessment of aims, establishing further accountability, and give overall cohesiveness or parity between the aims of the Department for Culture, Media & Sport and its sponsored bodies.

English Heritage established a Funding Agreement with the DNH for the first time in 1996, and for reference purposes it has been reproduced in Figure 4.4 from the 1996 Corporate Plan. The Corporate Objectives that can be identified from 'English Heritage Aims & Outputs' (Figure 4.4) in the style of Argenti's explanations already outlined before, have been essentially distilled to a minimum, with three new objectives (called 'aims' in the Plan) that do not appear in the list identified in the National Heritage Act (HMG 1983). Those original aims have therefore also, in comparison, been subtly altered. The corporate aims that can be identified from the 1996/7 Corporate Plan comprise: 'Secure the heritage'; 'Increase understanding, enjoyment and pride in the heritage'; 'Be the national focus in advancing knowledge, standards and skills in archaeology and building conservation'; 'Increase English Heritage's influence and win support' and 'Maximise funding for the heritage' (Figure 4.4).

Thus it can be seen that for some reason, the statutory corporate objectives, as laid out in the National Heritage Act (HMG 1983), have been altered and expanded. As will be seen from the more central strategic analysis covered below, what were originally corporate strategies have been 'promoted' to corporate objectives, in the light of the organisation's analysis of itself and its 'environment' (which will be further explained below) through the strategic planning process. At this high level of corporate objectives, aims and raison d'être for the organisation, a simple explanation for the change can be proposed: in 1996/97, the establishment of a Funding Agreement between English Heritage and the Department of National Heritage, (and increase in the cohesiveness between the respective aims

Figure 4.5 *The Department of National Heritage's Aims. (from DNH 1996 a, v)*

OUR AIM IS TO ENRICH PEOPLE'S LIVES
To meet this aim we will seek to:
- Encourage high quality and diversity in current creative activities
- Safeguard existing creative achievements and promote understanding of the past
- Extend opportunities to enjoy an appreciate rewarding leisure activities
- Promote the contribution all our sectors make to national prosperity and prestige
- Carry out these activities with proper stewardship of the resources available

of the DNH and English Heritage), caused a change in the outcome of the planning process within English Heritage, formalised in its Corporate Plan. For terms of reference, the Department of National Heritage's aims and objectives are presented below in Figure 4.5. These have been unchanged since the reformation of the DNH as the DCMS.

Figure 4.6 *English Heritage Corporate Plan 1989-93 Central Statement. (from English Heritage 1989 a, 3)*

1.1 The role of English Heritage is to bring about the long term conservation and widespread understanding and enjoyment of the historic environment for the benefit of present and future generations using expert advice, education, example, persuasion, intervention and financial support.

1.2 In pursuit of this, our aims are:
- to work with the public, private and voluntary sectors to increase resources for and commitment to conserving the historic environment
- to ensure the flexible and responsible use of resources, taking account of long-term conservation priorities
- to secure the best possible protection, care and use of the historic environment, and to ensure recording in cases of unavoidable loss
- to establish high standards based on our own research and practical experience, and that of others, and to uphold those standards in our judgements and in the example we give
- to give independent, authoritative information, advice and assistance reflecting the standards we have set
- to help people to enjoy and understand the historic environment, and to see the need to protect it
- to be open, responsive and fair in all our dealing
- to attract and keep the best staff for the job and provide appropriate training and development to promote their effectiveness and job satisfaction
- to manage our resources effectively, efficiently and economically

---

The first formally published Corporate Plan for the organisation (English Heritage 1989 a), covering the period 1989-93, whose introductory part of the Central Statement is reproduced in Figure 4.6, can be considered to be radically different from the corporate aims identified most recently by the organisation. This is, however, in words and format, rather than in spirit. The nature of the organisation as a public body, funded by government and established by statute (the National Heritage Act 1983) codifies the organisation's spirit as its corporate objectives. It is the process of management, and the effects of the shift to greater strategic management with its ethos of having an eye on the future, freeing an organisation to 'control its destiny by looking ahead' (Longman 1991, 2), that has changed the presentation of the organisation's corporate objectives, resulting in greater clarity and therefore the ability to achieve defining itself and reaffirming its abilities. Further comments about the implications of the establishment of funding agreements by a sponsoring department for an organisation such as English Heritage, and the assessment of corporate strategy, will be made later.

In the three-year period 1990-94 to 1992-96, the objectives, aims and strategies are mixed, and though labelled as 'The Role, Corporate Aims and Objectives of English Heritage' (reproduced in Figure 4.7, and identical for each of the

three years 1990-94, 1991-95 and 1992-96), in the terms of corporate management as outlined by Argenti (1989) such a table does not suffice for the identification of the corporate objectives. Argenti argues that there should be only be a few corporate strategies; 'if [the organisation's] aims are not clear, attractive, challenging, simple and dynamic then they wilt.' (*ibid.* 99) The organisation thus has a clear need to define itself and its own established position. The seeds of change in identification of the corporate objectives seen in the 1993-97 Corporate Plan coincided with, as can be seen from Figure 4.8 section 1, a fundamental review of the strategies employed by English Heritage to achieve its corporate objectives. However, the section labelled, 'Corporate Objectives 1993-97' (English Heritage 1993 a, 5) mixes strategies (i.e. means of achieving the objectives) with objectives.

The Corporate Plans for 1994-98 and 1995-99 show much clearer demarcation of the objectives, stated in the 'Central Statement' (English Heritage 1994, 2; 1995, 4): 1994-98 can be seen to be transitional from previous plans whilst 1995-99 sees the clearest demarcation, with role, aims and means identified. The Figures 4.7 – 4.10 below, directly reproduced from the relevant Corporate Plans, show the changes seen from 1990 to 1995. Objectives and strategies are mixed in the box labelled as 'Corporate Aims' for the 1993 and 1994 plans, and objectives are distinguished as 'principal aims' for the 1995 plan. If comparison is made to two years' Corporate Plans for 1994-98 and 1995-99, obvious developments are seen in the corporate objectives, and the start of the changes which result in the 1996-2000 Corporate Plan are seen.

The corporate plans of English Heritage and other organisations are meant for management purposes rather than public dissemination. Information about the organisation, its aims, results and work are presented in the more accessible format of the Annual Report and Accounts. Using Argenti's philosophy behind determining corporate objectives, such documents are not, however, particularly useful for analysis. He sees them as part of a marketing process, which must be distinguished from the corporate and strategic planning process, with its own philosophy. This contrasts with Blockley's assessment of management in archaeology, where terms of marketing and strategic planning are confused (1996). Marketing is fundamentally about selling the products or services that the organisation produces: it therefore must be a specific undertaking within the overall management and setting of strategy for an organisation. Therefore, the identification of mission statements within such documents as the Annual Report must be treated with care. There is concurrence here with Argenti's argument that, 'mission statements are nothing to do with corporate planning, they are PR statements... Mission statements should neither be outputs of the corporate planning process, nor the inputs; they should be seen for what they are: Public Relations.' (1989, 67)

Identification and use of explicit mission statements, and development of implicit information about the organisation in them, is a recent phenomenon of marketing. They are highlighted here for the purposes of identifying where

Figure 4.7 *English Heritage Corporate Objectives: 1990, 1991 & 1992. (English Heritage 1990 a)*

The Role, Corporate Aims and Objectives
of English Heritage

The role of English Heritage is to bring about the long term conservation and widespread understanding and enjoyment of the historic environment for the benefit of present and future generations using expert advice, education, example, persuasion, intervention and financial support.

In pursuit of this, our *aims* are:

1. to work with the public, private and voluntary sectors to increase resources for and commitment to conserving the historic environment;

2. to ensure the flexible and responsible use of resources, taking account of long-term conservation priorities;

3. to secure the best possible protection, care and use of the historic environment, and to ensure recording in cases of unavoidable loss;

4. to establish high standards based on our own research and practical experience, and that of others, and to uphold those standards in our judgements and in the example we give;

5. to give independent, authoritative information, advice and assistance reflecting the standards we have set;

6. to help people to enjoy and understand the historic environment, and to see the need to protect it;

7. to be open, responsive and fair in all our dealings;

8. to attract and keep the best staff for the job and provide appropriate training and development to promote their effectiveness and job satisfaction.

9. to manage our resources effectively, efficiently and economically.

The *key corporate objectives* for English Heritage for the Corporate Plan period, unchanged from the last plan, are:

1. To carry out work to improve our knowledge and understanding of the state of the historic environment in England in order to be able to assess more precisely the need for action.

2. To decide on and implement changes relating to the structure of the organisation to improve its overall effectiveness and efficiency.

3. To have produced a Properties in Care estate which is well repaired, efficiently managed and continues to earn an increasing percentage of total costs and which makes maximum use of external resources.

4. To improve general understanding of the role we are playing in protecting the historic environment, particularly by informing people better what our aims and objectives are and what significant steps we take towards achieving them.

Group objectives are given in the body of the plan:

Conservation group on page 14

Properties in Care group on page 19

Central Services group on page 33.

Figure 4.8 *English Heritage Corporate Objectives 1993-97. (English Heritage 1993 a)*

Corporate Objectives 1993-97

1   To make the most important parts of the heritage more accessible and more enjoyable.

2   To identify the most important historic structures and sites which are at risk and, using the help and efforts of others along with our own resources, to ensure that action is taken to safeguard their future in good time.

3   To attract maximum funding from all sources for conserving the historic environment:

a. To increase our efforts to gain extra resources for conservation by encouraging legacies, gifts and sponsorship for identified regional or specialised buildings or sites.

b. To propose allocations from the National Lottery and Millennium Fund for conservation of the heritage.

c. To explore with major private foundations and others the setting up of a Conservation Fund which would harness private resources to enable English Heritage to take emergency action to save outstanding properties where other Agencies are unable to intervene.

d. To seek other ways of strengthening the capacity of the private sector to deal with local problems for which local solutions are right.

4   To intervene directly in exceptional cases and emergencies, acting quickly and decisively to resolve particular problems where no-one else is able or willing to do so.

5   To give greater priority to our education and publishing programmes in order to further the understanding of the importance of the heritage by opinion formers, specialists and the general public.

6   To advise Government on legislative changes to provide a stronger protection for the historic environment and to encourage local authorities to use fully the powers that exist.

7   To continue to improve our efficiency and standards of service to the public and other users of our services.

8   To recruit, train and manage expert, qualified staff to deliver our promised service.

Figure 4.9 *English Heritage Corporate Objectives 1994-1998. (English Heritage 1994)*

CORPORATE AIMS 1994–98

1. To make England's heritage more accessible, enabling people, now and in the future to appreciate and enjoy the extent and variety of our historic surroundings

2. To identify and seek to conserve the historic structures, sites and areas which embody our heritage and, where these are at risk, to ensure that action is taken to safeguard their future

3. To secure maximum funding for conserving the historic environment

● by increasing the profit from our income-generating activities

● by encouraging sponsorship, legacies, gifts and other private contributions

● by identifying and promoting heritage conservation projects suitable for funding from the National Lottery and Millennium Fund and other national and European sources

● by seeking other ways of enabling the private sector and local government to deal with problems for which local solutions are right

4. To provide authoritative advice, set standards and undertake research on key issues through the retention, development and flexible use of our own professional skills and to use these skills to intervene directly, quickly and decisively to resolve particular problems where no-one else is able or willing to do so

5. To increase awareness of our heritage and the need to preserve it, using our education and publishing programmes to increase commitment to our cause

6. To provide a stronger protection for the historic environment by monitoring the effects of current law and advising Government on desirable legislative changes

7. To continue to improve our efficiency and standards of service to the public and other users of our services

Figure 4.10 *English Heritage Corporate Objectives 1995-1999. (English Heritage 1995)*

PART ONE : CENTRAL STATEMENT

1. INTRODUCTION

1.1 English Heritage is the national body created by Parliament in 1984 charged with the protection of the historic environment and with promoting public understanding and enjoyment of it. We are the Government's official adviser on all matters concerning heritage conservation, provide substantial funding for archaeology, conservation areas and the repair of historic buildings, and are responsible for some 400 historic properties in the nation's care.

1.2 English Heritage's principal aims are :

● To secure the conservation of England's historic sites, monuments, buildings and areas

● To promote people's access to, and enjoyment of this shared heritage

● To raise the understanding and awareness of the heritage and thereby increase commitment to its protection

1.3 We also seek to make our pursuit of these aims more effective by :

● securing maximum funding for the historic environment

● improving the efficiency of our operations

● giving the best possible service to those with whom we deal

1.4 The principal means by which we will pursue these aims are :

● by advising Government, owners, local authorities, and others

● by identifying sites, buildings and areas meriting special protection

● by giving grants for repair and conservation projects

● by undertaking major conservation projects ourselves

● by presenting the historic properties in our care to the public in a manner which will enhance their enjoyment and understanding of this country's past

● by organising special events, exhibitions, educational and publishing initiatives which will raise awareness of our heritage

● by commissioning and undertaking archaeological and other research projects to increase our understanding of the heritage and develop technical solutions to key conservation problems

● by maintaining and developing our own expertise in order to take the leading role in all aspects of heritage conservation and management

● by setting standards and using our skills to provide training for others

● by consulting widely on our plans and policies and communicating our work effectively to the public at large

1.5 English Heritage's Role

We will seek to acquire, retain and develop the expertise required to take the national leading role in the conservation and presentation of our heritage. We also aim to act as a catalyst in recruiting the skills, enthusiasm and resources of others to our cause. We are increasingly an expert purchaser, rather than a provider of services - payroll costs currently represent only 22% of our expenditure. Much of what we achieve we achieve through, and in partnership with local authorities, private and public owners, the voluntary sector and fellow professionals in other organisations.

possible discrepancies in management analysis may occur. The most recent developments in marketing technique are more obvious, as the activities of the organisation are tailored to its identified customers; for example a catchphrase used by the chairman of English Heritage, subsequently adopted on the cover of the 1995/96 Annual Report, 'England's heritage is yours. Enjoy It.' Other mission statements may often prove more of a confusion with corporate objectives and such an example is seen in the English Heritage Annual Report and Accounts for 1992/3, reproduced in Figure 4.11. In the 1988/89 Report and Accounts, use is made of the Central Statement, already considered in Figure 4.6; this is reproduced in Figure 4.12. Other marketing activities, considered as a strategy to achieve corporate objectives, will be further considered in the strategic analysis later in this case study, and elsewhere in the thesis.

Comparative heritage agencies and corporate objectives

Though there are certain differences in corporate objectives for other heritage agencies at the equivalent scale of English

Figure 4.12 *English Heritage Mission Statement 1992, (English Heritage 1993 c)*

OUR MISSION The magnitude and importance of England's historical and architectural heritage are exceptional. Our built heritage is one of the nation's greatest assets and its protection and promotion generate significant economic, social and cultural benefits.

As the centre of expertise in all aspects of conservation and as the major single source of funding, English Heritage seeks to be involved whenever England's heritage is at risk. However, at a time when resources are scarce, our primary aim is to ensure that our funds and expertise are concentrated where there is greatest need.

In determining priorities we alone do not set the agenda. We consult extensively with Government, private owners, local authorities, developers and amenity groups and we attempt, at all times, to communicate efficiently and helpfully with the public to whom the heritage belongs.

We are extremely proud of England's built heritage and we believe that its conservation is a national priority.

Figure 4.11 *English Heritage Mission Statement 1988. (English Heritage 1989 b)*

PART ONE : CENTRAL STATEMENT

1. INTRODUCTION

1.1 **English Heritage** is the national body created by Parliament in 1984 charged with the protection of the historic environment and with promoting public understanding and enjoyment of it. We are the Government's official adviser on all matters concerning heritage conservation, provide substantial funding for archaeology, conservation areas and the repair of historic buildings, and are responsible for some 400 historic properties in the nation's care.

1.2 **English Heritage's principal aims are :**

● To secure the conservation of England's historic sites, monuments, buildings and areas

● To promote people's access to, and enjoyment of this shared heritage

● To raise the understanding and awareness of the heritage and thereby increase commitment to its protection

1.3 **We also seek to make our pursuit of these aims more effective by :**

● securing maximum funding for the historic environment

● improving the efficiency of our operations

● giving the best possible service to those with whom we deal

1.4 **The principal means by which we will pursue these aims are :**

● by advising Government, owners, local authorities, and others

● by identifying sites, buildings and areas meriting special protection

● by giving grants for repair and conservation projects

● by undertaking major conservation projects ourselves

● by presenting the historic properties in our care to the public in a manner which will enhance their enjoyment and understanding of this country's past

● by organising special events, exhibitions, educational and publishing initiatives which will raise awareness of our heritage

● by commissioning and undertaking archaeological and other research projects to increase our understanding of the heritage and develop technical solutions to key conservation problems

● by maintaining and developing our own expertise in order to take the leading role in all aspects of heritage conservation and management

● by setting standards and using our skills to provide training for others

● by consulting widely on our plans and policies and communicating our work effectively to the public at large

1.5 **English Heritage's Role**

We will seek to acquire, retain and develop the expertise required to take the national leading role in the conservation and presentation of our heritage. We also aim to act as a catalyst in recruiting the skills, enthusiasm and resources of others to our cause. We are increasingly an expert purchaser, rather than a provider of services - payroll costs currently represent only 22% of our expenditure. Much of what we achieve we achieve through, and in partnership with, local authorities, private and public owners, the voluntary sector and fellow professionals in other organisations.

Heritage, comparison can be made between the agencies' procedures of establishment. The greatest similarities in organisational terms are seen between English Heritage and Historic Scotland and Cadw: Welsh Historic Monuments, who act as the equivalent national heritage services (acting for the government) in the respective areas of the United Kingdom. Both of these institutions have been established through the government's 'Next Steps' reforms of the Civil Service as Executive Agencies, with full executive powers of government. English Heritage does not have the same powers and duties that Cadw and Historic Scotland have (Historic Scotland 1996, 5), and it therefore acts as the government's 'principal advisor' in England. The actual executive functions of scheduling or listing sites within England therefore remain with the Secretary of State for Culture, Media and Sport.

Implications of different establishment procedures

Whilst all government agencies and organisations concerned with heritage have adopted the preparation of annual corporate plans and reports, there are certain implications in strategic management terms for the differences in establishment of those agencies. Though at a smaller scale in size and economic terms, brief consideration of the Framework Document such as that for Historic Scotland, whose outline is seen in Figure 4.13, suggests that it may give a greater clarity and focus on the managerial style that the organisation must adopt. Whether an organisation is under direct government control or not, the preparation of a Framework Document may provide greater clarity than reference back to an Act of Parliament, though both Act and Document are equivalent in management and

Figure 4.13 *Historic Scotland Framework Document. (Historic Scotland 1994)*

HISTORIC SCOTLAND

1 STATUS AND ROLE OF THE AGENCY

1.1   Historic Scotland is an Executive Agency within The Scottish Office Environment Department (SOEnv). The Secretary of State for Scotland is the responsible Minister, supported by the Minister for Agriculture and the Environment.

1.2   This document sets out the framework for the operation of the Agency from 1 September 1994.

MISSION

1.3   Historic Scotland will discharge the Secretary of State for Scotland's functions in relation to the built heritage - that is, ancient monuments and archaeological sites and landscapes; historic buildings, parks and gardens; and designed landscapes. **Its mission is to safeguard the nation's built heritage and to promote its understanding and enjoyment.**

OBJECTIVES

1.4   In support of this mission, Historic Scotland will pursue the following objectives:-

A. To Protect Scotland's Built Heritage

1   To give statutory protection to monuments of national importance (by scheduling) and to historic buildings of special architectural or historic interest (by listing), and to protect them through the statutory consent systems.

2   To give financial support and advice to others to repair, manage, protect and conserve outstanding ancient monuments and historic buildings.

3   To protect the 330 monuments which are in Historic Scotland's care, together with the Palace of Holyroodhouse and the Royal Parks, and ensure their sound conservation and maintenance.

4   To ensure that archaeological excavations are carried out at sites threatened by development or natural forces.

5   To research issues and develop skills relating to the built heritage, and to raise the standards of conservation practice among owners and trade and professional groups.

B   To Present Scotland's Built Heritage to the Public

1   To encourage visitors to properties in Historic Scotland's care and ensure that they enjoy and benefit from their visits.

2   To encourage knowledge about Scotland's built heritage.

C   To Manage Historic Scotland

1   To maintain an effective and efficient organisation.

2   To continue to increase income.

establishment terms. The recent establishment of funding agreements between a sponsoring government department and its agencies or bodies benefit from having 'stand-alone' framework documents to which to refer. They provide exactly what the title suggests, the *framework* in which the agency can operate, as is seen in the case of Historic Scotland. English Heritage's corporate objectives have most recently become more thematic as it incorporated and aligned its aims with those of the DCMS, through the funding agreement reproduced in Figure 4.4, and such an exercise may prove a further useful strategic management tool for the organisation.

Strategy: delivery of English Heritage corporate objectives

Having established how English Heritage exists as an institution and within an environment of other public service heritage institutions, I will turn to the second of Johnson & Scholes (1989) three levels of strategy exploration, that of competitive or business strategy. I will analyse the objectification of heritage through English Heritage's actions as an agency of management.

It has been established that an organisation, 'can be considered as a group of individuals with a common purpose,' and that, 'these individuals, in both profit and non-profit-making organisations pursue a number of objectives independently but each has a common objective, survival' (Proctor 1982, 51). The corporate objective that is established does not rely on the Act, but the strategic objectives that drive the organisation do rely on the Act, because of their practical nature. The analysis of the second strategic stage therefore establishes how the organisation will go about delivering the corporate aims, assessing the organisation in terms of capabilities and the environment in which it operates in the present and forecasting the future within the Act's framework. This process of analysis is essentially concerned with the self-assessment of an organisation and its management; it then leads on to the third strategic level, operational strategies. This final level with a number of sub-stages, concerns itself with devolving responsibilities for achieving the corporate aims through individual's work, literally at the stage of 'what to do on Monday morning' (Barrow et al. 1993, 25) at the bottom of the pyramid of goals: delivery of the organisation's end products through action plans prompting action. This third level can be seen in operation at Brodsworth Hall in Chapter 7.

The human element and the culture of organisations

Johnson and Scholes's strategic analysis provides the areas that will be covered in the following sections of this case study (Johnson & Scholes 1989). This begins with recognition noted within the school of strategic management thought, that 'strategy formulation is a cultural process' (*ibid.* 37). In the previous chapter I outlined how the human element was left out in the first studies of the business environment, and has since been seen in certain

Figure 4.14 *The Cultural Recipe (Johnson & Scholes 1989, Fig. 2.4)*

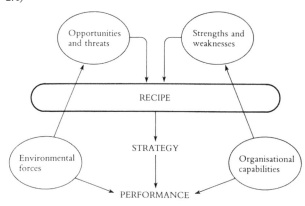

cases as a difficulty to be overcome in the creation of a perfect system of production. Johnson and Scholes further argue that, 'traditionally, strategy has been viewed as the response of an organisation to its environment', and that early strategy formulation omitted the 'major influence... of social processes' (*ibid.* 37). They identify this as the 'organisational culture' (*ibid.*), and suggest it comprises the ingredients for the organisational 'recipe', professional expectations and change (*ibid.* 40) (Figure 4.14).

Within English Heritage, the recipe or cultural context is an interesting case in itself for study outside the scope of this thesis. This results from the organisation's establishment originally as a central government department, part of the civil service, moving on to the creation of English Heritage with the status of not being part of the civil service, but retaining similar form and identified as a professional specialist advisor. Subsequent to this, though still essentially being a fundamental part of the public service, English Heritage has reconfigured itself to address its environmental position. Thus the recipe, as for many other public service organisations, has been in a state of flux, but is a key to the organisation with its professional status and need for a particular skill and knowledge base, with the variables altering as a result of internal and external pressure.

Tension exists within professional training where expectation has to be set against application of that professionalism within the acceptable corporate model for the organisation. This tension is recognised and to some extent is normalised through the corporate process, where the likeliness of expectations economic, social and political realities have to be assessed.

Between 1992–1996 general study of the attitudes to jobs and the organisation has been evaluated by English Heritage's Central Planning Team through a series of questionnaires (J. Hinchliffe, pers. com.). Though the results remain for internal information only, they would seem to show that employees are beginning to have a greater understanding of their own jobs and professional expertise, and the purpose of those tasks in relation to the organisation's objectives. Though such a link remains problematic in general management terms, such a study can help the exploration between the high-level objectives and the end product – the management process. The greater understanding of English Heritage within the organisation's employees is a further result of the strategic management process, and its emphasis on availability of information: in turn this greater understanding can have a settling effect on the recipe and form part of the dynamics of recipe change, as considered by Johnson and Scholes (1989).

The recipe of organisational culture at English Heritage forms a part of the organisation's strategy for dealing with the outside world. In particular, the government's Citizens's and Customers' Charter programmes can be mentioned here, as the recipe directly affects how well the organisation does its jobs, and is thus perceived by its customers, the public. A result of this was a centrally prepared statement of Values and Behaviours (English Heritage 1996 b), emphasising the organisational culture within and outside English Heritage. This is presented in Figure 4.15 below. A further, more detailed result can be seen in the 30 or more customer service standards that English Heritage aimed to fulfil as part of its customer standards initiative during the period in question.

It should be noted that the academic world is not necessarily seen as a customer for English Heritage because the organisation assumes that it is corporately representative of that professional world. Tensions created as a result of this are not considered here.

Figure 4.15 *English Heritage Values and Behaviours (English Heritage 1996 b)*

1   Customer Orientated
    We seek to be open, positive and friendly in our relations with people by:
    – treating others as we would like to be treated – delivering our Customer Service Standards – being ambassadors for English Heritage
2. Working in teams
    We seek to work together as one organisation with a common purpose by:
    – providing effective and pro-active leadership – supporting and trusting colleagues – encouraging flexibility and respecting different views
3. Valuing people
    We seek to enable people to develop their strengths by:
    – treating people fairly – valuing skills and individuals
    – realising people's potential – offering appropriate rewards and recognition
4. Open communications
    We seek to develop swift and open communications within and around the organisation by:
    – volunteering information – encouraging feedback
    – listening and sharing

English Heritage's strategic position: environment and resources

For the purpose here of analysing English Heritage and other aspects of the heritage, the socio-cultural environment is the most important, because the organisation is dealing with sociological and historical interaction, which produces the phenomenon of heritage. Furthermore, as a thematic and abstract concept, with relation to personal and national identity, and its explicit link with the process of history, the greatest influence that a heritage management institution such as English Heritage can have, is in the socio-cultural environment identified previously in Chapter 3.

Within English Heritage itself, as an organisation created in the form of a non-departmental public body (NDPB), the staff are no longer civil servants, though pay and conditions may be roughly comparable, as the majority of the organisation's staff were originally employed as civil servants in the Department of the Environment's Ancient Monuments and Historic Buildings Branch. There are several sources of labour supply for the organisation: as well as the specialist staff concerned with achieving English Heritage's corporate objectives, there are other less specialised support staff, needed to keep the organisation running on a day-to-day basis.

The specific niches of labour supply needed by the organisation are, as mentioned above, specialised and they include: archaeologists; architects; conservators; scientists; land agents; information technologists; personnel managers; communications specialists; photographers; marketing specialists and academics. Less specialised professionalism may be needed by staff employed in pursuit of the operations of the organisation, such as caseworkers, secretaries, custodians, customer service assistants, and computer operators. In order to fulfil its role, English Heritage needs to draw on these labour forces, and at the same time, as a result of its corporate objectives, promote specialisms through continuing professional development (CPD) of its labour forces. Therefore, in conjunction with the sources of labour supply that are already established outside the organisation, such as architects or archaeologists, there is a symbiotic relationship, as English Heritage promotes the work of those suppliers in pursuit of its own goals.

An example of this within the organisation has been seen, until fairly recently, with the running of the Fort Brockhurst Training Centre and the Historic Properties Restoration Group. Fort Brockhurst provided occupational training for conservation of ancient monuments and historic buildings. It also provided tailor-made training for other organisations, such as British Waterways (English Heritage 1996 a). This facility, through the strategic planning process, has been subject to review, and its activities are being curtailed as training can be provided outside the organisation in the future. One reason for this is that the in-house conservation and restoration labour force, Historic Properties Restoration Group, has been privatised and the major need within the organisation for training no longer exists. Conservation and restoration work on English Heritage properties are now tendered for in an outside labour market, previously operated less efficiently within English Heritage. It can be suggested therefore, that the training centre's activities and the reformation of the directly employed labour into a specialised company, which was subsequently privatised, further developed the market for heritage and conservation training. This continues to establish standards in conservation, which English Heritage maintains in an advisory role rather than through direct provision.

Sources of finance for English Heritage have, until recently, been limited. Greater internal management of strategy, exploring how best to achieve the organisation's goals, coupled with developments and pressure outside the organisation, mainly from the government, has started to widen these financial sources. The main source of funding for the organisation was in the form of grant-in-aid from the Department of National Heritage. For 1996/97 the base plan allocations were for an income (grant from government) of £126.3 million.

The corporate planning procedure acts in part as a bid for future funds each year through the PES (Public Expenditure Survey) carried out by the government and resulting in the bi-annual Budget. Projections are calculated within the annual corporate plan, allocating funds to the various programmes determined by the organisation to achieve its objectives over a three to four year period (which is general across government departments). Across government departments funding has been frozen or pegged below inflation, meaning cuts in budget in 'real terms' (English Heritage 1996 a). Therefore organisations like English Heritage, at arms length from government, and not determined as a core government activity through the political process such as health or education, have to look elsewhere to raise funds and make up any shortfall in income.

Other sources of funding have been developed internally through the organisation's work and objectives, or externally by changes in the environment caused by others, including other government departments. An example is the National Lottery. Money has become available from the allocations of lottery proceeds to 'good causes': one of these is 'the heritage', funded through the Heritage Lottery Fund (DNH 1996 a, 47). The amount of money available dwarfs the annual budget of English Heritage, and this source of funding is liable to dominate funding across heritage interests to a huge extent in the future. As a result of the overall objectives for English Heritage, it plays a part in allocation of moneys through professional advice to the Heritage Lottery Fund on heritage applications (NHMF 1996); it can also apply itself for lottery money to undertake projects which are the result of its corporate objectives, such as the purchase of pictures for the collections of historic properties, or restoration and presentation projects like the one at St Augustine's Priory (English Heritage 1996 c, 38).

Sources of finance are also available through other external funds, such as sponsorship and grants in the form of objects from the National Art Collections Fund, the government's Acceptance-in-Lieu scheme, or the National Heritage Memorial Fund. Sponsorship is used extensively through the Arts sector, encouraged by the government's Business Sponsorship Schemes, and Partnerships in the Arts (DNH 1996 a). This has spread across to the heritage sector,

particularly in the case of charitable trusts: the National Trust makes extensive use of business sponsorship for its work (National Trust 1996). English Heritage has been able to organise sponsorship through the special events programme, the concerts programme and through the membership scheme on an English Heritage credit card and insurance offers.

Sponsorship can also be drawn on in the 'individual' sense: donations, legacies, gifts or fund-raising events. The charity sector relies most on this type of income, though increasingly public bodies, whose grant-in-aid may not allow them to carry out the objectives they wish to achieve, are beginning to utilise this form of income. The membership scheme and the formation of the American Friends of English Heritage for example harness such funds (English Heritage 1990 b). Much effort is made to diversify such funding sources: recent development has been seen through increased media use of sites in film and television locations.

English Heritage, in the discharging of its own responsibilities, and programmes to achieve its corporate objectives, is able to draw on sources of finance from this 'internal' work. Obvious examples include charging for certain advice and work it undertakes in a professional capacity; money raised through the education service provided centrally and at its properties; efficiency savings (expected and scrutinised by government as part of its desire to reduce overall public expenditure); membership income and publications. The major source of finance raised within the organisation is through its presentation of historic properties and trading activities. In the light of Department of National Heritage figures suggesting that tourism is responsible for 7% of the country's Gross Domestic Product (GDP), with spending figures in tourism of around £12 billion pounds (DNH 1996 a), English Heritage's portfolio of 408 historic properties is well placed to act as a major force in English tourism, thereby providing a potentially huge income source for the organisation. Figures provided by English Heritage show the capitalisation that is made of the tourism sector, with a rise since its establishment in 1984 from an income of approximately £2.6 million (HBMCE 1985) to almost £18 million in 1995 (English Heritage 1996 c).

The sources of materials have to be considered in a more abstract fashion than other sources in the proximate environment (previously considered in Chapter 3). English Heritage is not a manufacturing organisation in the strictest sense, though in this thesis, in its consideration of the transformation of heritage suggests that from a management perspective, heritage can be considered a product that has been manufactured or manipulated in a certain way. The end product therefore is the heritage product: the ancient monument, the grants to conservation areas, and so on. The raw materials, or the source of the materials, must therefore be the thematic subject that can be labelled as 'heritage' by the management process. Thus, it is variable and expansive, causing at once opportunity and threat to English Heritage, which will be considered further below.

In its widest sense, archaeology, monuments and historic buildings form the majority of source materials for English Heritage to manage and/or label as the historic environment. These raw materials come from diverse disciplines: those that give rise to objects or other materials that form a part of the heritage identity. If something can be identified as heritage outside the organisation by another organisation, group or discipline then it may, in time and as a result of the expert nature of English Heritage, come to be considered as heritage falling within the bounds of what can be managed by English Heritage, as it continues to undertake its own research and identification programmes. This is a somewhat tortuous argument, yet serves to reflect well the nature of the phenomenon. Archaeology, as a study of part of the historic environment, has matured as a discipline and widened its concerns and remit, both in terms of timescale and physical evidence. Thus the heritage identity may be accorded to modern movement architecture, wartime defences, and designed landscapes and battlefields; all of which have been subject to investigation and protection by English Heritage in recent years. This source of material is also extended and altered by public support for aspects of the environment in which they live as being historical and part of the 'heritage'. Allied to this social change, affected partly by trends in fashion (Boniface & Fowler 1993), such public desire and support, linked with ideas about modern consumption (Urry 1995; Carter 1984), has enabled enterprises elsewhere like the 'Past Times' chain to succeed beyond all expectations.

The widening remit of the disciplines 'supplying' the raw materials of heritage, from greater thematic goals and cross-disciplinary interests, has also changed the perception of management of the heritage in the public sector. Management of the countryside is no longer the concern only of the Countryside Agency (formerly the Countryside Commission), nor protection of species the sole concern of English Nature. English Heritage as an owner and manager of land has signed a statement of intent with English Nature (English Nature 1992), entailing wider consideration of their work in the physical and natural 'environment'; and all three agencies are jointly working on landscape characterisation programmes and ideas of sustainability across the whole of the country (English Heritage 1997 c). Dubbed the 'New Map of England', (Countryside Commission 1994), the Countryside Characterisation Programme is collating specific areas of concern (heritage, land-use, flora, fauna and geology) to present a broader environmental picture and assessment of environmental 'capital' (Countryside Commission 1996; English Heritage 1997 c).

General increase in concern for the environment in which we live has direct implications for the heritage, usually to its benefit. Again it is not for this thesis to be drawn into wider debates about these concerns; others such as Adams (1996) or Wright (1993) consider these specifically. Threats to the perceived heritage resource, however, provides a source of materials for English Heritage, as previously ignored material items or sites, when under threat, take on a new guise to be considered as heritage and therefore worthy of

preservation. This can be related to Thompson's ideas about 'rubbish theory' (1979), and can be applied to examples such as wartime installations, and industrial sites and machinery like abandoned coalmines. Once again, these examples have been recently listed as a result of the Defence of Britain Project (CBA 1996) or English Heritage's 'Monuments Protection Programme' (English Heritage 1996 d), though previously left to decay.

Identification of the final major category in the proximate environment, customers and middlemen, can probably never be exhaustive. Many of the identified groups are self-explanatory as either customers or consumers (in the management sense of the word) of English Heritage's products, be it expert advice, grants, or provision of access to historic properties as tourist sites. Alternatively they form part of a chain dealing with English Heritage in its widest remit of protection and 'championing the heritage' (English Heritage 1996 c).

The major customer groupings can be divided in accordance with English Heritage's establishment as a public body: the organisation acts as the government's advisor, protecting the heritage for the wider public. Both are therefore English Heritage's customers: assistance in provision of statutory responsibilities of the government on the one hand; and carrying out those responsibilities for the inhabitants of the country as a public service organisation on the other.

Many niche groups can be identified within these overall headings, related to professional and non-professional interests in the corporate objectives of the organisation. These groups can be as small as an individual in receipt of English Heritage's services. Such a list includes: the education sector; tourists; members; souvenir trade; recipients of grants; architects; archaeologists; academic disciplines; organisations at the receiving end of the organisation's professional advice; local councils; heritage businesses; and contract services. The other proximate bodies such as government advisory committees, which influence management activities, provide interesting material for exploration. Consideration of trade union activity is always of importance in any public sector organisation, relating specifically to pay, and the terms and conditions of employment of the organisation's staff. This is vital for the smooth running of the organisation's internal management.

Competitors are less easy to identify, as by the law of market failure and government intervention, there is no specific market in national heritage management. English Heritage has no direct competitors therefore, and acts as a monopoly. The previous Conservative government's philosophy on market forces, and changes in the style of management of public sector organisations seen earlier, has enabled certain markets to be created as a part of those organisations' work. Competition and greater efficiency has been introduced into the public sector (Flynn 1990; Hughes 1994), as demands for efficiency reviews and market testing have been implemented (Cabinet Office 1997; Hoare &

Fennell 1997). The effects of this are seen within English Heritage: as noted above the contract works for restoration of historic properties has been privatised, and the various divisions within the organisation have been organised as 'business units' (English Heritage 1996 a). The varying departments and project teams now agree service level contracts within these units across the internal structure of the organisation.

The most direct competition is seen in English Heritage's provision of sites open to the public, its education and publication service and events programme. Here English Heritage 'products' are in competition with other tourist attractions and organisations – the National Trust is one such competitor, and the differences in the model between the two are explored in the Brodsworth Hall and Uppark case studies. Others include educational services and other publishers of heritage materials. It must be noted, that the organisation does still have certain specialist functions in these areas, where it still has no direct competition: one such example is publication of certain archaeological volumes resulting from the excavation of publicly-owned or publicly-funded sites.

Local communities have a direct influence on the organisation's activities in countless ways due mainly to the fact that the organisation now exists in ethos to serve the public. Greater recognition of this has been made recently within the organisation (J. Hinchliffe, pers. com.) as a result of government initiatives such as the Citizen's Charter (DNH 1996 d), and the gradual shift to a strategic method of management, which carefully identifies the customers and environment in which an organisation seeks to operate.

Though the organisation acts within the basic framework of the National Heritage Act and other supporting legislation pertaining to specific corporate objects (such as listing and scheduling sites), no single 'customer' is defined within legislation for the purposes of corporate conduct. The organisation itself has had to determine through strategic management and the reassessment of itself as a public organisation that the ultimate customer of the organisation are the inhabitants of the country, not the ancient monuments and historic buildings as may have been assumed previously. Thus, English Heritage's mission statement for 1997 for the first time stated its *customer* clearly, 'to champion our heritage for the enrichment of present and future generations' (English Heritage 1996 c). This firmly established heritage as a human categorisation, and explicitly of relevance to local communities. Developments in late 1997 and 1998 saw English Heritage restructure itself into regional teams. This correlated with the Labour government's intention of delivering 'local' government. The regionalisation agenda falls outside the scope of this study.

General Environmental Influences

The general environmental influences also affect the model. They are related to the primary concept of heritage before its objectification, combining both direct and indirect influence on the organisation, its operation and corporate objectives. More often than not English Heritage has a limited influence on the environment and its activities contribute to these general trends. Each of the major environmental trends is now looked at in turn.

The economic environment, though not at first obvious, is able to affect English Heritage in a number of distinct ways. The crucial economic factor that must be considered is the economy of the government and its ability and intention towards funding of English Heritage and other public service organisations. The politics of the annual fight over funds between the government departments is not relevant here (Hennessy 1988), but it must be noted that although 'heritage' considerations are important for national identity and the whole host of other reasons put forward by archaeologists and historians (Lowenthal 1985), it comes well down on a government's list of priorities, which accords generally with Maslow's hierarchy of needs (1970). Specific management of heritage may then be considered to be a luxury item for a country, and subsequently its core funding is always under threat. This threat must be combined with the general shift in management of the public sector, with increased pressure to manage less of it centrally, and those parts that are managed centrally in a more efficient way, entailing staff reduction and market creation through market testing and competitive tendering procedures. Targets for English Heritage, set by the central sponsoring body, the DCMS in this instance, are revised each year within the corporate planning and funding agreement discussions, and generally year on year expectations and targets are increased. A specific discussion of target setting for the heritage sector is considered later in this case study.

Such financial pressure through the grant-in-aid to English Heritage, puts great constraint on the organisation's management, and increases the need for strict and comprehensive planning procedures, as outlined in the corporate plan. Development could be charted through the corporate plans produced by English Heritage, analysed earlier in the chapter: initial plans over the four year period for planning gave basic planning of how the organisation was going to spend its grant-in-aid, division by division. This included general comments about effects of increases or cutbacks in provision of money for the various divisional programmes. A complicating factor that must be noted is that the majority of English Heritage's grant-giving programmes are organised over more than one year. Thus commitments made in any one year must be able to be fulfilled in the following years, regardless of whether the organisation has to allocate less funding to that programme due to wider organisational demands such as grant-in-aid reduction. The position is outlined in the corporate plan for 1989-93 as follows:

'We have considered the implications of a reduction in resources when looking at all our operational programmes. The general picture is that our major grant programmes could, if required, reduce expenditure by reducing the level of offers. The impact of this is not immediate as it depends on the rate of take up to produce claims for payment and the full effects of such reductions would not be felt until we were into the second and third year from offers being made. The corollary is that most of our grant expenditure in a given year relates to offers made up to four or five years earlier. We can do nothing to reduce these commitments. It follows that we would have to make exaggerated cuts in current levels of offer to attain real reductions in expenditure in the short term. That is why we seek to avoid such action. As an example of the longer term effort, a cut of 15% in grant offer levels implemented from 1990-91 would reduce grant expenditure in 1992-93 by £4.5 million.' (English Heritage 1989 a, 12)

Whilst over the projected planning period use is made of figures showing projected deficits, such as in the 1994-98 plan the organisation planning for a £4.95 million deficit in 1997/98, the figures must in fact balance each year, and such a deficit is not allowed by central government. The move to greater strategic management and planning uses such deficit planning as an aid to show reductions that must

be made in expenditure by the organisation, and as a case to central government for increases in funding. This is a process of tactical manoeuvring as usually the increase is not forthcoming and the Government expects management savings (through efficiency and payroll reduction) to be made and external income to be increased.

The organisation's independence from government has been utilised more over the period in question, and distinct changes have been seen in the tone and format of the corporate plan as a result of this. This is seen most clearly in the 1996–2000 corporate plans, as greater emphasis is placed on the implications of cuts in government grant-in-aid. This plan introduces the use of three different funding strategies to highlight the threats to the organisation's work in different circumstances, dependent on the outcome of its own and external funding being made available. A powerful summary introduction outlines English Heritage's case for funding. This has been reproduced in Figure 4.16 which illustrates the corporate plan as a tool used by the organisation in presenting its case to the Department of National Heritage.

Figure 4.16 *English Heritage Summary Statement 1996-2000. (English Heritage 1996 a)*

SECTION A: SUMMARY

This Four Year Plan takes us through to the end of the millennium. It is a millennium in which much of our visible heritage - England's historic towns, churches, cathedrals, industrial monuments and landscapes - was created. Our heritage is a prime national asset and a justified source of national pride. It is not only an asset in terms of our quality of life, but more tangibly in terms of the financial benefits brought by tourism - it is the principal reason people give for visiting this country. Meeting this need brings opportunities and benefits for local communities throughout the land in conserving and presenting their heritage. English Heritage's national role is to ensure that through the work of many people in partnership England's heritage is there to be enjoyed and appreciated by the public both now and in the future. The many activities summarised in this Plan are ultimately directed to this prime objective.

In constructing our **Base Plan** we have been strongly aware that this holistic approach is now under threat from lack of funds and that quality standards and previous commitments are increasingly at risk against the background of declining Government funding and a steadily rising workload. Developing all our potential sources of funding (including further advances in productivity) must therefore be of the highest priority over the next four years. Even so, any further reduction in the level of Government support will assuredly take us to a point where we must discontinue some activities. We have therefore developed for debate two alternative plans (a **PES Plan** and a **Heritage Plan**)

The key factors in planning our Base Plan work for the next four years are :

- the declining value of our Government grant :

  the loss of £44.7 million in real terms over the next four years

- our increasing workload :

  statutory casework growing by 10% per year

  grant caseload doubled in the last four years

  membership increasing by 7% per year

  visits to our sites at highest ever level

  a growing portfolio of building rescue projects

- our capacity to generate more income :

  maintaining the growth in income from visitors and

members (up 40% over the past three years; 25% growth targeted over the Plan period)

continuing to diversify our sources of income, including sponsorship

- the new opportunities for working in partnership with Lottery distributors and others :

  developing joint grant schemes with the Heritage Lottery Fund

  seeking Lottery support for visitor developments at our properties

  working with a variety of partners, including local authorities and the private sector, to achieve viable solutions for securing important historic buildings, areas and monuments for the future

  developing our collaboration with the Royal Commission on the Historical Monuments of England (RCHME)

- increasing productivity and effectiveness :

  identifying and eliminating unproductive costs

  reviewing the way we do things in the light of customer needs

Three Planning Levels

- The **Base Plan** seeks to prioritise the reducing Government grant and, whilst assuming steady growth in earned income and further productivity gains, still requires significant cuts to be made. There is no possibility of fully compensating for the loss of £44.7 million internally when Government grant represents more than 80% of our income

- The **PES Plan** is offered in the form of a 1996 PES bid which would allow us to maintain the current level of support for churches, historic buildings and conservation areas whilst maintaining our commitment to clear the backlog of repair inherited from Government

- An additional **Heritage Plan** is also offered which identifies bids, over and above the *Base* and *PES Plans*, worth up to £26.5m for visitor-related improvements to English Heritage properties from Lottery funding. The Heritage Plan also explores the implications of working in partnership with the Heritage Lottery Fund to the overall benefit of the heritage by providing consistency and stability within a national strategic framework.

There are other economic factors that are less crucial than the consideration of grant-in-aid for the organisation, though they are becoming more important as English Heritage looks elsewhere to develop sources of funding and these vary quite widely. Tourism is perhaps the next largest consideration, having a direct influence on income for English Heritage from its properties in care. The organisation must present and interpret its properties in such a way that visitors want to visit them, and enable the sites to compete in the wider tourist market. Figures produced suggest that, 'the 407 historic properties in our care receive 10 million visitors per year' (English Heritage 1996 a, 17). There is performance against other organisations and sites within the English tourism market, and general trends world-wide for tourism in Britain (Prentice 1993), that have to be taken into consideration, as affecting potential earnings for English Heritage. As heritage largely falls into the 'leisure' market (Prentice 1993; Veal 1994) there are general economic considerations within this market for supporting specifically heritage concerns. Therefore, competition may be seen between sport, the arts and media as sectors within this market, all with economic effects.

Lesser factors include the following: the lottery, as a source of funding for the heritage, dependent on the lottery operator's performance; the building and construction industry, including roads and statutory planning responsibilities, and their ability to affect heritage sites necessitating protective or investigative action – a big increase could put a huge strain on resources; agricultural policy, where a similar change may affect archaeological and other sites entailing greater work and expenditure for English Heritage; and local authority economic policy – the ability of local authorities and other regional public bodies to provide heritage services delegated to and expected of them, highlighted in local government reorganisation.

Legal factors in the general environment can be affected by English Heritage, acting in its capacity as the government's expert advisor on heritage matters. English Heritage's independence enables it to give greater consideration and response to such consultation documents as 'Protecting our Heritage' or 'Portable Antiquities' (DNH 1996 b; DNH & Welsh Office 1996), than Historic Scotland for example, which issues such consultation documents itself, acting for the Secretary of State. Therefore the legal factors include: English Heritage's own position as an independent public body; its establishment and functions on a statutory level; the general legislative framework for heritage in which it can operate and influence; its financial ability to operate within such a statutory framework (related to the general economic environment); and the policy of government departments through intent to change or create new heritage legislation – such as proposed changes to the National Heritage Act (HMG 1983) currently under consultation, and the creation of new Acts including the Railway Heritage Act (HMG 1996), or National Heritage Act (HMG 1997 a).

The political environment is similar, in many respects, to the legal environment, there being only a technical difference in whether the government is carrying out legal duties or policy intentions with regard to the heritage. Consideration must be given to the general policy of the government in respect of the country's heritage – entailing the development of policy through such means as the creation of a Department of National Heritage, and the non-statutory expectations that can be placed on English Heritage. Examples of this were seen in the Government's general environmental initiative, 'This Common Inheritance' (DoE 1990 b). Further political considerations include the 'quango' status and attitudes to accountability that such a status entails, and the relation to other heritage bodies. Balance also has to be made between undertaking government responsibilities for the heritage, retaining full independence and expertise in the field, and gaining public trust and support for its position.

Socio-cultural considerations of the heritage range from the abstract to the particular, as reflected in the range of writing on the subject, and from critique (Hewison 1987) to theory (Shanks 1992) and practice (Davies 1985). English Heritage has to acknowledge this within its corporate objectives of the conserving and promotion of understanding, and there are inherent needs for an understanding within the organisation of those socio-cultural arguments and trends, from the general to the particular. In pursuit of this understanding (for its own purpose and in pursuit of external objectives), English Heritage is increasingly an instigator of debates and discussion. Such discussions addressed by the organisation through conferences, management programmes, research, CPD, education, publication and survey include: the concept of leisure; environmental or green concerns; countryside appreciation; personal participation in activities; prices; choice; social characteristics; history; emotion; identity; education; value; specialism or academy; tourism; and membership of society groupings. Exploration of these various headings are usually best made at the lower level of service delivery and the implications of it, i.e. at the point where the activities of English Heritage affect other people, outside the organisation in the wider world. The ramifications of such study have great relevance, however, at the highest level of strategy exploration and objective setting.

The final general environmental consideration (technology) is highly specific to the activities of the organisation, and its ability to carry out its function. Linked explicitly to the sources of labour needed to carry out the organisation's work, technology provides the means of doing so. It can range from the simplest to the most complicated, and includes such areas as: development of GIS; computer simulation; non-destructive action; media and communications; management and accountancy systems; monitoring; conservation method; and delivery of service. Many of these headings would fit under the other groupings of environmental influences, but specific consideration must be given to the technological aspect of any operation: the best way of carrying out a task and machinery needed to do it.

I have highlighted features of the strategic position of English Heritage in its environment. Management and its actions thus transform heritage through various means. In its objectified state the phenomenon can be addressed in the different environments identified, and subsequently transformed in the second stage of the model back into an intangible concept. Management techniques such as SWOT analysis consider these transformations and, at the same time, English Heritage's competitive position is assessed in business terms, leading to strategic options and finally programmes of action to achieve the corporate objectives. It can be seen that, when strategic management is adopted, at each step the focus narrows, constantly scanning the future and reviewing previous steps.

Environmental Nature

In taking, 'an initial view of the nature of the organisation's environment' (Johnson and Scholes 1989, 53), I have assessed how stable or subject to change that environment is. For heritage, and English Heritage as an organisation, this is relatively straightforward. The nature of the environment is relatively static in terms of management institutions (i.e. there are unlikely to be large public bodies established, similar to English Heritage); but the subject matter, or more general environment that determines what heritage is (comprising the socio-cultural factors described previously) does show signs of change. The subject matter is an intangible abstract concept, and thus organic in development. Hence the tension between concept and object and the need for sustainable management systems to adapt this object in line with the conceptual change (at the second stage of the model).

Johnson and Scholes (*ibid.*) conclude, that 'if the environment is in a dynamic state or shows signs of becoming so, then a more future-orientated perspective is more sensible.' Heritage management operates in just such an environment, and in terms of strategic management, this future-orientated perspective is just what English Heritage attempts to take through its research programmes – end products of the entire corporate planning process. Even after 12 years of existence and over 100 years of government involvement in heritage through archaeological and historic environment legislation, exploration is still being made into what the historic environment consists of.

Competitive rivalry must be considered in the light of market testing and outsourcing of work by the organisation. It is a recognised principle within current public sector thinking that where the government can withdraw from providing a service that can be better provided in a private competitive market (working in the public interest) then it should do so. Heritage is no exception. Thus, as has already been discussed, with the creation of the Historic Properties Restoration Group and its subsequent privatisation, initial market establishment and support (in conservation services) has now been abandoned by English Heritage, and it buys in such services through competitive tendering. A different form of market creation has been undertaken through the devolved management of certain of the historic properties under English Heritage guardianship. Whilst not subject to such competition as is seen in the service sector,

identification of others who can manage the properties better than English Heritage can, has led to management hand-overs, though retaining supervision in case of problems. The fundamental *raison d'être* for English Heritage remains in the category of market failure, and thus the organisation has a monopoly and is subject to no major competition. Acting as a public service organisation it is difficult to see how any other scenario could work, though there is a continuing trend to identify areas where competition or new markets can be established. The demands for continuing year-on-year efficiency savings from central government targets contribute to this trend.

Strategic Choice

The combination of all the above assessments of the various environmental influences, issues facing the organisation, and the social responsibility instilled by the nature of the establishment of the organisation provide for the final stage of major assessment: strategic choice. What does English Heritage do with the heritage objects it creates? Johnson and Scholes conclude that, 'objectives and, indeed, strategies are better thought of as the product of a complex interplay between: the expectations of individuals and groups; the values of society; organised groups and the dominant culture of the organisation.' (*ibid.* 140) The strategic options available are those possible actions that support the corporate objectives of the organisation. The reliance in English Heritage is thus the expert nature of the organisation enabling it to identify and protect heritage in England. The specific environment in which any choice must be taken is dominated by that of the legal framework, the public sector ethos, targets set, historic decisions made by the organisation and the finances available for implementation of a choice. The final action, i.e. choice made and acted upon, will of course have resulted from the entire analysis made above, creating a management structure which is able to internally deliver choices which can be assessed.

Strategic management and the necessity for understanding

No consideration is needed here of the final stages of the decision-making process that English Heritage undertakes to produce its strategies and products at the end of the day. That is not to say that these processes are not important as they explicitly objectify the heritage, rather that for the purposes of this case study it is the principles of the initial high-level objectives and strategies and end-of-day delivery of programmes and products that are important and show the institutional transformation. The mechanics of every decision made by the organisation cannot follow a fixed recipe due to the variables identified in the high-level analysis. Thus there is no minute step-by-step process: the generalised steps followed in principle for strategic management of the organisation are scaled down and manipulated to suit each situation. The intangible nature of the heritage means that the final transformative mechanism that turns a strategy into a specific task, as part of a programme that delivers that strategy, depends on expert individuals that make up the organisation.

Personal expertise and knowledge is therefore essential in the organisation, and it should be recognised generally that an exploration, such as that carried out above, of the strategic management process of English Heritage, underpins the necessity for each individual to have an understanding of the entire background to the management process in which their work and organisation operates. Internally recognition is made of this expert nature, seen in greater staff development and training, and encouragement to participate in external heritage fora. Within any organisation such as English Heritage, working in a 'public' capacity as a result of market failure, recognition must be made of why and how principles of management are followed: this relies on individual involvement and expertise. Heritage management produces a very special kind of product, and its nature can only be understood by looking at the principles of the manufacturing process – the management of the organisation itself rather than management simply as a means to achieve something.

Strategic management: organising the institution

English Heritage has undergone a great deal of restructuring, and it can be seen that such change is inevitably continual. The strategic management process, with its inbuilt monitoring and weighing of choices, means that such organisational change is necessary for the organisation to achieve those corporate objectives in the changing conceptual environment. The process does not therefore advocate change for change's sake: restructuring processes are clearly aimed at constantly adapting the organisation to its environment.

This constant scanning of the environment is easier within smaller focused groups reflecting corporate aims as noted above: generally the process means an increase in the divisional groupings, in effect moving from a monolithic structure to a devolved 'team' (Johnson & Scholes 1989) structure. English Heritage has thus seen a change from three core groups in 1989 (Conservation; Properties in Care; and Central Services) to seven by 1995 (Conservation; Historic Properties; Research and Professional Services; Major Projects; Development and Marketing; Public Affairs; and Corporate Services). Consolidation of strategy within the organisation has since regrouped it with five departments in 1996, reflecting overall the developed corporate strategies more closely: Conservation; Historic Properties; Major Projects; Public Affairs; and Support Services. Future consolidation in 1998 occurred through the establishment of regional management teams to carry out all corporate objectives in a 'one-stop shop' fashion, leaving a central policy-making core (J. Hinchliffe pers. com.; Alexander 1998). This has since been affected again by wider internal reorganisation and regionalisation agendas.

Information has been established already (in Chapter 2) as the key element in the transformation and strategic management process. As decisions (based on information) move responsibility for achieving the corporate objectives down to the bottom of the organisation, these corporate objectives in turn can only be supported by the delivery of specified tasks. Such tasks support further levels of strategy at a lower level than the organisation's corporate strategies: hence the importance of an organisational structure that can support these lower level strategies. The organisational form allows movement of information quickly, and the strategic approach allows specialist groupings to be established to tackle specific management needs, address 'new' transformations, and reassess strategy at all levels of the organisation. As noted previously however, maintenance of the organisation both as a professional institution, and within a professional framework (archaeology and conservation), creates tensions that must be addressed within the operation of the institution. As a corporate body, a corporate approach must be taken in all of its work: at the same time, individual concerns, preferences and expertise must be allowed consideration, and in some cases developed. Therefore the culture of the organisation remains at the heart of its effective management.

Actual transformation through the delivery of objectives in the Corporate Planning Process

A combination of the devolving of decision-making within English Heritage and the establishment of strategic teams reflecting this management process produces a hierarchy of strategies. Each level may be called something different to prevent too much confusion, though each can be considered in the abstract as a strategy. The breakdown of strategic management delivery in English Heritage is shown in Figure 4.17.

The high level corporate objectives are determined by the statutory establishment of English Heritage: reference is therefore made to the National Heritage Act. At the next level down, the organisation sets its own strategies, which are applicable to the whole organisation. These can be sub-divided into Programmes allocated between the various Divisions in the organisation. Each Department therefore takes these Programmes and sub-divides them again. Teams and individuals are provided with specific day-to-day remits for a particular part of the objectification process. At each stage it can be seen that the strategy becomes less abstract and more practical, and so the transformation is achieved from the intangible concept to the tangible object or product – the end result of a person's action. As noted at the start of the chapter, the institution determines the kind of transformation, and the precise nature or result of transformations are seen in the day-to-day tasks of English Heritage staff. Some of these are explored in the following case studies.

Referring back once again to the historical developments seen in the English Heritage Corporate Plans, it is seen that the format used to pre-set a system of strategic management is radically different from the traditional plan. It can be seen that full description and budgeting of 70 management programmes in the 1989-93 plan (English Heritage 1989 a)

Figure 4.17 *English Heritage Programme Delivery 1996. (English Heritage 1996 e)*

PROGRAMMES (to deliver the strategies)	
STRATEGIES	**PROGRAMMES**
1. CONSERVING **To secure the heritage through the creative and targeted funding of repair and restoration**	1.1 Giving grants for the repair of historic churches
	1.2 Giving grants for secular historic buildings and monuments
	1.3 Giving grants for the repair of historic cathedrals
	1.4 Giving grants for conservation areas
	1.5 Giving grants for historic parks, gardens and landscapes
	1.6 Undertaking building rescue projects
2. CONSERVING **To secure the heritage through the innovative management of our properties and collections**	2.1 Conserving our properties
	2.2 Managing and maintaining our properties
	2.3 Managing and developing our collections
3. CONSERVING **To secure the heritage through our influence and strategic advice**	3.1 Identifying the heritage
	3.2 Advising government, local authorities and owners (including statutory controls and advice to Lottery)
4. ENRICHING **To increase understanding, enjoyment and pride in the heritage**	4.1 Developing our properties
	4.2 Presenting and interpreting our properties
	4.3 Welcoming visitors to our properties
	4.4 Educating and publishing
	4.5 Mounting special events and concerts
5. BRAINS AND SKILLS **To be the national focus for advancing knowledge, standards and skills**	5.1 Advancing archaeology and archaeological science
	5.2 Carrying out technical research
	5.3 Providing professional construction services
	5.4 Providing occupational training
6. CHAMPIONING **To increase our influence and win support**	6.1 Increasing awareness and support
	6.2 Promoting the heritage
	6.3 Developing membership services
7. FUNDING **To maximise funding for the heritage**	7.1 Improving productivity
	7.2 Maximising grant-in-aid
	7.3 Maximising our net earned income
	7.4 Attracting sponsorship
	7.5 Maximising Lottery and other public funding
	7.6 Developing new sources of funding
8. QUALITY SERVICE **To deliver a professional, flexible and customer-friendly service**	8.1 Achieving quality standards
	8.2 Developing our people
	8.3 Developing internal communications
	8.4 Developing business planning
	8.5 Supporting our frontline work

has been reduced to 8 corporate objectives supported by budgets for 34 programmes in the 1996-2000 plan (English Heritage 1996 a). The corporate planning procedure, resulting in the presentation of the Corporate Plan, is a synthesis of the highest-level strategies and delivery action. Each of the Divisions, organised as Business Units with their own budget and planning systems, produces a Business Plan that feeds into the Corporate Plan, sub-dividing the strategic information into more detailed team plans and budgets. Thus the information and decisions and support for strategy are passed as far down the organisation as possible. At the extreme case each staff member may have a personal job plan with tasks and time allotted to them; these feed into team plans and the lowest level of financial budgeting; and so on.

As a result of strategic management therefore, the final corporate plan becomes a tool at the highest level of a family of planning procedures in the organisation, which can be used externally to present a picture of its management framework, and results of its delivery of service. This supports the change in style and tone of the Corporate Plan, which has been discussed earlier.

Targets and results: the monitoring procedure

Targets and the monitoring of results are the actual measures that can be used to see whether an organisation is achieving its objectives and overall aim. An intimate problem with public sector management, and especially with heritage management, is that measurement of it can prove difficult. Profit-making organisations have an immediately identifiable corporate performance indicator (CPI) (Argenti 1989) in profit itself. An organisation can be seen to be achieving its purpose if it can function at a profit. Money is the major international valuation mechanism that is measured and compared worldwide. The Corporate Performance Indicator for a public sector institution however is more difficult to assess, as its operations (resulting from market failure) cannot necessarily produce profit. It may not be possible even to find a CPI: there is no universal indicator to establish if the government is achieving the aim of protecting the heritage; relative values and equivalents are used, which can determine a 'yes' or 'no' result for the aim.

For government and public service accountability, simply answering 'yes' or 'no' to whether an aim has been achieved is not good enough. There must be some comparative mechanism as a basis on which funding for strategies and organisations can be achieved. Costings for employing staff to undertake a job cannot be used, as there is still no measure of whether the job is or can be achieved. The Government's main aim is to control its own spending, and if possible reduce it therefore: targets for delivery and efficiency savings are set for its departments. Whilst central government departments have always been set targets, this has not always been the case with public bodies. As a result of the greater demand for the three 'Es' (economy, efficiency, effectiveness) in management, increasingly targets have been set for sponsored bodies to perform their functions in a better way. English Heritage has been no exception: whereas previously targets were set internally to improve the management of operations and to raise income, targets for accountability are now set externally as well by the DCMS. Such practice might seem of relative importance, but it has been emphasised as recently as 1996 that, 'neither Ministers collectively, nor Parliament, currently have the information needed to judge how executive NDPBs overall are performing.' (Cabinet Office 1996 b, 2)

Whilst thematic targets have always been set in the statutory duties for the heritage (for example to schedule ancient monuments), explicit targets have been introduced only in 1996 through the Funding Agreement system. This follows the lead of the Next Steps programme for performance measuring of created 'business units' in government, such as Historic Scotland. The Funding Agreement between the Department of National Heritage and English Heritage has already been reproduced in Figure 4.4.

It can be seen in the Funding Agreement that no reference is made to an overall Corporate Performance Indicator for English Heritage. It is acknowledged that the situation of market failure and the multiple objectives for the heritage render one impossible to identify. Therefore, lower level strategies and programme deliveries are given targets, which can be established in terms of economic or numeric value, and can be used as representative of a performance indicator.

The idea of a performance indicator for heritage management might seem like a 'force fit' situation, using numeric values as indicators that do not specifically indicate whether that management is doing it well. It is the nearest that can be established however, and roughly correlates to performance within the statutory framework for heritage management and establishment of English Heritage as a management institution.

The specific high-level targets set by the DCMS may be altered each year in terms of figures, though for the sake of

accountability the exact specifications of the targets remain similar. The targets are in the Funding Agreement section 'Aims and Outputs' of Figure 4.4. Furthermore, whilst some of the externally-set targets may be very specific, such as 'enter into a further 30 local management agreements', or 'increase earned income from £17.6 million to £19.0 million,' whilst others may be more general, like 'ensure that any increases in payroll and running costs are offset by efficiency savings, other economies or are self-financing.' In order to achieve these general targets, supporting targets are subsequently set internally, directing allocation of resources to specific programmes which will support target achievement, and thus in turn affecting strategy (as an direct environmental influence on operation). The example target of increasing income and making efficiency savings are incorporated into the review of results presented in the Corporate Plan by English Heritage. This is shown in Figure 4.18, and can be seen to break down the general target into very specific targets across the institution, which are built into the business and operation plans produced by the individual Departments. Targets are therefore imposed from above and directly focus strategy decisions quantifiably, whilst supporting possibly unquantifiable corporate aims.

The Corporate Plan as a tool is also used therefore to present very specific results and target setting as a support in the strategic management process. At a corporate level it can be seen how individual actions and projects fit into the organisation's overall corporate objectives, and that measurement can be made of them for purposes of accountability. Such measures of performance are an aid to external monitoring, and essential for internal monitoring and determining how to proceed in pursuance of overall and specific aims.

Conclusion

It is my view that the context of the decision-making process in the objectification of heritage is identified in strategic management, and this has been the focus of this chapter. I have placed emphasis on the specific instance of corporate strategy and objective setting at English Heritage as the mechanism of production for certain public heritage objects. The various environmental analyses allow an organisation, such as English Heritage to assess exactly what its own 'heritage' is identified as; and what it, as an institution, can achieve through corporate strategy and objective setting to objectify that public heritage. I have shown how English Heritage exists as a public institution, and how the shift to a strategic management perspective questions why the organisation exists (such questions themselves being a part of keeping a strategic check on corporate activities). I have explored how this approach has re-examined the notion of the public institution and market failure and how new management style allows markets to be created. As a result English Heritage has abandoned operations in certain areas, such as directly employed conservation services, and identified who its customers really are – each an effect of the explicit objectification of heritage as a resource.

Figure 4.18 *Extract from Review of results 1995/96. (English Heritage 1996 a, 28)*

Promoting the heritage

3. MAXIMISING FUNDING FOR FRONTLINE EXPENDITURE

3.1 Income from Visitors and Members

Our performance in generating income from admissions, sales and membership is as follows :

Income from Admissions, Sales & Membership

£,000	92/93 Actual	93/94 Actual	94/95 Actual	95/96 Actual	% growth in last 3 yrs	96/97 Target
Admissions	5,883	6,890	7,147	7,558	*28.5%*	7,782
Sales	3,499	4,221	4,497	4,791	*36.9%*	5,342
Membership	2,432	2,876	3,178	3,550	*46.0%*	4,112
TOTAL	11,814	13,987	14,822	15,899	*34.6%*	17,236
% growth per year	16.8%	18.4%	6.0%	7.3%		8.3%

3.2 Efficiency Savings

In order to achieve a balanced budget for 1996/97 efficiency savings of 850k had to be found within the spending plans proposed last year, in addition to the £3.7 million efficiency savings already incorporated in the Budget (and set out in our 1995-99 Plan). Savings on systems support and office services in the 1996/97 Budget exceed this figure by £983k :

Efficiency Savings in 1996/97 Budget

£m	Budget	95 Plan	Saving
Systems Support	1.14	1.48	0.34
Office Services	7.15	8.64	1.49
TOTAL	8.29	10.12	1.83
Target	–	–	(0.85)
Additional Savings	–	–	0.98

Visitor/membership income

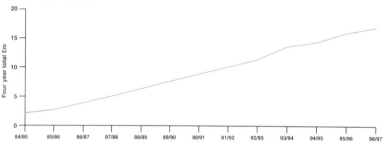

Frameworks, ability and intention to act result from the corporate processes employed in the strategic management of the organisation: English Heritage transforms the heritage by virtue of its corporate responsibility for the heritage, and its position as the 'country's leading heritage organisation' (English Heritage 1997 a). The actual transformations occur through non-corporate, individual actions on a day-to-day basis, where specialists within the agency produce specific results. These can, however, be classed as heritage objects and part of a suite of corporate results produced by English Heritage as a public institution. The encounter with the heritage objects 'transformed' by such organisations as English Heritage, The National Trust and others are explored in the remaining case studies. The mechanism and effects of the transformation by use of management tools is thus further addressed.

5 Transformation of heritage into archaeology and vice-versa: The Monuments Protection Programme

The context for the MPP

In the hierarchy of case studies, which has been identified previously (Chapter 1), the Monuments Protection Programme (MPP hereafter) follows on from the analysis of English Heritage as a whole. MPP can be classified as one of many 'management actions' or projects instigated by a management institution, in this case English Heritage, functioning to fulfil the duties placed on such an institution externally. Such management projects are numerous, ranging widely from the protection of ancient monuments in the case of MPP, to remedial works on site – excavation and survey, to presentation and enhancement of individual sites or other heritage features in the wider built or natural environment. Each individual act of management or project has the aim therefore of supporting the overall mission of the institution. Within the MPP, the archaeological resource is the subject of management policy rather than archaeological policy in the first instance. Each project, functioning as its own managerial unit, can be analysed much as was done for the whole institution before, though in this case a different approach will be taken. Consideration of MPP will be thematic, looking at the implications of the project in the light of the model of transformation.

Each of the three main themes raised by the project follow on from each other in a logical way: these are the transformation from concept to object in MPP; the idea of MPP as a management project; and the wider effects of MPP in archaeology and the wider world. Three sub-themes, each interlinked, form a part of the wider consideration of MPP as a management project: these are the ideas of time; space, site and scale; and 'ring-fencing', a function of this particular management process. Instances of MPP 'in action' are illustrated by reference to three archaeological sites. These have each been identified, interpreted and managed by English Heritage in a different way, even though all have been assessed using the standard of the MPP scheduling programme. Such differences in management at the site scale further emphasises the need to explore the initial transformation within management as a process, identifying the variety of contexts that the site exists in and is challenged by, and subsequent action taken. It can be seen through the exploration of management here that the variety of outcomes is designed to serve a similar purpose, that of protecting the country's archaeological resource.

Hadrian's Wall stretching across Cumbria and Northumbria, Baconsthorpe Castle in north Norfolk, and St. Mary's Abbey in West Dereham, Norfolk are all identified as archaeological sites. The processes employed by English Heritage in its statutory duty to protect archaeological sites (now encompassed by the MPP) have previously assessed these sites to be of national importance in the country's archaeological resource and recommended that they be given scheduled status. This has been undertaken by the DCMS or previous Government departments responsible for this task. Having objectified each site through the scheduling process, however, each site has been subsequently managed in a different way by English Heritage.

Figure 5.1 *Hadrian's Wall illustration from cover of guidebook. (© English Heritage)*

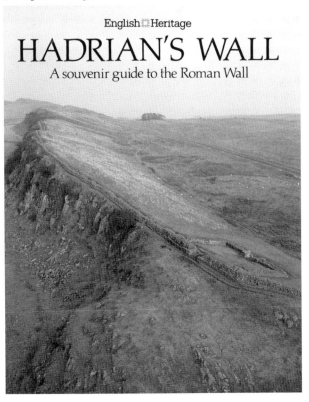

English Heritage

HADRIAN'S WALL
A souvenir guide to the Roman Wall

Figure 5.2 *Western section of Hadrian's Wall in Management Plan Summary. (English Heritage 1996)*

THE BOUNDARIES OF THE
WORLD HERITAGE SITE

When the World Heritage Site
was designated in 1989, it was
given no precise boundaries.
After much consultation we have
proposed that the World Heritage
Site itself should be
restricted to the
archaeological core
of the Hadrian's Wall
corridor and its extension
down the Cumbria coast.
This will need to be
confirmed by UNESCO.

■ Hadrian's Wall World Heritage Site
☐ Setting of World Heritage Site

In the rural areas, the Setting will allow local planning
authorities to protect the World Heritage Site from
inappropriate development. It will also establish an area
within which to target support for positive landscape
management and enhancement.

The World
Heritage Site
therefore forms
a linear zone
from Wallsend to
Bowness-on-
Solway with
separate islands
for outlying
archaeological
sites (shown in
red on the map).
In order to
protect the
World Heritage
Site, each local
authority has
agreed a Setting
or buffer zone to
protect its main
linear parts
(shown in pink
on the map)

In the urban area of Tyneside and Carlisle, the buffer zone
will protect the known archaeological remains and provide
the chance as opportunities arise to look for them elsewhere
when their position is uncertain.

HADRIAN'S WALL
WORLD HERITAGE SITE

MANAGEMENT PLAN

Hadrian's Wall is in the joint ownership of many different individuals and organisations, including the National Trust and English Heritage. It has been further designated of World Heritage Status. Figure 5.1 and Figure 5.2 show use of the Wall in both management and tourism literature. In recognition of this, English Heritage has taken a proactive approach to the site through co-ordination and development of a Management Plan for the Wall (English Heritage 1997 b). Management activity is therefore continuous due to its enhanced status, and English Heritage established a management office and staff posts to deal solely with this site.

Baconsthorpe Castle, a ruinous site in north Norfolk, has been taken into Guardianship by English Heritage, and is open to the public. The site's layout can be seen in Figure 5.3 showing the official schedule for the site, and in Figure 5.4 the site is presented as a visitor attraction in English Heritage's national site gazetteer. It has no visitor facilities and is not a 'key' English Heritage site, as it does not receive many visitors and is not a large site. Though recognised as nationally important through the site's scheduled status, at a future stage it may be handed over to another manager through a Local Management Agreement in accordance with English Heritage policies for its Historic Properties Division (English Heritage 1997 a). The site is currently maintained by English Heritage contractors; grass cutting and masonry consolidation is undertaken, and the site is regularly inspected by English Heritage archaeological and administrative staff, as part of the Historic Properties Division portfolio of sites. The site therefore already

partly fulfils one of English Heritage's economic strategies, reducing the 'cost' of the site for the organisation.

The site of St Mary's Abbey at West Dereham, also in Norfolk, though scheduled and including substantial standing ruins and earthworks, remains in private ownership. The schedule plan for the abbey is reproduced in Figure 5.5. There is no active management or consolidation of standing structures by the owner and, as the site stands on private land, there is no public access. As the site is scheduled, it is on the inspection rounds of local English Heritage Field Monument Wardens, though visits to the site are infrequent with at least a year between visits.

The characteristic that the three sites share is the objectification through the process of identification and assessment by MPP and legal protection through scheduling. Information and assessment of relative value are therefore key issues in management of the sites, as is the kind of management itself and the effects such actions have. The case study explores this through analysis of the conceptual and actual effects of MPP as a management and objectification process.

The Monuments Protection Programme has developed as a project over 10 years since being introduced by Darvill, Saunders and Startin (1987). A history of the project is unnecessary here as the project has been a talking point for archaeologists and heritage managers ever since due to its scope and the effects it has had, and most notably

Figure 5.3 *Schedule Plan for Baconsthorpe Castle. (© Crown Copyright)*

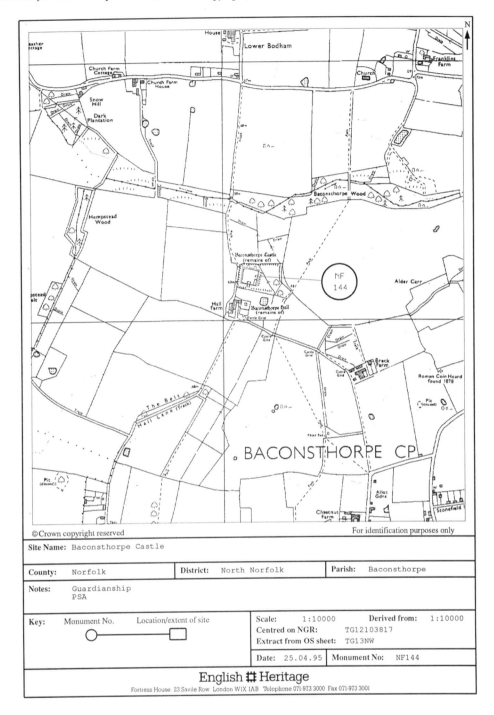

those effects re-evaluating the project's ultimate aims. The MPP of 1997 is not therefore the same project as the one of 1987, and some of the reasons for this lie within the institutional management structure of English Heritage and the shift already described (in Chapters 3 & 4) to a strategic management policy. The MPP engages with the model on two levels. Its primary intention is to undertake a systematic academic assessment of the archaeological resource, but it also operates as part of the overall management strategies of the organisation through objectification of the heritage. Therefore, even though the MPP is not driven by economic principles, it can exist as part of a corporate organisation as a result of its systematic decision-making giving it the form of strategic management.

Legal protection of archaeological sites (scheduling) is considered in detail by many texts on heritage management and is not considered here. It is perhaps worth noting that full explanation may be gained from either the legislation itself: the Ancient Monuments and Archaeological Areas Act (HMG 1979), or technical explanation in such texts as Breeze (1993) or McGill (1995).

At the time of English Heritage's creation a review was being undertaken by government of the effectiveness of legislation enacted five years previously. Meanwhile, internally, the Inspectorate of Ancient Monuments was looking carefully at the procedures employed in a process and duty that dated back to 1882, as a precursor to the new

Figure 5.4 *Entry for Baconsthorpe Castle in English Heritage members' handbook. (© English Heritage)*

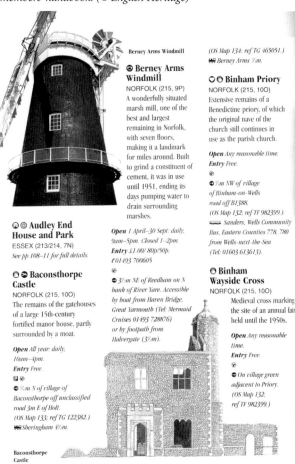

management institution about to be created for England's historic environment – English Heritage. Wainwright (1984) in his presidential address to the Prehistoric Society reflected on the joint conclusions of such scrutiny. On questioning whether standard criteria had been applied to the selection of ancient monuments, Wainwright explained that whilst the legislation enacted since 1913 had stipulated that the criterion be monuments of 'national importance' (*ibid.* 8), it was only since 1983 that a more detailed breakdown of that criterion had been proposed (DoE 1983). He furthermore asked two questions and set about answering them from facts available in the public domain: 'Is the data adequate for analysis?' and 'Is the list representative?' (Wainwright 1984, 8) The answer to the former question was a resounding 'no', and the later more reserved, though pessimistic, 'suspect not, but unable to demonstrate' (*ibid.*).

It has been recognised from respective analyses of environmental legislature (Adams 1996) and the 'social context' for preservation (Carman 1996) within the subject, that archaeological sites have always been fortunate in the support given to their protection by fairly comprehensive legal measures. In a period of bureaucratic scrutiny by the government of the 1980s, aiming to lessen prescriptive legislation and 'red tape', such powerful measures enacted for a possibly ephemeral concern of the government, warranted review and pressure for justification and/or change.

Such is the broad 'environmental analysis' for MPP as a newly established project. A necessity for conservation as a

result of law and social concern, and a need for justification of better management from government, weighed against an existing schedule inadequate in many respects for archaeology as a discipline or justified for continued support. It must further be noted that all of this applied only to 'ancient monuments' as defined by law: 'historic buildings' have remained a separate concern within the planning system, most specifically the Planning (Listed Buildings and Conservation Areas) Act 1990 (HMG 1990), previously enacted in 1953. What is being dealt with therefore is a very specific part of the process of assessing the heritage environment that MPP undertakes, that of scheduling archaeological sites or uninhabited buildings: the archaeological parts of the built environment rather than the historic part.

This division between the archaeological and historic recurs throughout MPP as a project and, as will be seen, becomes a greater concern as the project has developed beyond the scheduling function originally assigned to it. Only since 1983 have specific criteria been applied to scheduling procedures: specifically these cover survival/condition; rarity; fragility/vulnerability; diversity; documentation; group value; and potential of ancient monuments (DoE 1983). Essentially these practical scheduling criteria all pertain to physical aspects of the monuments, and specific archaeological or conservation features, and there is little scope for wider interpretative historic appreciation of a site, though the legislation does provide for this in its broad definitions. English Heritage, in its own establishment, defines ancient monuments in a different way and this divergence may have caused some confusion or possible inability to undertake full protection of sites. Such an issue has been raised as a result of MPP's work in establishing wider contexts for archaeological protection as part of other countryside initiatives. In altering the way sites are perceived, the rigid physical criteria by which sites are identified have come under review along with the wider remit of the legal framework. A note to this effect is made in a recent government consultation, 'Protecting our Heritage' (DNH & Welsh Office 1996), and is reproduced below.

> "Ancient Monument' is defined differently in the 1979 Act and the *National Heritage Act 1983*. A monument is an 'ancient monument' for the purposes of the 1979 Act if it is a scheduled monument or a monument which, in the opinion of the Secretary of State, is of public interest by reason of historic, architectural, traditional, artistic or archaeological interest attaching to it (section 61(12) of the 1979 Act). An ancient monument for the purposes of English Heritage's general functions in the *National Heritage Act 1983* is 'any structure, work, site, garden or area which in English Heritage's opinion is of historic, architectural, traditional, artistic or archaeological interest' (section 33(7) of the *National Heritage Act 1983*)...' (*ibid.* 41)

Whilst briefly considering definitions, it is worth considering the use of the term 'monument' at this stage also. As noted by Carver (1996) and others, archaeology, and most

Figure 5.5 *Schedule plan for St Mary's Abbey. (© Crown Copyright)*

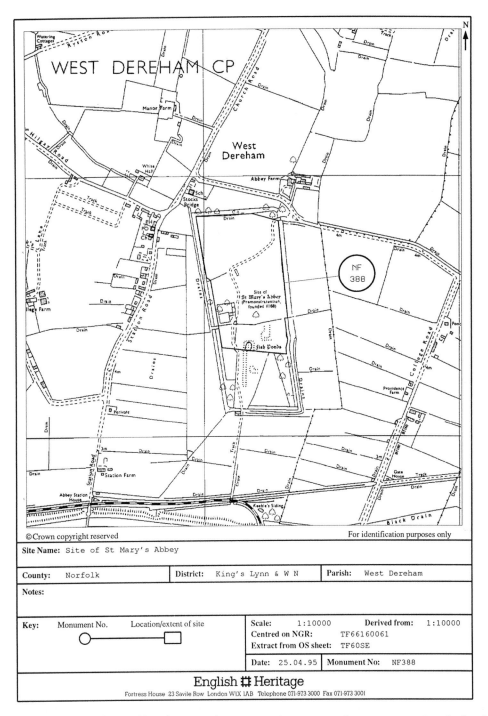

notably public archaeology, in the form of legislation and government management, has concerned itself with the monumental. The title of the project under consideration calls itself the 'Monuments' Protection Programme; legislation defines ancient 'monuments'. As a result of this, unwittingly perhaps, we bring preconceived ideas and apply them to the archaeological resource. The concept of site has become central to MPP. Monumentality and the inherent problems such a term brings with it will be further considered in due course.

I must here acknowledge the original aim of MPP. I have touched on ideas above, highlighting developments since MPP's inception, without spelling out the project's first stated

goal. This is not without reason, as I wished to introduce a wide context in which to place the project. I am not analysing MPP as a project from a management perspective, nor do I wish to review the project and score its successes or faults. Through the consideration of the six themes and sub-themes described at the outset, I intend to analyse the philosophy of the project, looking at areas that are not addressed by the project itself as part of its work or management. Thus, the model of transformation may be illustrated here in a different way suggesting that a management project, whilst transforming archaeology physically, may also transform the discipline's own perceived view of archaeology as a discipline and furthermore, resulting from its own internal project management, transform itself.

MPP's history of development is better charted elsewhere, the best review being Fairclough (1996, published as English Heritage 1996 d). Below are reproduced the principal objectives of the project at its outset, from Darvill, Saunders and Startin (1987).

'Its principal objectives are:

1   to review and evaluate existing information about sites of archaeological and historical interest so that those of national importance can be identified;

2   to make recommendations to the Secretary of State that those monuments identified as being of national importance should be protected by law, or that some alternative action should be taken;

3   to collate information on the condition of those monuments so that the resource requirements for future preservation, and the priorities for action, can be assessed.' (*ibid.* 393)

Since the Monuments Protection Programme has been introduced in the context of legal, professional and governmental concern for the archaeological resource, the aims above might indicate a relatively simple procedure. An understanding of the management process as has been gained from the previous case study however, shows that just such a simple procedure becomes complicated in practice. Such complication is not introduced for its own sake to perpetuate the management function: the developed function of the strategic management process identifies, through environmental analysis, a scenario that may not have previously been seen, but which may be affected by the project. Such identification and analysis by the MPP's managers, resulting in sub-projects to answer questions raised by MPP's overall aim, provides essential justification for itself and its purpose. A themed approach enables the wider picture to be questioned, perhaps impossible by the project management itself. Thus the question can be posed: what is the MPP doing?

MPP: a transformation from concept to object

The Monuments Protection Programme illustrates the proposed model of transformation from concept to object in one obvious way, and in a variety of other, less visible means also considered here. Though acting as heritage management in practice, prime consideration has to be given to how the project is 'acting' as management rather than how it is managing what it is doing: tautology perhaps, though important to distinguish. The process of scheduling, then, is unimportant; as it is the means by which the project allows scheduling to take place that form the more subtle transformations within this case study.

The overriding transformation that is visible and forms a prioritised aim of the project and the institution running it is to create an archaeological resource worthy of protection. This transformation is more suited to the corporate analysis already carried out and as we have moved down the scale

to a specific management project, a more relevant aim and transformation must be distinguished: one which has relevance to this project only. Again, this is fairly visible as the end goal for the MPP: to review the resource and identify sites of national importance, and recommend some sites for scheduling by the Secretary of State, by reviewing existing information and assessing future requirements for preservation. This aim, an amalgamation of the 'principal objectives' noted above, applies only to the Monuments Protection Programme. No other functional management project of English Heritage at this level on their perceived hierarchy has this aim. Tasks or management projects undertaken within the remit of MPP will thus treat such a project-specific aim as their 'corporate aim', and each in turn will have its own unique aim at its level of the organisational hierarchy. Essentially identification of this aim shows the intricacies of management of this project. Each task within it may thus be distinguished from any other task within the organisation.

The transformation at this stage is not particular to MPP however. Though the project's aim is unique, the transformation that occurs in the practical management of the project is shared with other projects within English Heritage such as World Heritage consultation with UNESCO for Hadrian's Wall, or Historic Properties management at Baconsthorpe Castle. Archaeology, or the concept of its existence in the world around us, is transformed into sites, 'interpretations' and the legal constraints known as scheduled ancient monuments. The MPP is one way of achieving this transformation, and though unique in itself is not the only way of achieving this particular transformation.

I have suggested that the MPP does contain a series of other more subtle transformations, and these may be teased out by management of the project in practice and the development that it has undergone in order to find the best way of achieving its aims. I suggest that whilst some transformations are posed as questions to solve by use of management, other transformations may prove to show themselves as illustrative of the process after the event of management. To use an analogy from chemical reactions, there are by-products of the main transformation – which, in themselves, may be other transformations. These should be acknowledged and understood – assessment of the environment after management and gauging the effects that any particular action has had may thus inform future choices, building a corpus of knowledge and realisation.

The MPP through its three-stage process of characterisation, discrimination and assessment, creates physical entities or scheduled ancient monuments. Or at least, this would be an assessment of the preliminary results of the project: once the term 'monument' has been questioned, it can be found that other transformations begin to take place, where a scheduled ancient monument is not the only eventual outcome. The realisation of this, through the awareness of MPP management, affects the project through opening new possibilities and raising questions to answer and justify. The importance of information comes to the fore – whereby the physical structure of Hadrian's Wall can be assessed as being part of a wider Military Zone, and St. Mary's Abbey forming part of the Premonstratensian religious order.

The ideology, which becomes clear from the project, therefore suggests that there are three different kinds of transformation taking place, each a result of different management sub-processes. Like Carman (1996) or Thompson (1979), it can be suggested that these transformations are in terms of physical change; change as moral entity; or change as an entity of knowledge. The key is this term of 'monument': not so much in terms of its definitions under law, but realisation of the nature of a monument as something that may be identified and called an ancient monument, or something else. An alternative term that perhaps may not be so confusing in this case is 'site'. The implication within the legislation that MPP started working in as a framework, is that physical entities already existing within the environment may be identified as sites, and then, through application of a management procedure within a legal framework, be transformed into a protected site or scheduled ancient monument. Hadrian's Wall exists as a linear masonry and earthwork feature; Baconsthorpe Castle exists as a ruined fortified manor house; and St. Mary's Abbey as a set of disparate earthworks bounded by the remains of an enclosure.

It has been established that heritage is an intangible concept. The management process undertaken by MPP, coupled with knowledge and debate within the archaeological discipline, has shown that the site itself is a concept that is intangible until it can be defined clearly. The outcome of the management process however, tends to select one particular form of a site in order to accord definition to its physical existence. It is this form of site that is identified through systematic identification as a particular form of archaeological site.

Furthermore, a protected site or scheduled ancient monument, the end product of the transformation from the concept of an archaeological site, has undergone further transformation. The site becomes protected: there are certain actions that will or will not happen to it: its continued existence as a part of the changing landscape has been prescribed physically as a result of that legal protection. Such protection under the Ancient Monuments and Archaeological Areas Act 1979 may provide for other physical changes, i.e. what can physically happen to the site once objectified and re-conceptualised as important. This is a further step in the management process, not specifically part of MPP. A scheduled site may be excavated, conserved, opened for access and so on, under provisions such as Sections 17 or 24 in the Act. Thus Hadrian's Wall is consolidated and surveyed, and the sections in private ownership become eligible for Ancient Monument grants. Baconsthorpe, on the other hand, was taken into guardianship, conserved and opened to the public by English Heritage.

Because of the concept of 'monumentality', the site, its identification and protection by law in defining a 'monument', is the smallest building block of archaeology that can be dealt with in this public management sphere. However, though the term 'site' is used freely, tension is found here between the legal unit of site, the professional conception of site, and the legal constraint of site.

The nature of law as an accepted social construct (Giddens 1993) means that there is a framework for the physical nature of a site or monument, though once a 'ground-rule' such as this has been spelt out, there is scope for wider discussion of what constitutes a site within the context of that legal framework and the environment of the institution. The notion of 'ring-fencing' may be applied therefore to sites, and this will be further considered as a separate theme later in this case study.

There are three changes (physical, moral and knowledge) that dictate the other transformations that may occur, though again allowing scope for variability in such transformation from concept to object. *Physical* change, as we have already seen, is visible: a scheduled site is protected in the environment and changes by its different treatment, so that the environment around may alter in a different way to change 'allowed' on the site. This is the case even at St. Mary's Abbey where inspections are undertaken of the scheduled site to ensure that it is not being harmed, though little physical intervention management is carried out. The *moral* change that occurs is the acceptance within society that legislation can be applied to an entity accepted and acknowledged as being an archaeological monument. This is largely unseen – and takes the form of professional or managerial opinion, justified through such process as the MPP through 'system-aided judgement' (Darvill et al 1987; Darvill 1988). A site is here identified, and that site may become a protected site.

The third change is that of *knowledge*. This takes the form of accepted wisdom and experience, backed up where possible and appropriate with system-aided or scientific judgement. Thus a physical landscape entity may be recognised through the management process of MPP to be an archaeological site, and through classification and subsequent legal classification, justified as of national importance. It may also become knowledge of a different kind, part of the bank of archaeological knowledge in the discipline through analysis. This knowledge is in effect an object: the scheduled ancient monument represents a piece of information, relevant to the archaeological discipline in particular, and elsewhere classified as knowledge. The site of St. Mary's Abbey is not just some earthworks but the remains of an identified Abbey with particular religious links and history. It *is* St. Mary's Abbey, a Premonstratensian foundation, founded in 1188 (see Figure 5.5).

Once objectified, the archaeological resource may of course undergo further change, but not as a part of this management project. Once the site has been protected, the aim of the project has been successful, and the transformations in this context come to a halt. It is at this point, that the collection of objects (collectively as data) can return back into the form of concept for another series of transformations in other management contexts (management agreement, Guardianship property, World Heritage Site). The hierarchy of data collectively adding to information, which collectively adds to knowledge, is a cumulative process, itself a psychological and sociological concern and too complex for consideration here. It can be suggested that where physical management is the transformative process, the model sees continual transformation: from concept to object in the first stage, and object to concept in the second. Thus heritage may be a scheduled ancient monument; a result of the transformation from concept to object, and that Scheduled Ancient Monument is of national importance (object transformed back into concept). Baconsthorpe is of national importance as an example of a unique fortified manor house, whilst Hadrian's Wall is of importance as a unique linear defensive feature and an original boundary of the Roman Empire.

Project management at the MPP

The time, effort and economics invested by English Heritage in the Monuments Protection Programme were large by archaeological standards. As a project with specific aims and a budget, a complete management structure had to be constructed, reflecting those aims whilst working within the institutional arrangements of English Heritage. The costs of establishing the project were expected to be substantial, but there is a general expectation in management that these costs lessen as project management settles into a routine. The project still however remained a major resource implication for English Heritage, costing hundreds of thousands of pounds as the central core of its archaeological programme.

Those costs are related more to the work involved than the cost of getting the work done. Much of MPP's research and survey work has been contracted out from English Heritage as the precise definition and scope of it have become determined (English Heritage 1996 d), i.e. it was unknown at the start of the project precisely what it would entail. In short, it can be said that in order to protect the heritage resource, there must first be a firm understanding of it, what has already been identified, and exactly what there is. Whilst it has been argued strongly that archaeology is a non-renewable resource (Darvill 1987), as MPP began its work it was soon found that there was no firm idea of how many archaeological sites there were in the country, no exact position known for many, and, as a result of general trends affecting archaeological interpretation, new sites were coming to be considered as of archaeological interest every day. The argument that the resource as a whole is finite is still held in many places, though it must be recognised that as a result of MPP's attempts to understand the resource, such a tenet is becoming harder to justify. There will be a limited number of Neolithic long barrows in England, but until we have the technology to identify every example of every class of monument with complete certainty, it cannot be argued that the resource is finite. This is especially

true if one considers that the timescale of archaeology is increasing, backwards on an evolutionary perspective and forwards on a socio-historic perspective: new types of Palaeolithic site are being uncovered through survey and excavation, and new classes of site from recent history are establishing themselves as worthy of research and in some cases preservation. The archaeological resource, far from running out, is constantly renewing itself and may, in itself, be considered to be sustainable.

Startin laid out four stages for testing the methodology of the MPP at the outset of the project (Startin 1987): 'establishing the countrywide database on which evaluation will be founded; improving documentation and mapping procedures within English heritage; evaluation of the data to select monuments for scheduling; and making recommendations to the Secretary of State.' (*ibid*. 32) The second and fourth stages were relatively simple operations in the management processes internally established already at English Heritage. These could be adopted and adjusted for use by the MPP: this can be seen in the weighty Scheduling Procedures Manual, revised and issued for MPP (English Heritage 1993 e); and computerisation of mapping and databases (Clubb 1988; Clubb and Startin 1995).

Database assessment meant involvement of the Royal Commission on the Historic Monuments of England (RCHME), and development of 'systematic approaches for classifying and evaluating the archaeological resource.' (Fairclough 1996, 3) As noted above, MPP primarily established the fact that not enough was known about the identified archaeological resource: 'the systematic approach to SMR-based evaluation confirmed that only the better-studied classes of monument could be evaluated from existing data.' (*ibid*)

It is unnecessary to go into great detail about the process for evaluation of sites, other than to point out that the deficiency in information prompted a series of other projects to address such questions. It is not a poor reflection on archaeology, as much information has been gathered on sites with excellent documentation: but for the project to work in terms of management of rigid data sets, justified academically and managerially to a government overseer, new ways of looking at the information and curation of increased data had to be established first. Whilst there is full government support for protection of the heritage, such support must be justified economically year by year (DCMS 1998). Thus each project must yield tangible returns – in the case of MPP the target set by government for English Heritage is a minimum of 1,500 scheduling recommendations each year (English Heritage 1997 a). The MPP has to provide the information necessary to make these recommendations within the framework of law and statutory guidance. Further consideration of the frameworks for MPP, which contributed to the establishment of sub-projects, is considered in a separate section.

The crux of the underlying problem necessitating the sub-projects described below is set out by Startin's obvious comments (1992). 'Where we understand the nature of the archaeological resource, we know how to record it; we can define the 'user requirement'. However, we have difficulty recording what we do not understand and herein lies the challenge. It is not enough simply to record the easily recordable: we must attempt to record all the forms of heritage in order to provide a database which will support both further academic study and the needs of cultural resource management.' (*ibid*. 205). It may be noted that within this statement he treats the archaeological resource as objectified already.

Since archaeology exists as a professional academic subject, remains can be identified and analysed through professional judgement within the discipline. This is not enough however for the management process of a public institution such as English Heritage, ultimately answering to the government in terms of professionalism in management and economics. There must be a combination of system-aided judgement and professional judgement (as noted by Fairclough 1996). At the end of the day however, the system-aided approach may ultimately provide the most justifiable results in management and economic terms. The tension between the two is not easy to resolve particularly in MPP's case, where some unknown quantities are being dealt with.

Differently scaled evaluation projects form the solution to the dilemma of the archaeological resource. The MPP has used two scales: "SMR-based' evaluation using existing information contained within local authority records, and 'nationally-based' evaluation, using specially-commissioned and largely desk-based assessments of significant parts of the resource for which existing information was inadequate for MPP purposes.' (*ibid*. 3) As noted previously then, what at first seemed to be a relatively simple objectification procedure of scheduling ancient monuments became more complicated, albeit with greater justification, as a result of the management procedure. Nevertheless this has created a mass of facts and figures for interpretation.

The survey of information held in SMRs yielded new information for the project, revising its original estimates for the number of monuments needed to be scheduled to make protection representative (Wainwright 1984). Figures in English Heritage Archaeology Review 1992-93 (English Heritage 1993 d, 25) showed the following situation. It was established that there were 415,000 relevant records in the country SMRs; 215,000 of those (48%) referred to remains which might be identified as monuments under the 1979 Act. Of that 215,000, only 70,000 had been evaluated as falling within the approximately 200 monument classes identified for MPP purposes, acknowledging that some areas of recording remains insufficiently advanced. 30,000 of the sites may warrant scheduling, and these were divided into confidence groups depending on the information known about them.

Aside from assessments of known information, the MPP began to undertake new research for new information to aid its overall aims. These included research on how

best to manage the project and its aims, such as the MPP manuals (Darvill, five volumes 1988) explaining the project's relevance to sites in different settings and the ideas behind any assessment of the historic environment. Specific system-aided management documents include the SMR evaluation procedures, containing the scores for monument assessment criteria on a county basis, and a combination of system and professional judgements include the 225-plus monument class descriptions. For each identified class of monument (Darvill, Saunders and Startin 1987), 'these documents set out a synthesis of current knowledge,' 'helping to define national importance on the basis for example of rarity, archaeological potential and vulnerability.' (Fairclough 1996, 5) An example of the relevant class descriptions for the sites mentioned here, comprising academic surveys of form and function can be seen in Figure 5.6.

At the national scale, effectively new information is being created which may feed into the practical protection afforded at the site-based local level. The projects of assessment here comprise: industrial monuments; archaeological remains in towns (intensive and extensive urban area assessment); early prehistoric settlement represented by lithic scatter sites; recent defence sites; ecclesiastical sites; air photograph sites; settlement patterns; and historic landscape assessment.

In the three stage process used by English Heritage, and outlined in the first edition of Exploring Our Past (1991), this suite of projects address each stage: identification, understanding and recognition of significance, and protection. MPP itself uses the terms of characterisation, assessment and evaluation (Fairclough 1996). Whilst many of these sub-projects are yet to be completed, it is recognised that the results produced may not directly support scheduling action as protection. In other words, in the attempt to understand the resource, with the aim of using legislation to protect it, English Heritage and others have become aware that a single and very specific process of protection may not always be suitable. Scheduling works for discretely defined ancient monuments under certain conditions, usually in a countryside location, but for other remains scheduling may not be an option, or at least not the most suitable option. This has therefore created another area of study: assessment of the suitability of protection measures, and evaluation of protection under different statutory frameworks. As different sites come to be assessed, it is noted that scheduling now forms a smaller part of the overall aim of the project.

The Monuments Protection Programme has therefore mushroomed as a producer of information, and a number of transformations can be seen from the above. Most notably the project has itself been transformed from concept to object – an idea of protection to actual protection in management and assessment. Furthermore the concept of the archaeological site has been transformed into many different objects or types of site at different scales as a result of the assessment programme. Perhaps most interestingly, in terms of management of the sites in the

Figure 5.6 *Monument Class Description. (reproduced from English Heritage Web site)*

MONUMENTS PROTECTION PROGRAMME
MONUMENT CLASS DESCRIPTION
MONASTERIES FOR MEN (POSTCONQUEST)

AUGUST 1989

1 Definition	2 Date	3 General Description	4 Distribution and regional variation
5 Rarity	6 Survival and Potential	7 Associations	8 Characterisation criteria
12 Bibliography	13 Acknowledgements	14 Figures	

MONASTERIES FOR MEN (POSTCONQUEST)
Alternative, colloquial and related terms: Abbey; Alien Priory; Cathedral Priory; Cell; Convent; Priory
Ordnance Survey Map Terms: Abbey; Priory
RCHME Thesaurus Monument Type : Monastery.

1 Definition A monastery for men is a settlement built to house a community of monks or canons and, in some orders, lay-brothers. Monasteries are recognised through standing remains, earthworks and documentary records. Their main components provided facilities for worship, communal living and subsistence. These may include the church and domestic ranges grouped around a main cloister; a subsidiary cloister which might accommodate offices, an abbot's lodging, infirmaries, and an inner gatehouse; and an outer court for guest houses and ancillary industrial and agricultural buildings. This precinct was bounded by a wall or moat, pierced by an outer gatehouse and perhaps marked also by a gate chapel. Within or near the precinct, were mills, fishponds, and field systems. This class description discusses monasteries for men of traditional and Reformed orders (Arrouiasian, Augustinian, Benedictine, Bonhommes, Canons of the Holy Sepulchre, Cistercian, Cluniac, Fontevraultine, Gilbertine, Grandmontine, Premonstratensian, Savignac, Tironian, Trinitarian, Victorine). Cathedral monasteries, including their post-medieval development, are covered elsewhere. Friaries, Nunneries, Double houses and monasteries with distinct alternative morphological characteristics (Charterhouses, Preceptories, Hermitages) form separate class descriptions. Alien priories may be morphologically similar to monastic granges, which form another class. Monastic cells may closely resemble hermitages. The monument class of monasteries for men (post Conquest) encompasses foundations dating from around the Norman Conquest to the Dissolution of the monasteries (1535-40).

historic environment, a transformation has occurred in the concept of protection. Designation by a particular legal means (here the Ancient Monuments and Archaeological Areas Act 1979) has been transformed through the management process of MPP into an array of objects or means, including other legislative measures such as application of Listed Buildings law or planning guidance such as PPG16, and non-statutory designation. It is clear that the word 'monumentality', and the idea that such a term represents, has been effectively challenged in the course of MPP's assessment projects and their addition to knowledge about the historic environment. The effects extend beyond English Heritage's own management influence in the heritage environment.

Transformation in space, site and scale

There are five key themes, all of which are interlinked, and comprise transformations of a more unexpected nature than the norm. Three of the themes are treated together in this section, sharing characteristics on geographic and physical form. An understanding of these thematic units may provide answers to challenges lying within the standard model of transformation that have taken the management of the project and altered project procedure (management system) as a part of that project management.

It is unnecessary, as noted earlier, to comprehensively examine the historical changes in the management of MPP as a project. More may be learnt from a characterisation of the present situation, using current 'awareness' gained within CRM and the science of management. It is therefore prudent to pose the question: within the concepts of space, site and scale, what is the MPP doing? Working within the framework already established for the project, that of legislative protection for archaeological sites of national importance, such a question might be answered in a number of ways.

In achieving the aims of the project, namely protection for sites, there is an assumption that firstly we are able to determine what a site is, and secondly that we are able to formulate some form of suitable protection for such sites. The former consideration concerns us most at this point. Definition or positive determination therefore become key terms and illustrate the model in practice. The concept of site is defined; the space that site occupies and the space that is enclosed by the site (i.e. its features) is determined; and the morphological form in which that site is placed is also determined. Hadrian's Wall is an excellent example here. It can be divided into pieces of information comprising sites, features and units all part of the Military Zone. It can be seen that these three determinations or definitions occur at different physical scales. The features that make up the site are smaller that the site itself, which is smaller than the landscape in which it, exists. This landscape is part of the wider environment. Such an assumption becomes complicated when other scales are taken into consideration in this definition process. Questions raised by this have thus been incorporated into the sub-projects of MPP. It will be now shown how this happens.

There are a combination of different scales that can be worked with in defining the physical remains that can be considered archaeological, and therefore candidates for protection. Having broken through the idea of 'monumentality' discussed already, the field becomes wide open for the concept of what constitutes a site. There *is* a limiting factor, however. The legislation that allows for any kind of protection requires a specific label and line to be drawn on a map, therefore defining the site in geographic space. In reality there is also a limit on the size that the designated geographic space can be for obvious social reasons. A three-way pull is therefore established on the defined archaeological entity: the definition of the site in each case; the ability to limit such a site in a reasonable amount of geographic space; and the ability of any piece of legislation to protect such a site in that defined geographic space. These tensions are illustrated in Figure 5.7 below.

The concept of monumentality worked well for protection of single monuments in the countryside. Moving from monument to site demolished the special nature that seems to have been created for small single monuments, providing the closest opportunity to re-construct the archaeological resource from raw materials. The challenges of space, site and scale had only begun however, as the suitability of scheduling legislation for all sites was questioned. Early attempts to 'force-fit' the protective measures to the geography can be seen in the attempt to identify relict cultural landscapes (Darvill, Gerrard and Startin 1993). The field widened literally, as physical extremities of site have been challenged by the ability to find them. Cultural meaning in space has become a prime consideration – seen in MPP through the studies of industry, lithic scatters and the air-photo National Mapping Programme operated by the RCHME.

In asking some fundamental questions about the archaeological resource, MPP has transformed a way of thinking about archaeological sites. It has been recognised that landscape cannot be protected using the idea of 'relict cultural' remains, nor is archaeological definition and protection always the most effective means of conservation. Landscape has become a wider environmental consideration for archaeology, with characterisation more use than prescriptive identification or definition (papers in Fairclough, Lambrick & McNab 1996). Other agencies, whose perception of landscape differs to that of archaeology, may provide the lead – such as the Countryside Agency or English Nature now reformed into Natural England and the Commission for Rural Communities: though they too question the possibilities of protecting 'landscape' as an entity.

The question of space is paramount when concerned with landscape: bounded monuments depend on their class

– for example battlefields and parks may still be defined as physical entities – beyond this the concept of site becomes difficult to sustain. A variety of projects (ibid. English Heritage 1997 c, Fairclough 1996 b) have been established to test ideas on identification and protection here.

In considering the remains of industry, it is recognised that the extant resource presents a biased picture (Alfrey & Putnam 1992), as the successful mechanisms of production have been reused and reconfigured, whilst redundant technology has become industrial archaeology. The social context of industry has therefore been investigated in order to provide a better understanding of the industry, its remains and what to protect (LUAU 1995). In the urban situation, the complexities of archaeological deposits and the piecemeal provision of substantial information due to keyhole excavation, has led to two separate initiatives. Towns are now being subjected to Intensive and Extensive Urban Area Assessments (Startin 1991; English Heritage 1992 b), and generalised zones are being established, combining predictive modelling of the urban resource with known information.

Though the virtues of information production as a result of these initiatives are obvious, and may enable debate on the ways forward, it can be seen that at the same time as providing more prescriptive information at the small scale – clearly defining features and classes of site – at the large scale less prescriptive terms are being used, such as 'characterisation' or 'assessment'. This is the crux of the matter with implications for both archaeology and management as disciplines. Improvement in management technique shows clearly more options available as a result of providing more information to process: but this has a counteracting effect in archaeology. The more information we have, the less we know due to lack of comprehensive analysis – thus possibly preventing effective management. The ability to break the circle perhaps takes the form of an arbitrary decision, with the realisation that at some future point any decision taken may be criticised – hence system-aided judgement.

Sustainable approaches, implying the possibilities of reversing any procedure undertaken, may provide the safety net and therefore should be no deterrent to positive action. Within archaeology and the MPP itself, the debates about space, site and scale will continue inevitably, but the range of sub-projects addressing the problems inherent in space, site and scale, and the acknowledgement of sites within an environment, may tip the balance further away from the physical nature of the site.

The management process within MPP has further realised its priorities are to its customers – to people rather than monuments – as it is people, in particular communities, that created these features in the first place. The industrial protection programme has prompted this, identifying sites as part of a social and economic phenomenon, and archaeological remains as being representative of that. Consideration of archaeology and the changes in the

Figure 5.7 *Three-way tension of scale.*

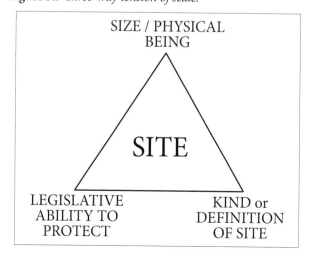

concept of time will assist in the enhancement of this kind of understanding, and this may eventually affect the range of sites within the 'prehistoric portfolio'. Time as a concept is further considered below. Thus as knowledge is enhanced about the social environment in which we live, space, site and scale may become clearer or less relevant in a holistic protection package. The alternative use of protective measures (rather than invoking the Ancient Monuments and Archaeological Areas Act 1979), may further bridge the divergence between museum and CRM practises. Hadrian's Wall is, for example, now promoted in another context as a long distance footpath as part of the Countryside Commission's National Trail network. An aware MPP management project, in questioning space, site and scale, considers whether we are attempting to recreate the museum experience in the landscape, i.e. without walls, and must find its answers from outside as well as within the discipline. Furthermore, it must continue the attempt to reconcile the existence of a modern landscape as a container of permanently placed ancient features.

It has not been the intention of this section to provide answers – analysis of space, site and scale has illustrated the increasing variables at play in resource management and the increasing complexity of the contexts for manipulating the variables, on a basic physical scale. The following consideration of the themes of time and 'ring-fencing' in the MPP process addresses further conceptual transformations before the concluding section may draw some clear themes from this, suggesting that we may be learning more about knowledge than what to do with it.

The MPP and the concept of time

It might be supposed that the concept of time would be easy to analyse under the auspices of archaeology. Archaeology and management as disciplines however tend to concentrate on points in time, rather than the ongoing march of time. Even MPP-prompted projects like the Monuments at Risk Survey (MARS) assess the survival of monuments at fixed points in time (by decade) (Darvill and Wainwright 1994 a & b). Archaeological classification of objects and sites distinguishes them by typology and period, and the formation process or transformation processes that physically take place on site as a result of their creation by human action fall to the scope of academic archaeology, rather than heritage management.

The MPP, through its projects, reinterprets the concept of site, as already seen, and further reinterprets what may be considered to be an archaeological site due to its implicit consideration of the passage of time. As pieces of information, archaeological sites become fixed in time. As they are classified, interpreted, features dated, and so on, dates and times are ascribed to each piece of data: the label attached to each object fixes it in time, and, as has been seen, in space. As the MPP has developed, in characterising the archaeological resource time has become an important management consideration as a tool or currency for scoring purposes, and also for more general character assessment.

Once the site has been 'created' however, time becomes less important as the site is fitted back into its modern landscape. Time is used by the MPP management process as little more than a justification that the site is of a certain archaeological class.

If we move beyond the information, however, drawing again on phenomenological research in archaeology, such as seen in Tilley (1994), and consider what happens at the site as it succumbs to being managed as heritage, interesting transformations again take place from the concept of time to the object of time. When managed as an archaeological resource, sites can be assessed and placed on two time 'scales': the first is the identification of the site and its ascription to a certain archaeological class, such as a monastery for men (Figure 5.2; Gilchrist 1989). The MPP has classified over 200 different kinds of archaeological site in this way, and has prepared a Single Monument Class Description for each (ibid.). The second scale on which the site is placed through the management process is a comparative measure between the site's creation and its survival at a point in the present. The function of time has created the site's 'condition' by virtue of its continued existence in the environment through time. The MARS project specifically looks at the environmental conditions of sites and their effects on site survival through time. Site survival does play a key role in conjunction with other scheduling criteria on deciding whether the site will be protected by law. Hence sites that are poorly preserved are less likely to be afforded protection.

The move beyond the management and information content of the site presents a more difficult concept of time. Kubler (1962) provides a background to this. He considers the site by virtue of its existence in both time and space, and the movement in time made by the site when the management process is applied to it in the present day. It is best explained step-by-step creating a picture of the site and its place in time, using Hadrian's Wall again.

The site (Hadrian's Wall) exists in the present time as a physical entity. It is therefore of the present day in the form visible on the ground, or by archaeological methodology or air photography, survey, excavation or events. The site has an existence in a particular physical form that is probably different to that physical form in which the modern 'site' was first created. The Wall now comprises ruins, museum archives, earthworks or excavated features. In effect, a site has decayed through time, and what is seen now is not the original site. As time has moved on, the site has been reconfigured physically due to its continuing physical existence in a changing environment. The site decays through natural process, or by human intervention, such as from visitors clambering on the ruins, or the Wall being a traditional source of building materials for the local area, or used as a hardcore base for later road-building. Furthermore, as noted previously, understanding of 'site' can be perceived differently depending on the site's value at a particular point in time (e.g. creation, alteration, spatial location or boundary etc.). The technical sense of monumentality has only been applied to the site in modern times.

Following on from this, it may be argued that as archaeology comes to study a particular site, that very process of assessment makes the site both ancient and modern at the same time. The site exists as a modern physical entity in the environment, but archaeology instils the site with another timeframe – that of recognising it as an indication of being not of our present time, but past time. It is a recognised frontier of the Roman Empire but also, at a later date, a national boundary between the Scots and the English. Historical and archaeological methodology, coupled with perception of physical existence in the environment, therefore suspends present time on an identified site, and through its classification process recreates the site as of ancient time (or backdates the construct) (G. Fairclough, pers. com.). Information in the site's physical form backs up this ascription in a scientific manner. The site at any point therefore exists in our perception in at least two timeframes: ancient and modern. Each of these has time-depth, needing further careful consideration. It is not presented in guides as a pile of stone, but as the remains of Hadrian's Wall, and a Roman defensive site and a national boundary: each have their own attached history.

What happens to the site after it has been identified and subsequently protected? Most specifically a 'ring-fence' is put around the site, and the implications of this will be further considered in the next section. With respect to the concept of time, however, a protected site is further transformed from existence in two timeframes, into existence in three or more. This results from the imposition of the protective measures themselves. The third timescale for the site is created because the imposition of protective measures has the ability to freeze the site at a point in time. Whilst the site continues to exist as ancient remains in the modern world, it also now exists as a site protected at a previous point in time, and its physical change, whilst not frozen exactly at that point will probably have been slowed. That is to say, that whilst no explicit physical protective measures may necessarily be used on the site once legally scheduled, there are certain physical eventualities that may be prevented from occurring – i.e. total destruction by continued natural forces, or human intervention in gradual decay. It can be seen therefore that space, site and scale are also affected by this ring fencing – again this will be considered in the next section. It must also be noted that any alteration of a site in the present will be considered purely as another 'historical event' in future assessment of the site (especially seen in the historic property case studies). Thus the Wall was consolidated and partly rebuilt in the nineteenth and twentieth centuries. What remains now is also of that 'time': with the remains of Housesteads or Vindolanda being an example of archaeological practice earlier in the twentieth century.

Essentially what has happened to the site once protected legally is that, whether physical protection is undertaken on the site or not, the site begins an existence in a timeframe outside that of its surrounding environment. This may not be visible at the site, and such a transformation is more clearly shown at sites in guardianship, which are opened to the

public, such as Baconsthorpe Castle seen here. A separate case study will also consider this aspect. The reasons for a site's movement in and out of different timeframes is due to our perception of the site, prompted by the second stage of the transformation from object back to concept – and it can be seen how this links with the MPP's questioning of the suitability and effectiveness of legal protection measures for sites, as well as looking at what constitutes a site itself. Comparison of ways of perceiving the world around us may provide the next logical steps in understanding the protection of cultural resources outside our own society. Such work is undertaken in phenomenological projects, clearly within the second stage of the model. An example worth noting of this may compare our 'Western' perception of 'site' and its existence in time and space and the lack of oral tradition linking site, time and place. The 'dwelling perspective' used by Australian aboriginal groups provides a very different way of looking at the environment in which a person lives, negating individual identification of features in need of protection, and providing lessons for a holistic and sustainable existence in our environment (Chippindale pers. com.).

'Ring-fencing' and the management process

The idea of 'ring-fencing' has been mentioned already, and is studied further here in order to show how it effectively explains the relationship between the MPP and archaeology more generally. The term can be used both literally and figuratively in the pulling together of concepts explored in this case study. Taken literally, a site that is ring-fenced by the MPP is set apart from its surrounding environment through its protection under heritage legislation. On a figurative level, ring fencing may be a result of an academic exercise to determine what constitutes the boundaries of any particular site. Ring-fencing therefore is an implicit process of management which makes something stand out; differences between one thing and another are accentuated by this ring-fencing, and it may be as simple as identification of a site or object and its classification using a label such as 'recumbent stone circle'. It allows us on a very basic level to say what something is, and what something is not.

As a result of this basic ring fencing, the literal identification of an object, some degree of transformation has already taken place for us to be able to give something a name. This transformation relies more on mental and psychological process, and so is not considered relevant for exploration here. Aside from these personal mental processes, the more general result of ring fencing brings an object into play under the remit of management. Management cannot work unless it has something to manage, and the primary ring-fencing process provides for this.

At the outset the management process identifies frameworks for operation: effectively another kind of ring fencing. These frameworks may be of a physical nature, or of a non-physical nature affecting the management process internally and externally. Again there are different scales seen here: ring-fencing identifies frameworks for the project and its own system of management; and ring-fencing is identified as that which is imposed as a result of the management of the project. Boundaries are thus created which establish where and how the project may or may not be managed.

There are various frameworks that are external to the project, but whith both direct and indirect effects on the management of it. The list may not be exhaustive, but includes: the academic framework; physical framework; geographic framework; associative framework; legal framework; statutory framework; interpretative framework; and social framework. Specific frameworks that may be considered as internal to the project, affecting its ability to function directly, include the management framework (considered in the previous case study); the framework of public institutional management; the legislative framework for protection of sites and the statutory duties of English Heritage as an organisation; staff and organisation; technology; information and knowledge available both with the discipline and held as data by the RCHME for example; management systems; and the economics and time constraints of project management. Most notably from the identified aims of the project, the legislative framework and procedures are placed at centre stage as MPP, in not only assessing the resource but the management of it, addresses the context of law, ultimately questioning the established concept of monumentality.

The reassessment of the legislative protection for sites and archaeological finds has effects outside the project, and allows the parts of the archaeological research programme of English Heritage to be geared around it as questions raised by MPP need to be found answers. Furthermore, as has been seen already, this reassessment of legislation has challenged scheduling under the Ancient Monuments and Archaeological Areas Act 1979 as the best way of protecting archaeological remains. It has been shown through the various research programmes, such as the industrial monuments assessment and the lithic scatters study, that certain 'sites' are unsuitable for scheduling, and that scheduling is unsuitable for certain sites: depending on the context these are not the same as each other. There has therefore been consideration of the relative values of statutory protection, and non-statutory designation, where a change in the wider social context and acknowledgement of the heritage resource allows for equivalent protection measures without need for recourse to statute law. Again, Hadrian's Wall can be used as an example, where the entire military zone is not scheduled, but is afforded various degrees of overall protection through identification in the widescale countryside management plan (English Heritage 1997 b).

The MPP as a management system has also re-evaluated the process of valuation as part of system-aided judgement of sites for scheduling. Combining past policy capture (Fairclough 1996) and professional assessment, a system-aided approach has been established, which can justify itself in as scientific a manner as possible. More general valuation

of the past has also been affected; a consideration central to this thesis in suggesting that management, as a discipline adopted within an archaeological context, is responsible for such a change. Lipe's consideration of value within cultural resources remains as the most succinct explanation of its relevance. The systems of management have their necessity, in that '...such contexts or frames of reference are likely and certain to shift – emphasising the relativity of resource value' (Lipe 1984, 2): the process of management is justified, as it balances tangible interests within a framework of intangible properties.

The divide between public and private is not considered within the project management of the MPP, though it is considered here as part of the context for the model of transformation. Lipe points out that, 'the general point is that any serious consideration of the past removes us from the immediate concerns with the here and now of our private, individual wants and needs, and the demands of our immediate circle of kin and associates. It plunges us directly into the larger common world which exists in the stream of time and hence bridges the mortality of generations.' (*ibid.* 10). The sites and objects which we are dealing with here already exist conceptually in the private sphere as relevant to wants and needs: MPP as a specific project in heritage management takes what exists privately and philosophically and moves it into the public sphere. Ring-fencing publicly acknowledges the site, and gives preference to that public sphere over the private. The site becomes an object moved into the public/social sphere away from one kind of philosophical existence into another kind of physical existence.

Another example may be used to illustrate this idea: an unprotected site may not be known about other than locally, if at all. The site however does exist in the environment as a concept. It is part of the heritage. Once protected or ring-fenced by the management process of identification, attention is focused upon it in the public sphere. The site has gone from a private to a public sphere – from concept to object; and in that objectified form in the public sphere it may be acted upon by forces that would previously have had no direct effect on it through their actions elsewhere in time and space. Hadrian's Wall as a site has been objectified and exists in the public sphere – it may thus be manipulated as an object by almost anybody in the world, and fitted back into his or her own private conception of heritage. If it were unprotected, and unidentified by a public institution, the site could only have been affected by local human or environmental influences, and would not be seen to be objectified as a heritage resource. The part of the Wall that runs through a farmer's field is now no longer just in his 'ownership'.

Lipe's consideration of values, and more recent assessment by Darvill (1993) of existence, use and option value, therefore has more resonance with the proposed model than Carman's (1996) re-use of Thompson's (1979) 'rubbish theory'. Carman proposes that valuation of cultural objects comes through their manipulation by law, and that protected heritage objects exist as 'other' beyond everyday comprehension. The associated research projects of the MPP, and the model proposed in this thesis have proven that this cannot be the case. Valuation comes before the imposition of law, due to the established framework for public institutional management of heritage in the UK. Valuation is inherent in the process of creating and feeding sites and information through the system of management, and the primary stages of such a process subsequently allow the application of relevant legislation in the later stages (as it must be remembered that the actual act of scheduling is undertaken outside English Heritage's remit, by the Secretary of State for Culture, Media and Sport). The application of law gives value in just such a legal framework, though valuation as 'heritage' occurs prior to this point. And, as has been noted, MPP is placing less emphasis on scheduling as an end product: rather it is now treated as one of a number of suitable protection measures. The legal 'value' is being altered by the management process of assessment.

It is difficult to see how Thompson's 'rubbish theory' (*ibid.*) can therefore be applied now to the archaeological resource. The identification and assessment of sites within their landscape in terms of space, place and time, surely suggests that by virtue of their survival, they have not been thrown away at all. Thompson maintains that in order for a site to have been thrown away as rubbish, it would necessarily be found to be destroyed. Excavation is the most frequent cause of this, and rubbish theory may therefore come to be limited to application in museums and excavation archives, where sites are recreated through academic exercise, and argued by Carman as becoming 'other' (1996, 25). The sites' status is altered in public acknowledgement only, as having heritage value. Legal protection has relevance for certain management situations only, in a physical sense – in a general perceptual sense, such legal status is a minor consideration when compared to the very act of acknowledgement by identification.

Ring-fencing, through its setting apart of information about sites, as well as the sites themselves, serves another purpose. It allows improvement in the manipulation of those resources in management: meaning that as there is greater acknowledgement of the different types of information held about sites (physical, moral etc.), there is greater variability possible in any one management process. As variables are increased, so choice increases between them, reaffirming the valuation function within the management system. Moreover, greater variability of choice results in greater particularity as an end result: so choices that can be made in the management system may produce an end result (here being protective measures) that is more relevant to a particular site. Generalised routes for conservation of sites may be drawn from the variable options presented: these have been ranked by English Heritage in preference, and outlined in its guidance for funding of archaeological research (English Heritage 1991 b). The three stages, which are deemed to be applicable across archaeology are: identification, recording and understanding as most preferable; exploitative management; and preservation

by record as least preferable. This final option covers excavation, and destruction of the site, which may only be reconstructed as an archive and excavation report existing within the museum context.

The move to and fro between generality and particularity is also seen in the kinds of protective measures used for sites. As has been seen the use of any protective measure, such as scheduling, affects the site existence in space and time. Protection covering the 'particular' tends to do this more than that which covers the 'general'. A good example of this is seen in the difference between scheduling as a 'particular' action, the effects of which have been looked at previously, and a 'general' action such as designation of the Wall within an Area of Outstanding Natural Beauty or Environmentally Sensitive Area. It can be noted that the 'general' measures that can be taken are in terms of subject matter and geography. General environmental or archaeological designations tend to have less direct effect on any site, yet may still provide adequate protective measure. At this physical level, where geographic protection may be at a broad scale, the idea of 'ring-fencing' becomes less obvious. In the Historic Landscapes Assessment project (McNab & Lambrick 1996), the idea of ring-fencing becomes redundant as a 'tapestry' is created, mapping the full variety of interests in the environment – natural, man-made etc. The concept of an enclosed space is effectively done away with, as a holistic protection in the environment is made possible. This is seen in the management plan for the Wall Zone, which tries to represent and incorporate all owners and interested parties, not just archaeological managers.

There are some final considerations to be made of the ring-fencing idea – what MPP's management does to affect the archaeological resource in its widest context. First and foremost, the management process employed with an aim of protection, and containing in it a valuation function, allows the resource to be treated as just that – a resource. In the equivalent of a feedback loop, MPP's process of management allows the identification of a resource, so that resource may be managed by MPP. In transforming sites from concepts to objects, MPP creates a resource that may be treated as a scientific sample, and therefore managed, measured and valued scientifically.

Secondly, the ring-fencing process, in showing the variety of information that the resource contains, also shows what information is not contained in it. Thus the management process had the original aim of scheduling a representative sample of sites, but found at the outset that it had not known the extent of the resource to begin with. Effective management has therefore thrown up questions arising from a lack of knowledge about an aspect of the resource. These have been answered through the sub-projects set up.

Thirdly, ring fencing has identified clearly the division between public and private, concept and object, and the role which management plays in enabling transformation between them. Added to this, through identification of public and private heritage, it helps us formulate and articulate responses to the way in which we live with and manipulate such a heritage resource. Sites are therefore completely transformed in MPP at the first and second stages of the model: as information resource with physical existence in the first stage and then valuation as conceptual monuments or heritage in the second.

The Monuments Protection Programme does not undertake any kind of ring-fencing in a vacuum however, and the final section turns to the effects of this management project beyond the bounds of protection: the effects of MPP in the wider world.

The Monuments Protection Programme and the Wider World

Having assessed some broad themes raised by the work of MPP, in conjunction with an understanding of the various aspects of the project provided by reviews such as Fairclough (1996) or Wainwright (1994), the relevance and effects of the project in the wider world can be considered.

The concept of sustainability is beginning to affect many kinds of management practice. 'There is widespread recognition that we must ensure the outcome of today's decisions do not compromise the quality of life in future generations.' (Land Use Consultants 1996, 1) Archaeology, existing as it does in the world around us, is a particular consideration of sustainable policy for the environment. In being treated as a resource, discussed earlier, sustainable management thinking makes further use of economic terminology and assesses the overall environmental resource in terms of capital. There are considered to be two kinds of environmental capital: constant environmental capital and critical environmental capital. Constant capital may be 'traded' within 'groups of assets' (*ibid.* 7). Critical capital, on the other hand, 'comprises particularly significant or fragile components of the constant capital which are considered, individually, to be valuable, irreplaceable or essential for life. Small changes (loss or damage) to these key features could have serious effects on the system as a whole, or on future understanding and enjoyment.' (*ibid*) English Heritage, English Nature and the Countryside Commission are increasingly working together in this area, towards a holistic and realistic vision of environmental protection and management (1996).

Clearly archaeology as a resource of sites and monuments fits into these ideas well: moreover, it is obvious that MPP's comparative valuation systems can assess which capital group the resource fits into. Use of sustainable management's standard terminology, applied across the field of 'environmental' studies and management, increasingly will enable progress on the ideological vision of a holistically managed sustainable existence for us all.

The MPP has effects of a less ideological nature as well, most notably in the discipline of heritage management. The aims of the projects, and the sub-projects that have been established resulting from questions raised within the management system, have focused attention within the commercial archaeology sector on the increasing complexity of managing archaeology as a resource. Greater time is being spent on the establishment of management systems and processes. These serve various purposes including the running of contract projects from MPP, such as Lancaster University Archaeological Unit's specifications for MPP Industrial Monuments (1995), or Bournemouth University's MARS Project (Darvill and Wainwright 1994).

Revision or expansion of management systems is also necessary to deal with the information being produced by MPP. This affects the archaeological community generally through its effect on academic thought: more information and analysis needing to be incorporated into theory and practice. It also affects the handling and storage of that information, acting as both archive and resource. Institutions, headed by the RCHME as the national archive (for England), are spending increased effort to standardise data manipulation (RCHME 1994), and make that data available through the National Monuments Record, and the county-based Sites and Monuments Records (SMR). At this local level, the increase in information is sustaining the raised profile of archaeology brought about by its statutory inclusion in the planning process as PPG16 (DoE 1990).

As information has become more readily available and in greater amounts to the 'managers' of the resource, so too has the necessity for more widespread public provision of information. This matter is addressed for MPP by a detailed report (Chitty 1995), suggesting an eventuality of at least 20 different publications in at least 4 different media. This refers to information provided centrally by English Heritage, and does not therefore consider the dissemination of further information arising from use of MPP's own production of information. It can be seen how the ripples in research will therefore spread widely.

The expansion of knowledge enabled by MPP's research results are already affecting central research frameworks produced by English Heritage (English Heritage 1997 d) – ultimately governed by academic and practical questions and problems of analysis of the archaeological resource. There is an inevitable knock-on effect into research frameworks outside English Heritage (Olivier 1996), as the practicalities of funding such projects may be influenced by outside forces.

An intriguing aspect of MPP's effects on archaeology as a discipline is that it is enabling the subject to be reassessed in terms of what may be considered to *be* archaeology. The subject's limits are therefore expanding into areas previously considered to be a part of the environmental sciences (now aligning archaeology with them), and expanding the chronology of archaeology to recent times, reinforcing it as an historical and socio-economic discipline. Examples seen of this are seen in the Historic Landscape Assessment project's links to English Nature's 'Natural Areas Concept' (English Nature 1993), and the Countryside Commission's 'Countryside Character Programme' (Countryside

Commission 1996), and joint consideration of sustainability (English Heritage, Countryside Commission & English Nature 1996; English Heritage 1997 c). On the ground, this is seen in the inclusion of hedgerows in landscape assessment, or the man-made effects on the landscape caused by historic industrial sites. The expanding chronology of archaeology is seen through projects including the Industrial Assessment Programme (Pearcy 1992; Cherry 1995 and Stocker 1995), or the Defence of Britain project, looking at both wartime and recent military sites (Schofield and Lake 1995).

The identification of sites, and provision of information about them, has indirect effects on tourism and public involvement in ownership and access. Increasing numbers of sites are becoming interpreted through the work of MPP and reassessment of the schedule of ancient monuments, and there is provision under law for Section 17 and 24 funding and access development (HMG 1979), to enable increased physical access to such sites. Interest thus generated reinforces archaeology as a material consideration in tourism and development policy (DNH 1997; Harland et al 1996). Tourism as a heritage consideration will be explored in a separate case study.

Effects on legislative protection for the heritage have been mentioned already, and the management process of MPP has intimate links therefore with government policy and intention for archaeology and its management. The MPP, in questioning the use of law as a protective measure, through comparative assessment of different legislative and non-statutory tools or designations, prompted a governmental review of heritage protection (DNH & Welsh Office 1996).

Public and private provisions of management systems for the heritage are also called into question, though as a contentious issue, and no specific analysis of it is made by MPP or in this study. It does remain, however, a consideration that may be addressed, most likely by central government. MPP in prompting such a review has been used by the existing management agencies such as English Heritage, RCHME and local authority SMRs to reaffirm their own position (e.g. RCHME 1996), and the increasingly important status of 'heritage' as a social, political and economic concern. At the most basic level, MPP's effect across the various management institutions is seen in enhanced or improved protection of the archaeological resource and provision of information about it.

In conclusion, it must be stated clearly that MPP has been the central focus of the case study, and I have therefore suggested possibilities of where it has affected 'heritage' within and beyond its own remit. At no point do I wish to suggest that the MPP has been solely responsible for every change seen in heritage management in the last 15 years: the project must be placed in the context of increased ability to use management as a tool to manipulate archaeology as a resource, or most recently as 'capital'. The scale of MPP as a project must not be underestimated in either physical or academic terms: sites are being scheduled at an increasing rate of up to 1800 per annum (taking the current total to over 14,000 scheduled monuments), and the money invested in the operation of the project and its supporting research runs into millions of pounds. The effects of MPP are therefore substantial and contribute in a major way to the archaeological resource, and the ways of managing it as such, in a wider environmental, economic and social context. In central argument of this thesis, key themes may again be drawn out from the MPP, which illustrate variable and new kinds of transformation, resulting from increasing use of management as a discipline for developing systems of operation and delivery.

Conclusion

The preceding sections have concentrated on various thematic ideas arising from the Monuments Protection Programme. It has already been noted that the practical aspects of the project and scheduling as a form of protection are considered elsewhere (Startin 1993; English Heritage 1996 d), and it has been the aim of this case study to explore the relevance of the proposed model to a specific management project. Following the pattern of other case studies in this thesis, key themes are therefore listed here, which summarise MPP as both illustrative of and justification of the model of transformation.

The MPP clearly objectifies the heritage in two similar fashions: the project's aim is to undertake an academic assessment of archaeology: this is necessarily objective in intent. Secondly it aims as a piece of project management to manage a specific part of the historic environment (the identified archaeology) within the clearly defined framework of English Heritage's duties with regards to England's historic environment (legal, corporate and strategic).

The Monuments Protection Programme illustrates the model of transformation on a scale of transformations, in terms of size of coverage, and practical size. The MPP, effecting such a transformation, occurs as a specific management project operated by and within the larger management institution of English Heritage. Its remit and scale are controlled by that institution and may therefore not exceed, in practical size or scope, English Heritage as the managing agency for the project. The project thus operates to assist the fulfilment of one or more of the corporate objectives of English Heritage, itself acting within the framework of heritage management in England controlled by the Department for Culture, Media and Sport.

As with the corporate case study, at this different scale it can be seen that there is a clear transformation from concept to object occurring within the intent and operation of the Monuments Protection Programme. This transformation is instigated by and effected within processes of the management system. Heritage as a concept, and the conception of heritage, is transformed within the Monuments Protection Programme, producing a variety of heritage objects, defined as 'public' by virtue of the protective management afforded to them.

A particular context in which MPP is beginning to have a particular impact is that of codifying, sorting and increasing data and ultimately knowledge. As part of the management system in operation, sites and data that have already been identified are re-examined, and that data is added to by detailed investigation projects. As the body of data is built up, it is being sorted systematically, through the 'system-aided' judgement and criteria specified, and spin-off analytical projects are therefore enabled which may add to overall archaeological knowledge. These may be specific, such as geographical studies, or with wider remit, such as the lithic scatters analysis. There is therefore a transformation occurring here also, from the concept of archaeological knowledge – a context that MPP operates within – into data and knowledge objectified by the project. Information is a vital component in the transformation.

The use of management as a tool to effect the aims of MPP has increased the number of end 'objects' or products of that management system and the specific processes or operations within it. Such an increase in production of objects, and the assessment of them by that same process that created them, allows for problems and questions to be identified and furthermore creates the ability to analyse or answer such questions and problems (for example, the nature and development of the Military Zone around Hadrian's Wall). In practice, this is seen in the establishment of sub-projects within MPP to answer specific questions or address specific problems arising as a result of its operation. Specific identified areas of concern are tightly focused into a separate system of management, results of which support the aims of the overseeing project.

The transformation model is sustained, or is continual, due to the intangible nature of heritage as a sociological concern. Through MPP's specific identification and management, perception and conception of heritage is reconfigured continually, thus creating the scope for MPP to exist. As objects are re-examined conceptually, so management is prompted to objectify new 'information' or identify other physical objects as heritage.

As a result of this existence within an area of identified sociological concern (Hewison 1987), discrimination procedures and the assessment of 'value' have become increasingly important and, necessarily, more scientific. The management of heritage in the public sphere is therefore constantly justified within the management system in a number of contexts: economic, social, political, professional, and so on.

Whilst the concept of heritage is transformed into specific objects, another feedback loop is established whereby objects sustain the concept of heritage. It is argued by some within the discipline that the latter (object to concept) is the primary transformation. I would argue against this however: as any action must result from initial perception of the world around us, so the idea of heritage as a concept must come before the action of creating heritage as an object by use of management. After this point, the objects or 'products' may continue to perpetuate the concept understood as heritage.

The effects of MPP as a management system are seen across the discipline. Another transformation is effected, turning the concept of the historic environment into an object (archaeological management as a tool), itself acting within and supporting wider environmental initiatives. Archaeology therefore aligns itself through the ideas of sustainability, and assessment as a 'resource' within the context of the 'environment', as a consideration with parallels in other disciplines. The wider concept of heritage existing within the environment becomes transformed into a number of inter-disciplinary projects working towards a common broad aim. Archaeology is a specific 'slant', faunal protection or landscape identification another, focused on by other public institutions such as English Nature or the Countryside Agency.

Finally and fundamentally, MPP contributes to society's reflection on itself and the role of heritage within it. Though not effecting an explicit transformation in this context, such a large-scale project may help to enable a democratisation process of knowledge and participation in the heritage. MPP forces English Heritage, as management institution, and archaeology, as a discipline, to examine their own roles in the creation of heritage and their effects outwith their own concerns. Analysis of the themes raised by the project in this instance has the ability to highlight tensions within society, where they relate to heritage as a concept, and the relations between various other diametric concepts. Considered within this case study have been the opposites of concept and object, and public and private: others may include ephemeral and mainstream; the franchised and disenfranchised; ownership and access. Thus the management system of MPP, acting as a systematic and justified process, may contribute to the consideration people have of existing in the wider world, and the objects people consider as heritage existing in the wider world.

6   From fire to fake? Uppark & The National Trust

Problematic analysis and management

This case study considers a period straight after the re-opening of Uppark, following a devastating fire, during which a timed ticketing policy was introduced to control large-scale visitor flow. It addresses the difficult question of what management does when the individual site is encountered. The obvious can, of course, be stated in that the site is 'managed' – however, analysis beyond this shows a complex set of actions and organisational structures that need to be unravelled. The first stage of the model of transformation can be seen to be equally problematic in identification as the second (interpretation and presentation), as transformations from concept to object on sites are plentiful and constant. Analysis of the site, in this case Uppark, reveals key features about The National Trust (its manager), in both the perceptions of it from outside and the aims stated from within. Three strands of evidence are considered in the analyses of the historic sites in this thesis: the perceptions of the visiting public; the views of the managing agencies; and the views of the wider professional world in which both the site and the managing agencies exist. It can be seen however, that there is an unequal bias placed on these strands, as the views of the 'audience' are frequently given greatest importance. Whilst the National Trust opens its sites aiming for visitor satisfaction and English Heritage has a specific aim of public accountability both, as managers, are governed by the 'bottom-line' economics of operating in the tourism sector. Economically speaking, both managing agencies are concerned primarily with deficit limitation and revenue maximisation. These limits will be seen in the case study analysis.

Uppark has been chosen for study as it stands as a unique heritage object and is operated by the country's leading 'heritage' charity. In its presentation, The National Trust treats Uppark as a resource whose history is continual – literally to the present day – due to the fire and restoration completed three years ago. Furthermore, the house shows the typical complexity of history through ownership and effects on both local and national society. However, in terms of management, although Uppark has featured prominently in the media recently, little attention has been given to an analysis of the site in terms of heritage management, or the Trust acting as a charity within a market-driven area of tourism. The analysis of Uppark will explore further the material heritage object that has prompted such expressions as:

> 'In these days to be privileged to tread the short crisp turf of Uppark and muse in these exquisite rooms, so happy and so historic, is to steep every sense in England's *ichor*, distilled from her soil, her climate, her history and art.' (Hussey 1941, 566)

or:

> '...And again this definite estate of Uppark and the sharply marked out farms, villages and towns of the countryside below, caught me just in the proper phase to awaken a sense of social relationship and history that might never have been roused if I had remained in the catastrophic multitudinousness of suburban development.' (Wells 1934, 144)

or

> '...Repairing Uppark seems to have arisen from a combination of needs centred round the collective character and abilities of the Trust. Beyond the Trust's habit of not being daunted and its ability to protect, there has been a mingling of what a justly proud owner might have attempted, with feelings which are nearly beyond reach about English culture and noblemen's houses. Uppark is not exactly a national monument, any more than it is (or contains) a great work of art. Yet there are those in England to whom this place on the crest of the Downs feels like home.' (Haslam 1995, 73)

All of the analyses undertaken involve a degree of subjectivity in description of the object elements of Uppark. It is suggested within this thesis that the process of management creates through identification, manipulates, and establishes such objects. This is followed by the second stage of the transformation, in which subjective analysis is based, and those objectified elements become valued by virtue of their description and interpretation. In this case study therefore,

Figure 6.1 *Uppark house following restoration. (© NTPL/ Matthew Antrobus (35805))*

aspects of Uppark enrich and add to a wider perception of what the concept, *heritage,* is by the fact that they have been objectified, classified and managed in a certain way. Where the initial interest or value comes from in the first place is irrelevant for the purposes here of suggesting that specific activities promote Uppark's existence as part of the wider concept of heritage.

References and history aside, how can such a site be analysed in the light of the proposed model of transformation? It is intended, as already stated, not to present exhaustive historical explanations, nor to discuss the restoration project as this has been done elsewhere (Rowell and Robinson 1995). The site will be approached with all its 'supporting evidence' as a suite of objects, assessing how the house, as it exists today, came into being. The essential question that is therefore being asked of the site is, what does Uppark consist of? To answer this I have undertaken a combination of subjective and objective analysis to identify the objects that comprise Uppark and the concept that these objects have been created from. I have used anecdotal evidence in the analysis, which is noted where used; also the 'scientific' technique of ASEB Grid Analysis, developed by Beeho and Prentice (1995) is applied, which sheds further light on the transformations (plural) occurring at the site. Each case study therefore should speak for itself, illustrating the variety of transformation and showing that an understanding of the management of objects is essential for an understanding of the concept heritage.

Charitable works and country houses

There are few people in Britain who have not heard of The National Trust. Although we have probably all encountered the work of the Trust, there is still some confusion over what the organisation does and how it operates. There are some general misconceptions, such as that the Trust deals only with country houses, and there are major errors in understanding, for example the Trust being understood to be a government or government-sponsored body (Difference Engine 1994). The organisation of the Trust will not be subjected to the kind of analysis that has already been undertaken for English Heritage. It is the purpose of this case study to analyse the transformation of heritage with

regard to one of the National Trust's more famous properties (of late), Uppark, in West Sussex.

Consideration of the transformation of heritage at this country house will inevitably reflect on the organisation of the National Trust as a whole. The relationship in the management structures discussed previously may be seen in practice, as the operation of the site and the organisation are mutually supportive. The importance of the organisation and its place in the conservation movement in the country must not be underestimated (Jenkins and James 1994). Though charitable in status, and receiving no direct government grants for its work, the National Trust is the country's largest private landowner, farmer, and conservator of coastline, countryside, historic buildings and ancient monuments. During its centenary year in 1995, the Trust's expenditure was £158.2 million pounds, with 84% of that being spent on its properties (National Trust 1996, 26). The National Trust is unique amongst charities in having its activities prescribed by an Act of Parliament (various Acts dating from 1910, most recently the National Trust Act 1971), allowing it to declare its land and property holdings as 'inalienable'. The purpose of the Trust is further described in the Act and the Articles of Association as: 'the permanent preservation for the benefit of the Nation of lands and tenements (including buildings) of beauty or historic interest... for the purposes of public recreation resort or instruction.' (Cadogan 1995, 117) The history of the development of the Trust and its work have been discussed exhaustively during the centenary celebrations particularly, and also in previous years, by both admirers and critics (Chippindale 1997; Fedden 1968 & 1974; Gaze 1988; Jenkins and James 1994; Lees-Milne 1975; Murphy 1987; Newby 1995; Waterson 1994; Weideger 1994). Detailed information about the Trust's activities and finances are published by the Trust in its Annual Report (NT, annual).

For the purposes of this analysis, I would like to reiterate that the key features of the Trust considered here are the perceptions of the organisation held by the various visitors or audiences and the aims of management from within the organisation.

Uppark's ownership was transferred to the National Trust in 1954 by Admiral Herbert Meade-Fetherstonhaugh and his son Richard Meade-Fetherstonhaugh. The donor family have continued to live on the upper floors of the house and in other estate houses since then. The main show rooms open to the public are on the ground floor, along with the servants' areas 'below stairs' in the basement (Rowell 1995). Most notable in Uppark's recent history was the serious fire that gutted the upper floors, and badly damaged the lower floors, in 1989 (Sekers 1990 and Figure 6.3). After careful consideration and much public debate (Rowell & Robinson 1996), the house was restored to its condition the day before the fire, paid for by insurance, costing £20 million.

The histories of both the house and owners are the most obvious usable resource for understanding, both in terms of visiting and managing the estate. The history of the house

Figure 6.2 *The owners of Uppark. (Rowell 1995)*

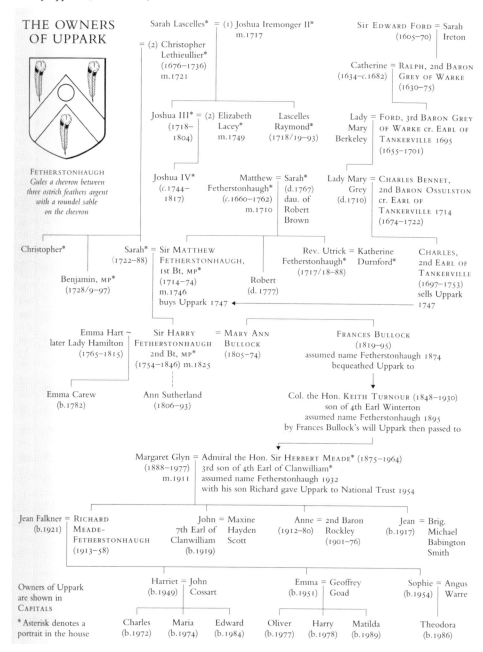

THE OWNERS
OF UPPARK

FETHERSTONHAUGH
*Gules a chevron between
three ostrich feathers argent
with a roundel sable
on the chevron*

Sarah Lascelles* = (1) Joshua Iremonger II*
m.1717

= (2) Christopher
Lethieullier*
(1676–1736)
m.1721

Sir EDWARD FORD = Sarah
(1605–70) | Ireton

Catherine = RALPH, 2ND BARON
(1634–c.1682) | GREY OF WARKE
(1630–75)

Joshua III* = (2) Elizabeth   Lascelles
(1718–   Lacey*   Raymond*
1804)   m.1749   (1718/19–93)

Lady = FORD, 3RD BARON GREY
Mary | OF WARKE cr. EARL OF
Berkeley | TANKERVILLE 1695
(1655–1701)

Joshua IV*   Matthew = Sarah*
(c.1744–   Fetherstonhaugh* (d.1767)
1817)   (c.1660–1762)   dau. of
m.1710   Robert
Brown

Lady Mary = CHARLES BENNET,
Grey | 2ND BARON OSSULSTON
(d.1710) | cr. EARL OF
TANKERVILLE 1714
(1674–1722)

Christopher*

Sarah* = Sir MATTHEW
(1722–88) FETHERSTONHAUGH,
1ST Bt, MP*
(1714–74)
m.1746
buys Uppark 1747 ◄——

Rev. Utrick = Katherine
Fetherstonhaugh* Durnford*
Robert   (1717/18–88)
(d. 1777)

CHARLES,
2ND EARL OF
TANKERVILLE
(1697–1753)
sells Uppark
1747

Benjamin, MP*
(1728/9–97)

Emma Hart ~   Sir HARRY   = MARY ANN
later Lady Hamilton FETHERSTONHAUGH BULLOCK
(1765–1815)   2nd Bt, MP*   (1805–74)
(1754–1846) m.1825

FRANCES BULLOCK
(1819–95)
assumed name Fetherstonhaugh 1874
bequeathed Uppark to

Emma Carew   Ann Sutherland
(b.1782)   (1806–93)

Col. the Hon. KEITH TURNOUR (1848–1930)
son of 4th Earl Winterton
assumed name Fetherstonhaugh 1895
by Frances Bullock's will Uppark then passed to

Margaret Glyn = Admiral the Hon. Sir HERBERT MEADE* (1875–1964)
(1888–1977) | 3rd son of 4th Earl of Clanwilliam*
m.1911   assumed name Fetherstonhaugh 1932
with his son Richard gave Uppark to National Trust 1954

Jean Falkner = RICHARD   John = Maxine   Anne = 2nd Baron   Jean = Brig.
(b.1921)   MEADE-   7th Earl of Hayden   (1912–80) Rockley   (b.1917) Michael
FETHERSTONHAUGH Clanwilliam Scott   (1901–76)   Babington
(1913–58)   (b.1919)   Smith

Owners of Uppark
are shown in
CAPITALS

Harriet = John   Emma = Geoffrey   Sophie = Angus
(b.1949) | Cossart   (b.1951) | Goad   (b.1954) | Warre

* Asterisk denotes a
portrait in the house

Charles   Maria   Edward   Oliver   Harry   Matilda   Theodora
(b.1972) (b.1974) (b.1984)   (b.1977) (b.1978) (b.1989)   (b.1986)

Figure 6.3 *The fire at Uppark in 1989 during the first restoration programme. (© NTPL/Andreas von Einsiedel (11401))*

is not considered explicitly here however, though sources of information (historical and otherwise) are drawn upon in the case study. Guides to the house, published by the Trust, provide both potted and lengthier accounts of the historical development of the house, its owners, contents and events, including the fire and subsequent conservation (Rowell 1995; Meade-Fetherstonhaugh and Warner 1964; Nicolson 1990; and Creed 1995). Other historical texts, published by the Trust and others, consider Uppark's history and people associated with it and the history of the local area (Country Life, various articles; Gordon 1877; Lummis and Marsh 1990; Pevsner 1965; Victoria County History 1973; and Wells 1908 & 1934). Figure 6.2 shows the family tree of the owners of Uppark. The size and complexity of the restoration project undertaken at Uppark between 1989 and 1994 has also warranted a separate volume, published by the Trust (Rowell and Robinson 1995).

Objects of heritage

Uppark is considered here as an object. Its value as a part of the country's heritage is a lesser issue in the practical day-to-day operation of the site as a tourist attraction. The actuality of Uppark's existence are those parts of the site that are 'graspable' by the visitor on his or her visit (Tinniswood 1989). Those parts of the site that can be 'consumed' (Urry 1995) must be considered, therefore, along with the problems that such consumption entails. It can be suggested that this section and the following ASEB Grid Analysis follows a scientific (from management terms) approach in establishing the contexts (or concepts) in which Uppark may exist. Uppark thus exists as a house; a tourist attraction; an example of conservation; a heritage site; a National Trust property, and so on. The house is one of 121 National Trust country houses open to the public, and during 1996 was fifty-fourth in the Trust's league table, with 76,217 visits. Uppark is one of numerous visitor attractions (sites, museums and historic towns) on the south coast, with easy access from both London and the north (via good motorway connections), and abroad (via Channel ports).

Uppark as heritage object in 1998

Basic details available to visitors in advance of their trips to Uppark come in the form of publicity material. This is produced for the region by the tourist board and by the National Trust, which in a series of separate leaflets highlights various places to visit in the area. Details for the property appearing in the Trust's leaflet for 'Great Days Out in and around West Sussex 1997' are reproduced in Figure 6.4. Interestingly Uppark does not always feature in the regional leaflets, for example 'Places to Visit in the South East' (National Trust 1995 a). Members of the National Trust receive an annual handbook (also available to buy generally), and this gives individual property details and further information. Members of the National Trust gain free admission to the property; this form of support for the Trust is very popular (Hanna 1995). The Trust sometimes advertises locally in the press, and in a separate development has launched a World Wide Web service, on which Uppark's details appear in a similar fashion to the members' handbook (UKIndex 1998; National Trust 1998).

The house is open for the standard summer season adopted within the tourism industry (April to October), for five days a week in the afternoon. Most notable about the admission arrangements for Uppark is the system of a timed ticket, for which the numbers are limited to 43 per quarter of an hour. This system is in operation at a number of very busy sites to limit numbers, prevent crowding and limiting inevitable damage. At Uppark during the summer tickets do sell out, though they can be booked in advance at extra cost. On purchase of a ticket visitors are given a foldout leaflet with a map of the site and further details about regulations at the site and other available activities (Figure 6.5). The Trust suggests how the visit should be approached: 'All visitors are advised to see the Royal SunAlliance Restoration Exhibition if possible before going to the house (allow at least half an hour). You may also like to visit the garden, woodland walk, and dairy as well as the National Trust Shop and licensed Tea-room while awaiting entry to the house.' (National Trust 1997 b)

Progression is therefore made from the car park to the ticket office and exhibition, housed in a temporary 'plastering shed' erected during the restoration project. The exhibition is on two floors and takes the form of a 'conservation site'; from floor to ceiling are display boards, reconstruction models, and remains salvaged from the house following the fire. The temporary nature of the shed (a modern corrugated metal structure) gives an idea of the field conditions in which the restorers worked. The interpretation uses frames built of scaffolding to further the effect and overall is very highly praised, receiving various awards including Museum of the Year 1996 (joint winner). Two different news videos at the start of the exhibition, playing constantly, relive the fire and the destruction of the house and this contrasts starkly with the family histories presented on the opposite wall. The exhibition immediately catches the visitor's interest and emotions and has been designed to provoke. As the visitor moves around the building separate sections cover the debate over the decision to restore Uppark and then the various conservation techniques used in the restoration, including structural work, painting conservation, plastering, gilding and carving. A mixture of commentaries on headsets and video footage is incorporated here. Upstairs on the mezzanine floor the exhibition concentrates on the conservation of the interior fittings of the house. There are numerous smaller displays on carpets, curtains, glass, wallpaper and so on. An area, which particularly attracts the attention of the visitors, is a 'play area' that, behind the fun aspect of activities to try out, portrays important craft and conservation messages. Moulds are available to experiment with plasticine; reconstructions can be attempted from fragments of plaster; salvaged materials can be inspected; wallpaper can be created by block printing; and patterns can be copied and completed by colouring in missing segments.

Figure 6.4 *Regional National Trust publicity leaflet. (© NTPL/ (left) Stephen Robson (39433)/ (top right) Matthew Antrobus (35822)/ (bottom right) Nadia MacKenzie (35261))*

UPPARK

Set high on the South Downs, Uppark is a fine 17th-century house that re-opened in 1995 after restoration following a major fire in 1989. The house, with outstanding 18th-century interiors and contents, has been fully restored to its state 'the day before the fire' and the garden re-planned and re-planted. Authentic and fascinating 'below stairs' rooms. The Royal SunAlliance multi-media exhibition tells the story of its rise from the ashes.

REFRESHMENTS: Light lunches and afternoon teas. Open same days as house 11.30–5.30. Kiosk near car park serving sandwiches, hot and cold drinks, open from 11.30.

SHOP: Open same days as house 11.30–5.30.

Lift to basement rooms in house. Exhibition (accessible by stair lift). Wheelchairs available. WC.

South Harting, Petersfield GU31 5QR.
Tel: 01730 825415;
Information line (24hrs):
Tel: 01730 825857

LOCATION: 5ml SE of Petersfield on B2146, 1½ml S of South Harting

OPEN: 30 March to 30 Oct: daily except Fri & Sat; **House:** 1–5; **Car park, woodland walk, ticket office, exhibition, garden:** 11.30–5.30; last admission to house 4.15. Print room open only on first Mon of each month. Admission to house is by timed ticket (incl. NT members) so visitors may have to wait before being admitted. Tickets will be marked with an entry slot (eg. 1–1.15), visitors enter the house during that slot, but may stay as long as the house is open. On Sun, BH and other busy days tickets may sell out. Some Sun & BH tickets are bookable in advance (small charge); tel. 01730 825415 during office hours Mon to Fri.

ADMISSION: House, Garden and Exhibition: £5; family ticket £12.50.

Figure 6.5 *Orientation leaflet. (© National Trust/J.P.Design)*

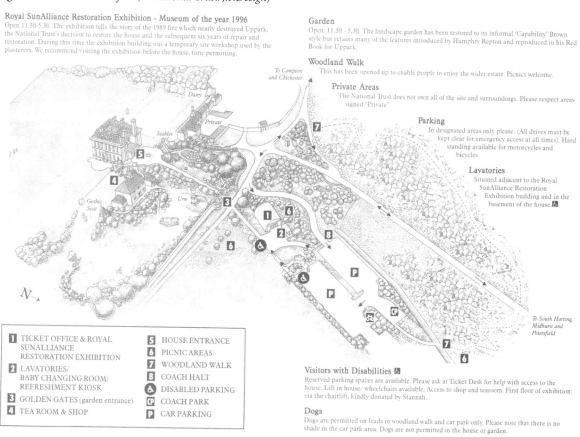

Royal SunAlliance Restoration Exhibition - Museum of the year 1996
Open 11.30-5.30. The exhibition tells the story of the 1989 fire which nearly destroyed Uppark, the National Trust's decision to restore the house and the subsequent six years of repair and restoration. During this time the exhibition building was a temporary site workshop used by the plasterers. We recommend visiting the exhibition before the house, time permitting.

Garden
Open: 11.30 - 5.30. The landscape garden has been restored to its informal 'Capability' Brown style but retains many of the features introduced by Humphry Repton and reproduced in his Red Book for Uppark.

Woodland Walk
This has been opened up to enable people to enjoy the wider estate. Picnics welcome.

Private Areas
The National Trust does not own all of the site and surroundings. Please respect areas signed "Private"

Parking
In designated areas only please. (All drives must be kept clear for emergency access at all times). Hard standing available for motorcycles and bicycles.

Lavatories
Situated adjacent to the Royal SunAlliance Restoration Exhibition building and in the basement of the house.

1. TICKET OFFICE & ROYAL SUNALLIANCE RESTORATION EXHIBITION
2. LAVATORIES/ BABY CHANGING ROOM/ REFRESHMENT KIOSK
3. GOLDEN GATES (garden entrance)
4. TEA ROOM & SHOP
5. HOUSE ENTRANCE
6. PICNIC AREAS
7. WOODLAND WALK
8. COACH HALT
DISABLED PARKING
COACH PARK
CAR PARKING

Visitors with Disabilities
Reserved parking spaces are available. Please ask at Ticket Desk for help with access to the house. Lift in house/ wheelchairs available. Access to shop and tearoom. First floor of exhibition: via the chairlift, kindly donated by Stannah.

Dogs
Dogs are permitted on leads in woodland walk and car park only. Please note that there is no shade in the car park area. Dogs are not permitted in the house or garden.

On the way out of the exhibition, longer-term conservation is described, focusing on the gardens and estate, along with acknowledgements of the size and complexity of the restoration project. The visitor is encouraged to join the Trust as a member, and help with the conservation projects on properties including Uppark.

From the exhibition the visitor walks towards the house, passing through the historic 'Golden Gates'. These act as a further ticket inspection barrier, guidebook selling point and the entrance to the gardens. Features within the garden include the planting regimes, statuary and Gothic Seat, which are highlighted in the orientation leaflet (Figure 6.5). The house can be circumnavigated on the outside (Figure 6.1). At the south front of the house, open downland is reached with views to the Isle of Wight. On the west side of the house are the stables and dairy, infamous during the history of the house when Sir Harry proposed to the dairymaid. Returning to the east side of the house, the former service wing and kitchen has been converted to a tearoom and Trust shop. The first floor of this building houses administrative offices for the property.

Entering the house on the north front, through Repton's entrance portico, the visitor can follow a clockwise route around ten ground floor show rooms, all restored since the fire (Figure 6.6). The basement may then be visited where the below-stairs lifestyle is on show. Six main rooms can be seen in any order, before the exit is made along the underground passage linking the old kitchen and the house. The visitor emerges therefore craftily in the shop. It is worth noting that due to the ticketing system there is no re-admission to the house, though the visitor can spend as long as he/she wants inside the house. The first floor rooms remain the private accommodation of the Meade-Fetherstonhaugh family, though the Print Room at the head of the main staircase is open once a month as a unique feature of the house.

Within the show rooms there are no interpretative displays. Stewards are available in each room to answer queries, and each of the rooms has a folder with before and after photos showing restoration work from the fire, and other historical details. The rooms are therefore displayed as the house would have been lived in.

The shop contains a typical array of Trust souvenirs, including site-specific gifts, and a range of books and other items. The tearoom is licensed and serves light meals and drinks. Other refreshments are available outside the exhibition building by the car park. Two picnic areas have been created on the site; one by the exhibition, and another at the far end of the car park, along the woodland walk. The walk takes in a wooded area of the estate, crossing the access road to the north of the house. Other areas of the estate are not open though, one mile to the north of the house, Harting Down has open access for walking.

Problems in local management of the site should briefly be mentioned. Most obvious is the popularity of Uppark due to media attention over the restoration. Before the fire Uppark

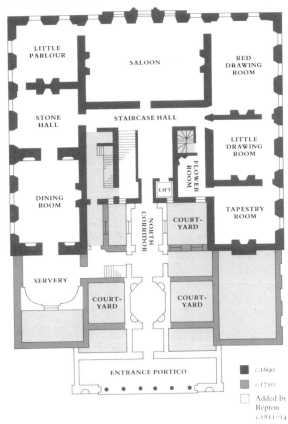

Figure 6.6 *Ground floor plan of the house. (© National Trust)*

received approximately 30,000 visitors per year; since the fire, this has more than doubled to over 76,000 (National Trust 1996). The site itself has not got any bigger, though facilities have had to be increased including further opening hours. Before 1989, Uppark was only open three days a week. The donor family have since had to make concessions about their original wishes. Pressure on the house is great therefore, both in terms of wear and tear and numbers of visitors wanting to see it. Introduction of the timed ticket system forces visitors to spend greater time in the grounds, again increasing wear. The shop and restaurant have been expanded and the exhibition, intended to be temporary, will probably become a long-standing fixture (Robert Dillon, pers.com.). Still the expectations of the site grow and as capacity is reached, the Trust adopts diversionary tactics to send visitors to other nearby properties and uses the tactic of increases in admission prices, used by many tourism operators, to deter the less serious visitor. Uppark remains a very popular site, as by virtue of the house's characteristics and its recent history, it has the ability to capture the imagination (Rowell and Robinson 1996; Creed 1995; Schouten 1995). This does not account for the professional interest shown in the site, which will be further considered below. At this point however, Beeho and Prentice's (1995) techniques of analysis can be employed to provide greater illustration of how Uppark 'becomes' heritage.

Brief comment on the visitor experience

The house is displayed and presented in a fashion typical of National Trust properties. Debate over this form of presentation continues elsewhere about displays of objects in different contexts and environments (Knowles 1993). It is not considered further here.

In presentation emphasis is placed on the costs of managing the property and the Trust's position as a charity. Support for the Trust is overtly solicited from the visitors to its properties. Reasons for this are given through stark contrast of financial costs: Uppark generates £260,000 a year income, but £350,000 is spent on operational and conservation costs. As with the majority of Trust houses, Uppark therefore runs at a substantial deficit and there is huge reliance on the support of the tourist industry and membership receipts.

Rowell (1995) provides further historical and artistic detail about the house and estate. I will approach the house objectively, describing the management and operation of it and assessing the values brought to the house and taken away from it by the visitor. In treating the house as an object encountered on a visit, this approach allows conceptual themes to be explored, provoked by human interaction with the surrounding place (Prentice 1993).

ASEB Grid Analysis – visitor reaction to Uppark

This technique, which makes an objective assessment of subjective matter, has been developed from the more traditional SWOT analysis (Strengths, Weaknesses, Opportunities & Threats), regularly used in the management sciences (Johnson and Scholes 1989) and the sociologically grounded Manning-Haas Demand Hierarchy (Manning 1986; Prentice 1993). Within the context of the leisure industry, it is emphasised that, 'the need to focus on consumer needs and motivations for product development in the commercial world is well grounded in theoretical work, notably in consumer behaviour literature focusing on products other than museum experiences' (Beeho and Prentice 1995, 230). The levels of the Manning-Haas demand hierarchy (Figure 6.7) are incorporated into the analysis, 'to provide a more consumer-based approach than that inherent in conventional SWOT analysis' (ibid. 232). It can be seen that the analysis shows where objective and subjective experience meet. It analyses the product and reveals where the transformation has taken place.

Information may be drawn out of it to identify areas where the transformation from concept to object takes place at the site-level. Beeho and Prentice tested the analysis on Blists Hill Open Air Museum (ibid. 236), and based their findings on semi-structured in-depth interviews. The analysis in this chapter is based on similar 'social' interviews undertaken with tourists at the site, incorporates anecdotal evidence and conversations with staff and other professionals who have been involved with Uppark and includes the results of visitor surveys undertaken on-site for the National Trust. The procedure is straightforward: 'the analysis is conducted by reference to each level of the Manning-Haas demand hierarchy in turn for each element of SWOT analysis. As such, analysis is undertaken for each row by each column of the matrix outlined in Figure 6.8, sequentially from cell SA to SB, WA to WB...' and so on (ibid. 233).

Methodology

The Trust is not in a financial position that allows it to act proactively in presenting all of its properties. Whilst certain projects, such as the Lifelong Learning/Minerva initiative, do attract investment by the Trust, other developments in interpretation take much longer to come to fruition where there is a clear public demand. As noted before, the Trust's position as a charity limits investment, which cannot be clearly justified. The 'coping' strategies therefore adopted in managing Uppark, in this instance, therefore justify the use here of a 'visitor-oriented' approach in analysis. The objective use of such analysis thus produces a structured use of commentary (largely subjective) on this site and from this I consider the various Stage 1 transformations that occur at Uppark.

My analysis has been undertaken through consultation with the managing agencies within the Trust, at site, regional and national level, where I have discussed views, opinions and perceptions of key individuals concerned with Uppark. I undertook fieldwork at the site, consulting management documentation, viewing the house in detail, and interviewing a selection of visitors (in an unstructured and informal manner) to gauge reaction to their visit and perceptions about the house and the Trust as managing agency. In the analysis I have also considered the views held by other interested parties within the profession, along with analysis carried out elsewhere, in the form of detailed visitor

Figure 6.7 *The Manning-Haas sequential hierarchy of demand. (from Beeho, A.J. & Prentice, R.C. 1995)*

Level of Manning Haas hierarchy of demand	Example (From Manning, 1986)
Level 1: Activities	Wilderness hiking
Level 2: Settings A. Environmental setting B. Social setting C. Managerial setting	Rugged terrain Few people No restrictions
Level 3: Experiences	Risk taking Challenge Physical exercise
Level 4: Benefits A. Personal B. Societal	Enhanced self-esteem Increased commitment to conservation

Figure 6.8 *ASEB grid analysis and cell identifiers. (from Beeho, A.J. & Prentice, R.C. 1995)*

	Activities	Settings	Experiences	Benefits
Strengths	SA	SS	SE	SB
Weaknesses	WA	WS	WE	WB
Opportunities	OA	OS	OE	OB
Threats	TA	TS	TE	TB

surveys (such as Tourist Board and Trust surveys). I have not undertaken a large visitor survey for the purposes of this thesis however and my questioning of visitors has been based on the Grid analysis already mentioned.

Though ASEB Grid analysis has weaknesses, developed as a social science tool, I have used it for a particular reason here. Subjective commentary provided by the different strands of evidence (including survey, professional opinion and management documentation) can be structured through use of the Grid analysis. Detailed commentary about the transformations at Uppark follows the use of the ASEB Grid's structuring of pertinent information.

Applying the ASEB Grid to Uppark

The strengths and weaknesses identified within a visit to Uppark are straightforward. Opportunities and threats are those perceived by both visitors and managers as perceived possibilities of further objects that could be encountered on the site and future developments and drawbacks which might affect the site. Again it should be noted that three strands of evidence have been combined in the analysis: those of the visitors, inevitably conditioned by the encounter with the site on a visit; The National Trust as manager, comprising various people's interests; and wider professional perception of heritage management.

1. Strengths

Strengths: Activities (SA)

Uppark is recognised as being a specific destination for a day out. Members of the Trust in particular, and many other visitors, have some knowledge of the house and its recent history (fire and restoration), which makes the house a 'novel' experience (Stafford 1989). Furthermore, there is some recognition of the ticketing system in advance and a part day or longer is anticipated at the site. The visitors can be divided between tourists and connoisseurs, or those who have come to the house particularly to see the conservation, or Uppark's architecture and furnishings. Ongoing restoration in the gardens and estate, coupled with the awareness of the enormous effort and professionalism that the Trust puts into gardens, further enhance the visit. The nature of the property therefore gives it a number of unique selling points (USPs) (Simon Bergin, pers.com.). A wide range of visitors comes to the site and there are a great number of repeat visits. The site may be further divided into distinct areas offering different activities: the house, garden (and dairy), exhibition, woodland, picnic area, shop, and restaurant: most achieve high satisfaction levels. A particular activity, which is a 'sport' for the visitors, is spotting the joins between original and conserved parts or items in the house. The children's guidebook encourages this hunt (Creed 1995 b).

Strengths: Settings (SS)

Geographic location plays an important part in this field. The setting of Uppark is considered to be authentic because there are neither modern intrusions within sight of the house,

nor any 'modern' landscapes visible in the gardens (Corner and Harvey 1991). The position of the house gives views over rolling Downs and clear line of sight to the Channel and the Isle of Wight. The lifestyles of the country house inhabitants is captured in the room settings, largely due to a lack of interpretation inside the house: visual stimulation and imagination is relied upon. Visitors particularly note the difference between the 'below-stairs' area of the servants, and the 'upstairs' lives of the Fetherstonhaughs. The range of visitors to Uppark allows frequent identification or abhorrence of one or the other lifestyle (Chase and Shaw 1989)! The setting of the house, with both gardens and woodland walks attached, generate repeat visits and the results of the restoration project are highly praised. Those visitors that had investigated the history of Uppark and its owners identified particularly with the romance of Sir Harry's proposal of marriage to Mary Ann Bullock in the restored dairy and the literary reminiscences of H.G. Wells about below-stairs life. His mother was first lady's maid and eventually housekeeper of Uppark and Wells spent many childhood years living in the house, visiting it in later life.

Strengths: Experiences (SE)

The visitor to Uppark experiences an individual response to the site depending on his or her own social nature. This obviously involves the subjective nostalgia (Chase and Shaw 1989). Obvious experiences, which are strengths, are emotional and reminiscent, appreciating the differences or similarities between the lives associated with the house and the situation of the visitor. An historical development is seen in both lifestyle and living, especially the contrasting below-stairs rooms: practical as opposed to furnished for show and comfort. The position of the site in the countryside and the provision of a garden and walks allows for physical recreation, which is appreciated (Prentice 1993). A visit to Uppark may also be an educational experience, formally and informally (Light 1995): both from a historical point of view, and from a modern example of preservation and craftsmanship employed on the site. The interactive nature of the exhibition about the restoration is a source of constant learning, provoking comments such as 'I never knew that', or, 'so, that's how that was made'. As far as the Trust is concerned, the management objectives are achieved, attracting tourists who pay for admission, in turn supporting the Trust's work, and also supporting the wider Trust objectives of preservation and education.

Strengths: Benefits (SB)

As with the description of Blists Hill by Beeho and Prentice (1995), the identified benefits stemmed from visitors enjoying their visit to Uppark. A privileged feeling was instilled in some cases through the feeling that visitors left the site knowing how the restoration was achieved. Furthermore, self-esteem was enhanced in the sense of patriotism, that the house was a part of the English heritage that was restored to its former glory after suffering a terrible fate (Lowenthal and Binney 1981; Shoard 1981). Characters identified in the history of the site provoked a greater awareness of historical development and events, such as Ford Grey's involvement in the Rye House Plot or the occasions of the Prince Regent's visits to Uppark (Rowell 1995). Comparisons are made with modern-day lifestyles and those illustrated in the house, and also the problems of conservation as a result of the house's history. Divisions of class within society can be challenged on site, firstly because the house was given to the Trust by a donor family who still lived there; secondly that the recent family members (Margaret Meade-Fetherstonhaugh in the 1940s) had made such an effort at conserving the interiors; and also a degree of pity that the fire totally destroyed the family's private apartments. Benefit is also seen in support for the Trust in its work, the crafts involved in the restoration, and the conservation/green movement more generally. The support generated and interest shown in the house, its contents and their restoration by visitors works both ways – between visitors themselves as they point things out, and also through interaction with the room stewards who are stationed in all of the showrooms and, as volunteers, enthuse about the house to all.

2. Weaknesses

Weaknesses: Activities (WA)

The house cannot cope with the number of visitors who would like to visit it: both in terms of sheer number and the conservation and damage aspects. This is not always appreciated and the timed ticket system is the one area that is criticised above others. The site can become crowded very easily, affecting visitors' enjoyment and ability to see items in the house and move about in the grounds and shop or be served in the tearoom. Walking between areas of the house is on gravel paths and the garden in inclement weather becomes very muddy. Dependency on the weather may also make walks in the wood and picnics impracticable and limit activities on offer. The size of the exhibition and the nature of the interactive elements may also sometimes prevent participation due to crowding or difficulty of physical access. The site cannot be developed further as the house is a listed building and the park is a registered landscape (English Heritage, 1987). Designations of the South Downs as an Environmentally Sensitive Area (ESA) and Area of Outstanding Natural Beauty (AONB) are a further consideration. The site has no further capacity for visitors; furthermore it has limited opening hours, coupled with a timed ticket system forcing visitors to be in the house at a set time. In line with national policy and other tourist attractions, admission prices rise annually, and are not at the cheaper end of the scale. Access to the site, located in the countryside on the top of a hill, may cause further concern: a car seems to be necessary for a visit. Signage may be difficult to see: both this, the pricing structure and lack of dedicated advertising may sometimes be used as a tool to deter over-visiting of the property. The tearoom and shop promote high quality goods in line with Trust policy and, again, may prove to be expensive. The site is not a museum: no interpretation is provided within the house, such as displays or video: little information of traditional didactic nature is obviously available inside the house.

Weaknesses: Settings (WS)

The term 'authenticity' lies at the core of the ongoing debate and opinion at Uppark (Cruikshank 1990). The Trust makes no apology for the fact that Uppark was badly destroyed by fire and has been restored: the visitor sees a modern copy of an historic house. This is further considered in the section of weakness of experience (WE). The site is quite difficult to get to and there is great competition from other, bigger and more family-oriented museums and attractions in the area. The nature of the site means that the Trust imposes numerous regulations for conservation reasons, and these may also affect the setting for visitors (Thackray, Jarman and Burgon 1995).

Weaknesses: Experiences (WE)

In questioning authenticity, an accusation of fraud may be levelled at the house and the Trust. What is seen in the house may be original, but the house itself is now only five years old. A most perceptive comment (Mary Baxter, pers. com.) suggests that the entire site might be seen as artificial. The house is a reconstruction and the family associated with it died out in the early nineteenth century when Mary Ann Bullock, as Lady Fetherstonhaugh, died in 1874. The owners since then have all adopted the Fetherstonhaugh name, but have little other connection with the house or its contents. Whether aware of the restoration work or not, as the grandeur of country houses is alien to much of modern life, the visitor may not actually see what he or she expects at the house (Littlejohn 1997). If the restoration aspect is considered this is almost certainly the case: there is no easy comparison of before and after other than photos held in the show rooms. The methods of conservation generally, and particularly those used on the site, may not be understood. The history and historical figures may not be engaged with and the lack of interactive presentation in the house (the supposed main feature of any visit) may bore the visitor. Elsewhere, in guidebooks, little is made of the social history of the house, as emphasis is (traditionally) placed on the architecture and fittings: the guides are therefore relatively 'highbrow', and require intellectual effort. The fact that the conservation project within the house is complete, and cannot be seen in action, and the timescale of restoration on the estate (growing life of trees and plants), mean that engagement with the conservation aspects is not necessarily easy or understandable outside the exhibition. Sites may appear to be geared, as a result of conservation regulations, towards education rather than enjoyment and an emphasis on being taught rather than learning for oneself. Games cannot be played in the gardens, in order to preserve the plants, and movement in the house is limited to the edges of rooms, confining energetic and boisterous younger visitors. Numbers of visitors may further make it difficult to see certain parts of the rooms, and prevent the appreciation of the house and its contents. For those who do wish to engage further in the history or people of Uppark, activity is limited to the books sold in the shop and no provision at this stage is made on-site for education or access to the conservation or historical archives. Objects within the house cannot be handled, and often details of the interiors cannot be seen as light levels are controlled strictly. Finally in this respect, Uppark has seen a fairly complicated history – it is difficult to get a firm grasp on all the people who have been associated with the house.

Weaknesses: Benefits (WB)

Uppark may be seen by some to be anachronistic in terms of both existence and presentation (Mandler 1996). The house and its contents bear little relation to modern lifestyle and the restoration means that the house's originality may have been lost. As far as the Trust is concerned, it may be felt that if the organisation could afford to restore Uppark then why not improve many of its other properties or rebuild certain ruins. Apart from the conservation issues, money is also an issue – with visitors wondering why they should give money to the Trust if as a charity it can afford such projects anyway.

3. Opportunities

Opportunities: Activities

Themes relevant to the national curriculum for primary and secondary school teaching in England are emphasised in those resources available for educational purposes, such as the resource guide produced by the Trust (Culpin 1995). This is divided between an historical overview of developments in country houses and practical aspects of the houses, including science, home economics and geography. A basic historical overview is available on the National Trust's corporate website [http://www.nationaltrust.org. uk]. Though it would be impractical to provide a full education service for the house, current strengths could be built on using relatively cheap computer technologies to broaden the house's educational use. Connoisseurs' tours are already occasionally run during the hours when the house is closed to the general public and this service, if extended, may prove popular for dedicated groups, such as Trust members or local societies. Equally, it may be possible for some provision of function facilities, as the Trust is increasing its participation in this area (National Trust 1997 c). Further opening of walks on the estate may provide further opportunity for activities during the busy summer months, or an extension of the 'open' season for the gardens and grounds into the winter when the tearoom could also be operational. The exhibition already gives a very broad introduction to numerous aspects of restoration and conservation and again, this could be developed through provision of 'master classes', or provision of contacts for participation in academic or practical conservation courses or causes (Prentice 1995). Special events or living history displays are another possibility, used frequently for both educational and leisure purposes (Light 1996), and the Trust's successful Young National Trust Theatre (YNTT) could be involved at the site. Essentially, the opportunities for Uppark do not lie in altering the current activities, nor would it necessarily be possible to do so due to conservation constraints, money and the donor family's wishes, which still need to be heeded. Current strengths need to be constantly built on to sustain the purposes of the Trust and provide the

'value' that the Director-General emphasises (Martin Drury, pers. com.; Lipe 1984; Darvill 1993). Most visitor comment suggested that there was a demand for greater interpretation within the house, including educational use for children, and the possible use of 'themed' events. The managers and professional opinion had the greater range of views with regards to overall opportunities, as these parties have greater knowledge of the site's limitations and potential.

Opportunities: Settings (OS)

It is important that the current setting for Uppark is not damaged in any way. Currently the house enjoys an unrivalled position and views across pristine countryside, with no modern visual intrusions. Hopefully, the Trust will work hard to keep this situation. Socially, opportunities for the setting may be enhanced by diverting people away from the house, by spreading the visitor load across the garden and estate walks. Within the house, the current programme of training for volunteer stewards and other staff in customer care needs to be regularly refreshed and provided, so that all visitors may benefit from the 'human element' in information provision inside the show rooms. Restrictions imposed by the Trust in management of the house are inevitable for conservation, practical and commercial reasons. It may however be possible to organise special photography or handling sessions at the house, or gardening 'practicals'. The literary connections of the house could be further built upon very easily, either through audio-visual means (perhaps film), or more traditional story telling, popular in museums (Morgan and Walton 1994). The increasing desire for interactive educational opportunities seems to be yet unfulfilled at heritage sites, currently, and specialisms already existing in the Trust could be promoted or demonstrated at the house (Underwood 1993): from professional standards to coppicing methods in woodland.

Opportunities: Experiences (OE)

Experience is a key concept at any Trust property; more often than not, a visit to a country house will mean an encounter with a 'different world' for the visitor, either in terms of economic, historical or social standing. This may be an experience that provokes the imagination or interest in the history or details of the house; alternatively it may be an unsettling experience, where the house is considered as anachronistic to modern day lifestyles. The latter experience needs to be addressed primarily by the Trust, as it aims to preserve the best of the country's heritage, without alienating any one group of subjects. Development of interpretation methods to provide easy ways in to understanding aspects of life on a country estate should be a prime consideration, as should emphasis on similarities between the house and modern life, and differences explained from a historical perspective. Further links may be established between the house and its landscape, promoting physical activities in different parts of the estate grounds and local area, showing the effect that the house and its owners had on the local community.

Opportunities: Benefits (OB)

As noted in Figure 6.10, the benefits seen in the demand hierarchy are both personal and societal. Opportunities and benefits arise from the experiences gained by the visitor on a trip to Uppark, taken home with them and forming part of the future life and activities of that person. Benefits can therefore be communicated by the Trust to visitors and others, for example through its membership involvement, and also by the visitors themselves, through improved commitment to subject matter such as history, or a will to get involved in the work of the Trust or some other conservation movement. Some of the wider opportunities and benefits of the Trust's work on a national scale have been assessed in the Countryside Review Group's work (National Trust 1995 b), and the core idea of linking 'people and place' may be built on.

4. Threats

Threats: Activities (TA)

The major threat to this site is the physical impact of increased visitor numbers: between the 1995/96 and 1996/97 seasons, numbers rose from 69,459 to 76,217 visitors, an increase of nearly 10% (National Trust 1997 a, 56). Such a sustained increase in figures, whilst good for the Trust in generating income and support, has the potential to do great damage to the site. The longer-term costs of increased wear and tear, and provision of further facilities, outweigh the short-term benefits of income. Furthermore, the sheer number of people visiting on a mid-summer afternoon already detract from the site; it may not be possible to visit the house if all the tickets have been taken and the queues can easily become unbearable, ruining any enjoyment in the visit. Different threats to the activities may be seen in the fact that the house is what people have come to see in all probability, and the other activities (walks, gardens, exhibition) are unwanted. The exhibition is a particular concern for the Trust; intended to be a temporary display, its popularity may force it to become a permanent feature, with the added burden of maintenance of the building and contents, and the need to refresh the displays. The dilemma which the Trust faces is whether it wishes the fire to be the main focus of visits to the house, or if that event should just become another part of the history of Uppark: in which case, a specific exhibition on the fire and restoration is unnecessary.

Less likely threats to activities at Uppark would be a downturn in visitor numbers making the operating deficit even higher; the house no longer attracting the volunteer help for staffing on which it relies substantially; or the cost of visiting the house (through admission price increase) deterring visitors from coming. Although a seemingly irrelevant concern, the tourist industry does lie at the mercy of the weather, and the ability to get to a site through transport links being operational. All are potential concerns for the Trust's management of Uppark and for the visitors themselves.

Threats: Settings (TS)

There are two substantial threats to the setting, one of which is identified by Beeho and Prentice (1995, 249), and the other is a more local concern for Uppark. Apart from the Trust's own mission for preservation, Uppark is open to the public in a competitive tourism field. Nearby attractions at Portsmouth, Chichester or Brighton, on the coast, may prove to be more attractive to visitors because of the concentration of activities available. Uppark's position makes it vulnerable as the house is the only thing to visit at Uppark – in other words, a specific trip has to be made to the site. The Trust has to ensure that people continue to want to make that trip, quite apart from the conservation restrictions already considered. The other threat is that posed to the scenic quality of the area, either by the creation of further visitor facilities by the Trust or other off-site developments that have a physical or visual impact. However unlikely in Uppark's case, there are development threats seen frequently along the South Downs (SDCB 1993) and the site's proximity to motorways, trunk-roads and sea-ports may affect it at a future date.

Threats: Experiences (TE)

It has already been noted that few people live in houses like Uppark, and most visitors do not enjoy the social and economic standing of its former owners. This is therefore a threat to any experience gained on the site, as the country house and all its trappings may be too difficult to comprehend for some visitors. Conservation techniques, including the closing of blinds to keep out sunlight, a particular problem given Uppark's hilltop location, may further be a threat to experiencing the site. Development in interpretation and education at the site is limited due to time and money investment that the Trust, as a charity, cannot necessarily afford: this further threatens the visitor experience and the development of management improvements at the site. A final consideration here is the sheer complexity of the site which can never be explained to its full potential due to the number of people in its history, alterations made at the house and estate, effect on the local community, conservation and restoration, and archive material available. This makes Uppark difficult to grasp as a single discrete object and as such the house may not correlate with the idea of a good (and simple) day out as tourism becomes ever more fragmented and tourists become more demanding in their needs (Urry 1995).

Threats: Benefits (TB)

As with the example used by the developers of this analytical technique at Blists Hill (Beeho & Prentice 1995, 249), 'the principal threat concerning benefits flows from that of experience.' The influence and lifestyles of the country house have been in decline for many years now (Littlejohn, 1997), and do not correlate with modern society. Country houses have to constantly defend themselves from being labelled as museums and treated as such – the Trust vigorously defends the position that its properties remain 'homes' (Jenkins and James, 1994) of families connected to the property's history, rather than museum set-pieces. A further threat to benefits gained at the site may rebound on the Trust's management itself. It may seem that the charity is too rich if able to restore the house, and that therefore it does not need public support; or that money given to the Trust by visitors might be spent better elsewhere. This is not a major worry, though the Trust recognises its precarious nature as a charity that may suffer from the whims of public concern, as seen in the dispute over hunting on Trust land (National Trust 1995).

My conclusions from the ASEB Grid Analysis are drawn out of its main body of text and, for the purpose of exploring the transformation of heritage, the following sections will place them in the context of the model. The Grid analysis fits the model by pinpointing the points of transformation within the site. Though the different participants in the site each have their own clear perceptions of it, they have, in fact, proved similar when structured within the Grid analysis. This is where the technique has the useful function of combining subjective views and presenting them in such a structured manner. The contradictory or unjustifiable viewpoints that have emerged (inherent within the grid cells) further show the variety in transformation of the site depending on the participants' viewpoint. The commentary that follows is that of the thesis' author alone however, as exploration of the model of transformation is correlated with those transformations occurring at Uppark.

Transformations in management: creating Uppark

Uppark is just one of a number of houses in the Trust's portfolio of properties. The concerns of one house cannot therefore outweigh the concerns of the whole organisation, and although each property has its own management considerations, they are operated similarly, with certain functions carried out centrally by the Trust (Thackray, Jarman and Burgon 1995). At the 'local' level of site analysis, it becomes easier to see how management tasks are divided and the way in which certain procedures create and manipulate the object, or house, whilst other tasks concern themselves with the placing of the object in its wider context, through presentation, allied to Stage 2 of the model, originally proposed in Chapter 2. Stage 1 of the model provides a physical object that can be identified as Uppark. On-site property management deals with keeping the property open to view and, perhaps more importantly, in a fit state to be opened to the public. It is worth noting though, that visitors only encounter the 'local', that is the site that is visited. Management decisions made elsewhere within the organisation may be unidentifiable at the 'local' level of the site visitor. However, perception of the general management of the Trust as an organisation is affected by that perception at the local level. Thus general expectations of the Trust are altered through local encounter. Local decisions affecting the site also in turn affect perception of the general management of the Trust. There are considerable ramifications in this, which the Trust is aware of, and which emphasise the need for understanding how management works from the top level of central administration down to the local level where contact is most frequently made with the outside world, here, the visitor.

Maintenance forms a large part of this remit: from cleaning of the historic interiors, to gardening, litter removal, provision of paths and roadways, and positioning signage. Opening the house itself forms another 'suite' of tasks: arranging staffing, selling tickets and arranging visiting times, security and room stewarding, and the selling of souvenirs in the shop and cream teas in the restaurant. Each of these must be carefully scheduled, executed and accounted for, both in terms of time, human resources and money. The transformations occurring here therefore turn a physical resource into a country house that can be visited and classed as a tourist attraction. Effective planning is recognised as essential (McInnes and Ader 1995). It can be noted that at this point marketing and provision of information has not been included: this is a particular task that is not delegated to the local level. Trust policy dictates what will be on show and how the house will be presented in the guidebooks, as well as how the site is marketed, with the input of specialists in the conservation, marketing and academic field. These tasks, contributing to and forming the objectified heritage themselves (such as a guidebook), largely support the second stage of the model – providing interpretation of the house and contents in physical terms as having historical value and therefore being a part of the heritage. This subjective or descriptive element recreates the concept of all that the country house was and is, and thus the concept of heritage – at the same time it is objectified through the management practices of opening the house as an available choice of leisure pursuit identified in the hierarchy of demand.

There are various limits placed on the style of management that can be adopted by the local site manager and by the Trust in more widespread management of its portfolio of sites. The bottom line is that the Trust operates as a charity with clear purposes, and with enormous financial constraints and burdens placed on it. Except in the most carefully considered cases, the aim of property managers is to control the operating deficit of the property and raise money wherever possible. This is the area of the Trust's operation that is least understood by the general public, though the economics of conserving and operating country houses as attraction is a vital issue (Lees and Coyne 1979; Thomas 1995; Middleton 1995).

Local on-site management, performing the vital task of opening and running the house, also has to provide a monitoring system on the fabric of the estate itself, a primary concern for the Trust, and the provision of an attractive tourist site, effectively presenting the property and enlisting the support of visitors for the Trust's cause.

The fire has created a great problem for the Trust, apart from the opportunities so obviously displayed in the restoration project (Rowell and Robinson 1995; Targett 1996). The management of the project has entailed a huge rise in 'ongoing' conservation costs; new building regulations and conservation standards have been met, and the accompanying service contracts and monitoring systems have to be paid for. And yet the improvements in services for the house can provide no easy proof of how well they are working, as the Trust is not going to start another fire to test systems fully, or deliberately subject an historic interior to damaging activities or natural effects. A professional transformation has therefore been witnessed in the conservation project with new standards being set, for example, in fire safety (Fidler and McCaig 1992), or restoration (Lewis 1992) – effects of which are applicable across the country's historic environment. The revision of Disaster Planning Manuals and their provision at all Trust houses are one small detail in a myriad of developments in professional conservation practice. Knock-on effects are seen from this – many practical, concerned with the identification and labelling of, and retention of heritage objects, which can subsequently be interpreted in the latter part of the model.

One feature of the management of the site reflects directly on the Trust as an organisation and the perception of it by the public. Uppark is owned and operated by The National Trust, and receipts from the property go towards the ongoing work of the organisation. This is identified through use of certain imagery and 'house style', in the form of labels and logos. Nameplates used at the property use a distinct typeface and identify the Trust either in name or by the use of the acorn and oak leaf logo. Guidebooks and leaflets are standardised across the Trust properties, and the easiest identification of the Trust as an organisation associated with property is in the shop and to a lesser extent in the tearoom. The Trust promotes site specific and Trust specific souvenirs and ,at all public information points around the grounds, it is made clear that the Trust is a charity and relies on public support. Recruitment of members for the Trust is undertaken around the property, and this provides further explanation about the organisation and its management objectives. The 'branding' used by the organisation therefore promotes association between heritage objects (those operated by the Trust), and also the ideals of conservation and preservation (stated aims or concepts for the Trust).

The becoming of Uppark: historical and social transformation

The historical aspects of the property are the most important at Uppark, though in the first three years following re-opening, the fire and restoration have dominated visitors' reasons for coming. The balance of emphasis is perhaps clearer to the Trust than its visitors however: interpretation of the fire is confined to the exhibition building, well away from the house and gardens. The house itself has returned to its original state and its 'history' thus continues uninterrupted. As far as the house is concerned, the fire has just become another event in Uppark's history. The physical happenings at the house (events, owners and contents) are objectified through conservation and display and therefore, in doing so, given historical existence and value.

The historical facets of a visit to the house are accessed through the architecture, landscape and objects within the house, as well as the archive material associated with it.

Thus the themes and picture of the country house estate is built up: as a family home; centre of an estate; associations with royalty; fitted with foreign artworks and furniture; gardens specifically landscaped; and so on. Links to America are found through Sir Matthew's investments in the colonies and the archaeological ruins of the Vandalian Tower in the grounds, named after the intended colonial settlement. Edward Ford appears in the Dictionary of National Biography as a respected inventor and academic. William Talman, the original architect of the house, is also linked to Dyrham, Chatsworth and alterations at Hampton Court. Further artistic details are considered in numerous Country Life articles (six from 1910 – 1995). Lifestyle, in particular, is considered by analyses of country houses in general (Beaulieu 1967; Tinniswood 1989; Littlejohn 1997), or by often-neglected aspects, such as the ladies of the house (considered in Lummins and Marsh 1990).

The distinction between fact and fiction is blurred at the house due to mixing of its effect and existence within the different contexts of social, political and economic worlds, and the perception of these in modern society. Uppark was built and furnished in a period of history associated with the rise of high culture and taste, where the seat of power in the countryside lay with the owners of country house estates. Modern-day reaction by visitors to this image is varied, causing further blurring of distinctions. There are both advantages and disadvantages in this for the house and, though unstated as a deliberate policy, the Trust does nothing to counteract this blurring of view. However, it should be realised that this is not a problem unique to this house, as sociological research (amongst other disciplines) considers how human perception is swayed by the medium in which any message is communicated. We may therefore classify this as the 'Cadfael & Cookson phenomenon', where portrayal of a fictional historical resource profoundly affects subsequent encounter with an objectified historical resource. A pertinent example shows how visitor figures to Trust properties that have appeared in fiction televised dramas (e.g. the BBC's 'Pride and Prejudice') have increased dramatically (National Trust 1997 a).

The historical considerations at Uppark lead easily onto greater imaginary explorations, through the fictional associations with the house. Though fictional associations are used regularly as part of the heritage (Herbert 1995), Uppark benefits from both fiction and non-fictional description. The writer H.G. Wells (identified most readily with his works of science fiction) spent part of his childhood at Uppark, and the house and its owners are described in his autobiography, with information suggesting that his mother was a terrible housekeeper, eventually being dismissed by Frances Bullock (Wells, 1934). Wells' fictional Tono-Bungay (1908) is set at Bladesover House, based on Uppark and its owners. The poet Dryden portrayed the infamous owner of Uppark, Ford Grey, as the character Cold Caleb in his satire Absalom and Achitophel (1681), by describing him as 'below the Dignity of Verse.' In 'The Last of Uptake', two aged sisters consider the house and its history before leaving it to be consumed by flames (Harcourt-Smith

1944). It features illustrations by Whistler, the most relevant reproduced as Figure 6.9, here. For this story, inspiration was taken from a number of country houses, Uppark being among them: the eventual fate of the house perhaps being too prophetic! These examples show the objectified Uppark further transformed into the physical reality of a book, fictional or otherwise: the contents of which act as Stage 2 of the transformation turning the reality back into heritage as a concept. Uppark, in taking on a fictional role, has its intangible nature reinforced.

Subjects and objects: information and education at Uppark

The continual circle of transformation from concept to object and vice versa is seen clearly as I consider what can be literally learnt from Uppark. Information about any aspect of the site exists as an object – the terminology used includes 'pieces' of information. The information itself is objectified by means of the medium in which it is transmitted to the 'reader' (Hodder 1986; Hooper-Greenhill 1994): thus knowledge about the history of the site may be in books, articles, or a page on the Internet. Information is also objectified as building blocks or resources supporting larger subject categorisations. Uppark, treated as a collection of objects or pieces of information, can tell us about the larger concept of Uppark as a piece of heritage, and also provide both general and particular historical insight, archaeological information, economic, geographic and so on. There is a two-way transfer of information, with general knowledge of the subject matter providing insight into Uppark, enabling further objectification through classification of information about the particular physical existence and characteristics of that object. An example could be the scagliola-topped side-tables commissioned by Sir Matthew Fetherstonhaugh for the Stone Hall. These were made by Don Petro Belloni in 1754, who worked in the monastery of Vallombrosa near Florence. There are only five documented tabletops made by Belloni, apart from the pair at Uppark. What do the tables therefore tell us? Amongst many pieces, information can be gained about their art style, manufacture and the craftsman, Belloni. Furthermore things can be learnt about Sir Matthew's finances, travelling and interest in furniture. Wider sociological information can also be derived from participation in the Grand Tour, the kinds of objects purchased and the styles that were sought. After their damage during the fire, further physical characteristics of manufacture were studied in order to reconstruct the tables providing yet more detailed knowledge, both about the tables, their manufacture, and conservation as a subject.

It can therefore be seen that the variety of subject classifications that can be applied to objects at Uppark reinforces both knowledge and the classification process: the transformation of the objects from concept to object and back to concept is thus implicit, yet continual. Educational initiatives, as noted in the Grid analysis, have not been fully developed at the site, though developments across the National Trust properties continue as part of its education

Illustration 6.9 *Illustration by Whistler, from 'The Last of Uptake'. (Harcourt-Smith 1944)*

"Suddenly a flame blossomed out of it like a lovely flower, was joined by another, and yet more, till there was a bed of great petunias. They swayed in the moaning wind, these flowery flames; next there came a low rumble, sparks like fireworks for a victory, and the whole of Uptake was roaring and crackling."

service and Minerva programmes (National Trust 1997 a). Amongst other applied initiatives, the Trust has established conservation workshops, one of which, at Cliveden, has since been 'privatised' as a business due to the amount of work generated for it (Rowell and Robinson 1996, 167).

Subject classifications can be easily identified at the site without any need for specific educational initiatives: any developments are likely to work along the lines of the National Curriculum targets, or established Further or Continuing Education interests. The children's guide to the house, without intending to be strictly educational, in highlighting interesting facts or fun activities considers a number of subject areas (Creed 1995). These include: history; family trees (and therefore personal and social education); geography; technology; social history; home economics; art; design; politics; conservation; maths; English language and literature; and the physical and biological sciences. If the activities in the books are undertaken, a variety of skills and techniques are encouraged: including discovery; observation; drawing; writing; and story telling. Attention is focused on objects or aspects of the house, and this reinforces knowledge brought to the house, as well as adding to it. The action of encounter with Uppark as an object helps develop the ability for the visitors to achieve the second stage of transformation for themselves. Further interpretation encourages new encounters with and creation of new objects. The Trust's position as a charity, with limited resources, prevents many major developments in this area. However, much work is undertaken by the Trust at a national level, along with other specific localised projects for which funding has been secured or set aside (National Trust 1998). It should be noted also that this is an area in which the Trust has no statutory duty, unlike English Heritage. Educational development is undertaken by the Trust as a recognised 'voluntary' duty imposed on it by the organisation's position in society.

I have said little as yet about the processes of conservation. It should be stressed that professional interest in Uppark is just as valid as that of tourists, if not more so, as it gives the Trust the ability to operate as a conservation organisation. The management of Uppark, and in particular the management of the restoration project at the house, has enabled new skills to be developed (Rowell and Robinson 1996), 'lost' techniques to be rediscovered, and further objective study of the site, adding to knowledge across a number of different subject areas, considered themselves to be professional fields. Such subjects are the ones which do not immediately occur to the visiting public, but which are relied upon for the continued existence and opening of the house. These include: project management; conservation; archaeology; restoration; fire and disaster management; engineering; fine and applied arts; interpretation; facilities and visitor management; and archiving.

Conceptualising Uppark as Heritage

A paragraph in the opening remarks for this case study is repeated here as a reminder of its purpose: *All of the analyses that have been undertaken have involved a degree of subjectivity in description of the object elements of Uppark. It is suggested within this study that the process of management creates through identification, manipulates, and establishes such objects. This is followed by the second stage of the transformation, in which subjective analysis is based, and those objectified elements become valued by virtue of their description and interpretation. In this case study therefore, aspects of Uppark enrich and add to a wider perception of what the concept 'heritage' is, by the fact that they have been objectified, classified and managed in a certain way. Where the initial interest or value comes from in the first place is irrelevant for the purposes here of suggesting that specific activities promote Uppark's existence as part of the wider concept of heritage.*

A number of conceptual values are carried within each object that forms part of Uppark, and also the activities or manipulation of those objects at the site. The generalised aspects of the heritage and its value are dealt with outside this thesis, and this has already been noted. However, there are distinct issues that the National Trust concerns itself with in its management, and therefore are pertinent to analysis of Uppark. Martin Drury, the Trust's Director-General during the mid 1990s was keen to emphasise the messages both implicit and explicit in the name of the organisation, 'National' and 'Trust' (pers. com.). Value is a part of the commitment that the Trust operates within, both practically through its charitable status and conceptually, as having a mission to protect those aspects of the nation that are valued in a certain way. The Trust takes a 'long view' of conservation and is less interested in topicality that does not endure. The fire at Uppark may be one such example of this, as has been seen in the analysis. Other conceptual issues which the Trust operates within, which guide the purposes behind its management and where Uppark can be seen as an 'object example', are concerned with the environment and people's place in it. Perhaps laying itself open to criticism as being

a 'green movement', the Trust tries hard not to highlight any one object amongst others at its sites, but to focus on understanding the contexts in which those objects exist. This is one reason for the complexity at Uppark: many aspects of the estate have been 'objectified' in unintentional and intentional ways, forcing management structures to consider many variables, seen in the Grid analysis.

The Trust operates within the field of conservation, and this places certain duties upon its organisation, aims and activities. Furthermore, its activities occur within the sphere of both the charitable sector and the increasingly market- (and profit) driven leisure and tourism sphere. The effects of the Trust's work influences various other spheres including historical, political (identity), museums and social, with the interaction of people and their values, central to the ethos of the organisation.

Suspension of time is also a relevant theme, though it has not been dealt with in this case study. Its exploration will be a focus of attention in the analysis of another country house, Brodsworth Hall, where suspension of time features prominently. At Uppark, such suspension, whilst certainly existing, has been limited in part by the perception that the historical events at Uppark have continued to the present day – through the destruction and restoration. A conceptual problem, which the Trust has to deal with, is the balance between the three-way pull of the house 'existing' as a differently classified object: either as a house (with family still in residence), a museum or a dedicated heritage attraction. Trust stately homes fall between all three, necessitating the organisation to convey more than just history. There can be seen a number of themes all of which have some bearing on the thinking within the Trust and which filter through to practical action in the operation of its houses such as Uppark.

Transformations and the Trust: reflections on Uppark

The variety of transformations seen at Uppark does not need to be reiterated. Some reflection does need to be made on what these transformations achieve. The objectification and management of Uppark is achieved through the fundamentally positive intent of management (discussed in previous chapters). Uppark's place as a heritage attraction necessitates an existence in a number of interrelated spheres. The cornerstone of this is public value, interest, and action in the form of visiting the site. Again the motivations for this are usually positive, either for education or pleasure (although school trips are not always enjoyed by the participants!). Schouten (1995, 260) has coined an acronym for encounter with a heritage attraction or museum. It is suggested that the visitor wants, and the operator tries to provide a 'UNIQUE' experience. That is, the encounter is Uncommon; Novelty; Informative; Quality; and enables Understanding and Emotions. Management activity at Uppark, through the manipulation of objects, provides this.

The existence and encounter with the objects at Uppark are symbolic. Heritage is objectified at the site, and the mosaic presented to the public represents more than just their physical existence. The house exists in the context of a country house, and the objectified country house, as Cadogan (1995) states is part of a large system. The house exists in the context of The National Trust. The house also exists in the context of heritage and tourism also. There is a complex interplay between these spheres of influence, where the country house is considered important in history and this particular country house is seen as important in history. Uppark exists both as an individual site, and part of a corporate entity, the Trust – there is interplay here between the site's individuality in history and in the Trust, necessitating constant valuation and re-evaluation of its objectified state. Transformations are, therefore, both internal and external, visible and invisible, constant and occasional. The house enjoys a dichotomous nature in its management and presentation, and this is part of its success. It displays family history to the public; moreover, it is a private house that has had effects on public life. In addition, the National Trust is a private organisation acting for public benefit, as a guardian of aspects of the heritage.

The becoming of Uppark, in the historical sense, was an inevitability but, in the sense of heritage, shows continual transformations of the kind this thesis proposes. There is seen at Uppark a reliance on the two stages of transformation, seen alone in the management of the site, before any intentions of presentation that have not been covered in detail here. Even the 'simplest' of management tasks may therefore present a challenge and entail transformation of a kind. The management of Uppark addresses such challenges, and the encounter with the site, by managers and visitors alike, promotes engagement with the object, and provides the basis for the conceptual to be reached, acknowledged and reinforced.

This case study has approached Uppark in a particular way, concentrating on the conceptual aspects of the house that have become objectified by transformation into physical objects or identified aspects of the house and its history. It has been treated as an object just as the Trust has treated it as an object, as if acting as a museum curator looking after its collection. The processes of management at Uppark objectify and then conceptualise the site through the first and second stages of the model of transformation in a mutually supporting fashion. The object 'Uppark' remains of primary importance in both management and presentation. Uppark has thus become a site understood as forming part of the heritage, and it has been analysed as the transformation of heritage in action. The case study concerned with another country house, Brodsworth Hall, owned by English Heritage, will approach the transformation slightly differently, discussing the Grid analysis in the light of a particular management regime that operates at the house, and its existence as a comparative novelty for the managing organisation to look after and operate. It will be shown how such differences alter the objectified heritage considerably.

7   Brodsworth Hall: a brand new time capsule

A home, not a time capsule

The publicity surrounding the opening of Brodsworth Hall to the public in 1995 was considerable. The house was heralded as remarkable (Taliotis 1995), and its worthiness for preservation was noted as long ago as the 1960s (Girouard 1963). The unique nature of this new English Heritage property was perceived as the display of a time capsule, depicting life in the nineteenth century, and subsequently, that lifestyle in decline. The Independent newspaper's headline for an article about the house declared it to be a 'Memorial to a vanished age of opulence' (Gillie 1990).

Brodsworth Hall has been clearly objectified as a 'heritage object' by English Heritage since its opening, most noticeably in the publicity material promoting visits to the site (Figure 7.1). The visitor is invited to 'step into another world and experience the unique atmosphere of faded Victorian splendour.' (English Heritage 1997 e) In any visit to Brodsworth, the visitor may 'view the house's rich interiors and full contents, only made possible by five years of intensive conservation. No sanitised exhibition or glamorous depiction of the Victorian era, Brodsworth Hall proudly bears the marks of over a century of being lived in.' (*ibid.*) The assumption may therefore be made that time has been suspended at the site, as the visitor has to travel back from present time in order to see this 'Victorian Delight in Yorkshire' (*ibid.*).

However, within this case study it will be shown how the transformations as identified previously for Uppark are, at this site, more complicated and difficult to assess because of a different management regime. Furthermore it will be seen how a style of presentation may prompt the 'time capsule' response (Milliken 1989, 6), when clearly the site is nothing of the sort, and labels attached to the site in its publicity may seem irrelevant upon a visit to the site. Though perceived as such, Brodsworth's 'UNIQUEness' is also questioned, suggesting that it is the activities of a particular management agency at the site that prompt such a response, rather than the house itself. It is worth noting that Brodsworth, unlike Uppark, is a new heritage attraction: site visits for the case study were undertaken during the second full visitor season that the house was open (summer 1997).

At Uppark a specific event, with subsequent management action, has altered the visiting experience for the site: at Brodsworth, the entire experience and organisation of site management is new.

Similarities to Uppark may be seen, however, in the property representing a 'major project' (English Heritage 1995) for its managing agency, entailing ongoing project management, quite apart from the provision and maintenance of visitor facilities. Finally, the analysis of Brodsworth considers closely the suspension of time at the site, its relationship with the way in which the site is managed, and the effects that this has on the overall objectification of the site as a heritage resource.

The heritage object: Brodsworth's 'becoming' as a site

The history of Brodsworth, and critical appreciation of its Italianate architecture, fine interiors, statuary, art objects and grounds, are well documented (Girouard 1963 & 1979; Pevsner 1974; Read 1989; Whitworth 1995). When Pamela Williams gave the house to the nation in 1990, with the wish that it be preserved as a country house collection, it passed to English Heritage to conserve and present the property. The interior furnishings of the house were purchased by the National Heritage Memorial Fund for £3.36 million, and English Heritage has spent an equivalent amount on a five-year essential conservation programme. Whilst the house and collection is largely secure, further maintenance and conservation requires another long-term programme, which has been put into effect. Both programmes have adopted a 'conserve as found' policy (Taliotis 1995), and whilst major works have been undertaken to consolidate the building and conserve and stabilise the contents, no large changes or redecoration have been undertaken. Surveys did reveal, however, that the house was suffering from decay in many respects, and since 1990 an attempt has been made to slow or stop these damaging processes. This halting of substantial decay, like the fire and subsequent restoration at Uppark, in itself therefore is a major part of the history and presentation of the house. Subsidence had caused Brodsworth to tilt by nearly 20 centimetres, rendering roof drainage useless, and a

Figure 7.1 *Property publicity leaflet.*

Discover a World of Victorian Grandeur

Step into another world and experience the unique atmosphere of faded Victorian splendour. Take a marvellous journey through the intriguing passage of time and enjoy this tribute to 19th century architecture and lifestyle.

View the house's rich interiors and full contents, only made possible by five years of intensive conservation. No sanitised exhibition or glamourous depiction of the Victorian era, Brodsworth Hall proudly bears the marks of over a century of being lived in.

Events at Brodsworth Hall

Step back in time at Brodsworth Hall and enjoy an exciting selection of displays, re-enactments, music and drama - all part of our main events programme. With something for everyone to enjoy, events are held on many weekends from Easter to October. Pick up your FREE events diary at any English Heritage site or call 0171 973 3396.

Opening Times

22 March - 26 October, Tuesday to Sunday and Bank Holidays 1-6pm, last admission 5pm. Gardens open 12-6pm. Guided tours are available from 10am for pre-booked parties. 8 November - 31 March 1998, Saturday and Sunday 11am-4pm, gardens, shop and tea rooms only (closed 24-26 December). **Telephone 01302 722598.**

Admission

House and gardens: adults £4.50, concessions £3.40, children £2.30. Gardens only: adults £2.50, concessions £1.90, children £1.30. Winter: adults £1.50, concessions £1.00, children free. 15% discount for groups of eleven or more.

How To Find Us

By car   In Brodsworth, 6 miles north west of Doncaster. West of A1 between A635 and A638
By bus   Telephone 0114 276 8688 for details.

English Heritage is committed to making sites accessible to people with disabilities. We advise visitors to call sites in advance or refer to the English Heritage *Guide for Visitors with Disabilities* available free of charge by telephoning the number below.

Find Out More

For further information on English Heritage membership and how to obtain free entry to over four hundred sites, please telephone 0171 973 3434.

ENGLISH HERITAGE

ENGLISH HERITAGE

Brodsworth Hall
A Victorian Delight in Yorkshire

Gaze at elegant hallways, the ornate drawing room, fascinating billiard room, servants quarters and old kitchen with it's clutter of original equipment and utensils.

Enjoy the collection of statues, chosen for their sentimentality or charm, and allow yourself to be enchanted by a house with a very special atmosphere.

Enjoy delicious refreshments and light meals in our Tea Rooms, or relax with your own picnic in the beautiful gardens.

Also, commemorate your visit in the Gift Shop where you will find a whole range of interesting souvenirs.

There are further intriguing exhibitions about Brodsworth Hall, the family who lived here and how they were served.

Experience the fine terrace, croquet lawn, quarry garden, fern dell and 'The Grove' with its tall sheltering trees and rose garden.
The charming Target House, where the archery targets were once stored, now houses an exhibition about the extensive gardens.

Although we welcome children at Brodsworth Hall, regrettably we cannot allow pushchairs or baby carriers into the house due to its fragile interiors.

tidemark can be seen around the ground floor where rising damp had met with leaking roofs. The sandstone structure has been consolidated, with parts replaced and repaired, and new services (electricity, fire detection, heating) have been added. The original design for the house, and the building as it stands, can be seen in Figures 7.2 to 7.4.

As well as damage caused by structural problems, Brodsworth's interiors 'had suffered from long exposure to sunlight, the accumulation of dust and dirt, and insect infestation' (Whitworth 1995, 35). The interiors have been left 'untouched' however, including all alterations made by the owners, and apart from essential repairs, left as the hall

Figures 7.2 – 7.3 *Brodsworth – original architectural plan, hall today & artist's interpretation.*

was found in 1990. The inventory prepared for Brodsworth's collections now contains over 17,000 entries, 'ranging from oil paintings and sculptures to household linen and kitchen implements' (*ibid.* 36).

The gardens and exterior of the hall are described as having a more 'robust' treatment (Carr-Whitworth 1995, 3) and are being cleared of undergrowth and replanted along original plans. This includes consolidation of statuary and buildings, and full survey, with eventual aims to open the stable block and other areas of the grounds currently closed. Brodsworth was formally opened by HRH The Princess Margaret on July 5, 1995.

The heritage object: visiting Brodsworth

The site plan is reproduced as Figure 7.4 and house plan as Figure 7.5. At the entrance gate to the site is a nameplate and display board with opening details (site open standard summer season from April to October). Visitors to the hall then drive up a half-mile stretch of unmade driveway to a large car park. At the edge of the car park next to the driveway is the ticket office. This is a newly constructed building of wood and glass, with an undercover 'open' front with a large desk for admissions. Part of this structure comprises a small sitting area where membership and other information about the organisation can be obtained. Each visitor is given an A4 foldout plan of the grounds (without details of the house), with brief notes about the conservation philosophy, regulations, and available facilities.

From the admissions area where a clear division is made between the site and visitor reception, the visitor walks 'into' the site itself, along the driveway up an incline to the front lawn. The hall is entered through the front door where tickets are checked and pushchairs can be left. Guidebooks are available here along with a free children's activity sheet. The visitor is left to follow the route around the ground floor of the house, and then to proceed upstairs, around the main and servants' wings, and then down the servants' staircase to the kitchen, larder, shop and tea-room housed on the ground floor of the servants' wing. In the main circulation spaces of the entrance and inner hall and the bedroom corridor, the original carpets have been copied and replaced, and free visitor circulation is permitted. Illustrations of the main hallway and drawing room on the ground floor can be seen in Figure 7.6 and 7.7. Within the other show rooms, drugget has been laid over the original carpet and the progress of visitors around the edges of the rooms, fenced off with low stanchions. In all 46 rooms can be seen, including bathrooms, and the original lift installed by the last elderly owner, which is still used for infirm visitors who wish to see the upper floor.

As noted already, the house has been left 'as found' and no redecoration or major movement of furniture has occurred. The gradual decay of the house can be seen in varying degrees as the visitor passes around the house, most noticeably upstairs in the 'Boat Bedroom' (Figure 7.8). Another of the family bedrooms has been turned into an exhibition on the Thellusson family, with albums and displays, which

Figure 7.4 *Orientation leaflet – site plan.*

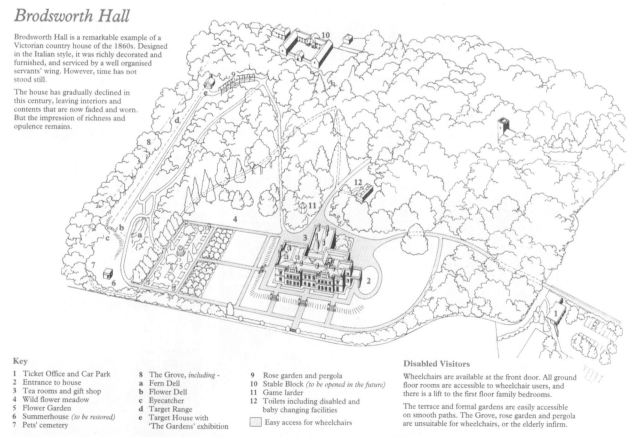

Brodsworth Hall

Brodsworth Hall is a remarkable example of a Victorian country house of the 1860s. Designed in the Italian style, it was richly decorated and furnished, and serviced by a well organised servants' wing. However, time has not stood still.

The house has gradually declined in this century, leaving interiors and contents that are now faded and worn. But the impression of richness and opulence remains.

Key

1 Ticket Office and Car Park
2 Entrance to house
3 Tea rooms and gift shop
4 Wild flower meadow
5 Flower Garden
6 Summerhouse *(to be restored)*
7 Pets' cemetery

8 The Grove, *including* -
  a Fern Dell
  b Flower Dell
  c Eyecatcher
  d Target Range
  e Target House with
    'The Gardens' exhibition

9 Rose garden and pergola
10 Stable Block *(to be opened in the future)*
11 Game larder
12 Toilets including disabled and
  baby changing facilities

  ☐ Easy access for wheelchairs

Disabled Visitors

Wheelchairs are available at the front door. All ground floor rooms are accessible to wheelchair users, and there is a lift to the first floor family bedrooms.

The terrace and formal gardens are easily accessible on smooth paths. The Grove, rose garden and pergola are unsuitable for wheelchairs, or the elderly infirm.

Figure 7.5 *House plan.*

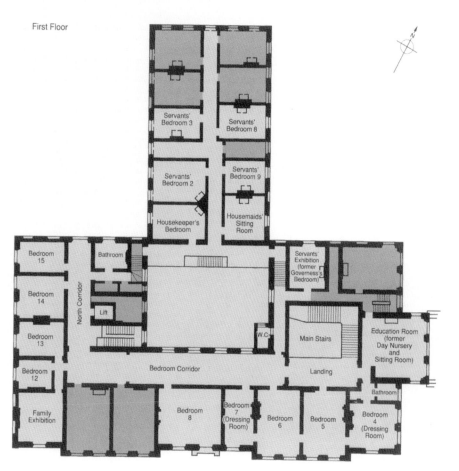

Figures 7.6 and 7.7 *Main hallway and drawing room.*

can be looked through. The room over the entrance hall has been turned into an education room, open to visitors and containing materials about the house, and space to sit and read. These include photographs of the conservation, copies of the original specifications for building the house, details of the conservation undertaken, and more on the owners of the house. There is also a dressing-up trunk, with nineteenth and early twentieth century costumes and hats to try on. Further round the upper floor the governess's bedroom has been converted into a static display about the servants who worked at the house. From this small exhibition the visitor moves on to the servants's wing, displayed as it was found, acting as storerooms for items from the house, and finally the kitchen and larder back downstairs. The kitchen, again,

Figure 7.8 *Boat bedroom, conserved as found.*

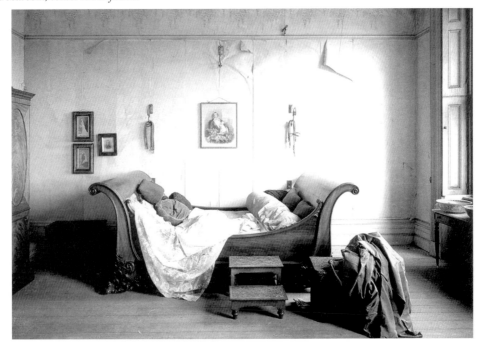

has been left as it was found, fitted with original stoves, and cluttered with nineteenth and twentieth century utensils (it is shown with the adjoining Billiard Room in Figure 7.9 and 7.10).

The ground floor rooms of the servants' wing have had their uses changed to a souvenir shop, and sitting areas for the tearoom. The service yard at the back entrance has further seating for the tearoom. The shop has a large stock of branded 'Brodsworth', 'Victorian' and 'English Heritage' goods for sale, along with other items, foods and postcards. The theme of the hall is reflected in the stock with items relating to Royalty (Victorian England), gardens, William Morris, and sculpture.

Figure 7.9 & 7.10 *Billiard Room and Kitchen.*

The visitor leaves the house by the tradesmen's entrance, and can progress into the gardens. A new toilet block has been constructed very close to the exit, secreted within woodland along the driveway, and hidden in any view of the house. There are specific features in the garden that are emphasised in the plan and guide. Two croquet lawns (still used by the local club) lie next to the west front of the hall; whilst further to the west are the replanted flower garden, fountain and seating. A wild flower meadow lies to the north and, beyond this, paths lead down to the quarry garden. In this area, known as 'The Grove', can be found the summer house with an exhibition on the garden's design and restoration; a large fern rockery with bridges and rock cascade (currently being restored); the archery target range; and the Rose garden and replanted pergola. A path leads down to the stable block from the Rose garden, though this has yet to be conserved and is not currently accessible. At the southwest extremity of the gardens is the icehouse and classical summerhouse on top of it, and the pets' cemetery, behind them. Though Brodsworth church lies within the area of the gardens, it is not accessible from them and can only be reached from the village.

The total area accessible to the public in the grounds and in the care of English Heritage is approximately 15 acres. There are no further parkland walks, as the rest of the estate and surrounding land remain in the private ownership of the donor family. Disabled visitors are able to access most of the house (including the upper floor, via the lift), and the main flower garden and lawns around the house, where the paths are tarmac. This category of visitor can be driven right up to the front door of the house, and may park there also. Other paths through the woodland areas and down to the Grove are gravel and have steep slopes in places, and are therefore less accessible.

There is no interpretation within the main rooms in the hall (except the two specific exhibition rooms), though volunteer stewards are stationed in most of the show rooms.

Grid analysis: identification of the heritage object

As with the analysis of Uppark, the use of ASEB Grid analysis (Beeho & Prentice 1995) identifies and structures the various 'objects' that comprise Brodsworth, and this is followed by more detailed comments on the site, which reflect the transformations that occur. The methodology used for the Grid analysis was identical to that undertaken for Uppark, using both unstructured interviews of visitors and staff, and assessment of management and other literature. The Grid cell assessments have been presented here in a briefer version than for Uppark, in order to limit repetitive analysis.

1. Strengths

Strengths: Activities (SA)
Like Uppark, there are specific activity areas at Brodsworth, which can be combined to produce a visit of suitable duration for the visitor. It is a new heritage attraction in the area. There is the house, the shop, restaurant, gardens, and The Grove. Within the house there are almost 50 rooms to visit. There are three separate exhibitions on the house and grounds, and activity sheets are available for children. The education room has a large amount of materials for study. The grounds provide walks in different settings of formal garden, woodland, dell, and landscaped rockery with equivalent varying planting layouts. Special events at the site, including inclusion in the annual English Heritage concert season (Russell 1997) provide a new venue for heritage activities.

Strengths: Settings (SS)
The environmental setting varies around the hall. Though there are gardens in the immediate vicinity of the hall, much of the original parkland is now farmed, and the surrounding area has a number of coalmines. There are large population centres to the north, east and southwest of Brodsworth, and the main A1(M) motorway runs within three-quarters of a mile of the house. The grounds, having been left to decay for so long, now contain important collections of wildflowers and other plants and wildlife. The hall itself is one of only a few large country houses in the area. Its setting is one which is expected by many of the visitors, who realise that such country house lifestyles no longer exist as they did in the nineteenth century. Brodsworth therefore fully represents the decline of the accompanying lifestyle. The interiors have been displayed as they were found, rather than tidying up or restoring the property to a particular period, and nearly all of the hall's rooms can be visited, unlike many country houses, which show only a few rooms. Brodsworth is favourably compared in this light to the nearby National Trust house, Nostell Priory. The setting of Brodsworth is further noted for its incongruity with the surrounding industrial nature of the landscape, and proximity to 'civilisation' (cities and motorways).

In management terms, Brodsworth has been successfully developed and operated utilising a large body of volunteer stewards: this is one of the first instances of this for English Heritage, whose properties are usually staffed by paid employees. As a conservation project, Brodsworth has also helped the organisation develop its expertise in the field of country house management and museum collections, where the National Trust has usually been assumed to be the 'lead' organisation.

Strengths: Experiences (SE)
Brodsworth is one of only a few 'heritage' properties in the surrounding area, and is beginning to act as a 'haven' for both short-distance as well as long-distance visitors, similar to Cusworth Hall, operated by the City of Doncaster local authority. Brodsworth provides the opportunity to mix physical exercise in the grounds, with a cultural experience in the house (and participation in special events), where a variety of different kinds of history may be seen. The hall provides specific opportunities for shopping, eating in the restaurant, and also specialised educational visits. Distinct experiences are available for the enthusiastic group of

volunteer stewards who devote time to assist in staffing the property. The enthusiasm of the staff in providing information is a noted feature in visitor perception about the property.

Strengths: Benefits (SB)

Again, Brodsworth is one of only a few heritage properties in the local area, and the only English Heritage furnished country house in this part of the country, the rest being ruins. The managing agency (English Heritage) has therefore raised its profile in the area, and made a significant contribution to an under-developed area in terms of tourism. The house further provides a specific regional resource in terms of education, and an example of expertise in conservation. The presentation of the house gives a unique insight into Victorian lifestyles, as well as the decline of that kind of social system.

2. Weaknesses

Weaknesses: Activities (WA)

Brodsworth is relatively isolated, both in terms of geographic location and other nearby tourist facilities. Cusworth Hall, already mentioned, is closer to Doncaster and substantially developed for tourism, and can be seen to be in direct competition for visitors. The National Trust property, Nostell Priory, with a large park to walk in and a variety of facilities, provides similar competition. The only other English Heritage properties in the area are two ruins of religious buildings and Conisbrough Castle. For members of English Heritage, this may prove a drawback in terms of the range of properties that can be visited in the area. Brodsworth as a property is quite small in comparison to some other country houses, and although most of the rooms are open, the visitor capacity is quite low due to professional conservation restrictions, due to the narrow paths that the visitor route takes round the rooms. Though the rooms can be visited, most of them cannot therefore actually be walked around. Outside the hall, though there is variety in the gardens and Grove, areas of the grounds are inaccessible to the less mobile, and the driveway from the ticket office to the hall is quite long. For the more able, walks are limited to the gardens: there are no estate walks as the land does not belong to English Heritage and has been turned over to agricultural use.

Weaknesses: Settings (WS)

As noted above, most of the original Brodsworth estate is now farmed and English Heritage looks after the small central portion only, containing the house and formal gardens. Brodsworth is therefore divorced from its proper environmental setting as an estate. As one of only a few country houses to visit in the area, during the height of the summer the property becomes very crowded, with queues for both entering the car park and the hall itself. Brodsworth has not survived as a pristine country house collection: its presentation is thus one of the country houses in decay. In terms of management, restrictions are inevitable, but more obvious due to the hall's fragile nature. Light levels,

as noted with Uppark, are a constant problem, where the balance is drawn between conservation and the ability to see anything. The costs involved in the conservation and management of Brodsworth are considerable, and the property's development programme is ongoing: development of further visitor facilities, and the opening of other parts of the property (further bedrooms, stable block, summerhouse and ice-house) is a gradual development, and thus it may be difficult to sustain interest in the site with 'new attractions'. The use of volunteer room- stewards, whilst successful, needs careful management to maintain proper custodial support for the permanent staff, and for presentation of the property to visitors. A particular weakness for the management is the lack of ability to attract increased visitor numbers travelling on the A1(M). As the trunk route is motorway at the junction from which Brodsworth can be reached, English Heritage cannot put a brown tourist attraction sign on the motorway. This is a vicious circle: the site must have at least 100,000 visitors per annum to allow it to have a motorway sign – but, of course, cannot attract those numbers of visitors without the sign.

Weaknesses: Experiences (WE)

Brodsworth has survived as a country house in decline, and this decline is a very obvious feature of any visit. Thus appreciation of the hall's artistic, historical and landscape merits are always mitigated by the overriding decline and decay from which the property has suffered. The site cannot be appreciated as the centre of a large estate, because much of the estate cannot be visited and has not been interpreted. Though there is specific interpretation of the Thellusson family and the servants, and a separate consideration of the gardens, there is little interpretation of the conservation of the house or of its architectural/artistic features and furniture, as would be expected for many other houses. The guidebook is very brief and concerns itself with a social history of the hall. As with other country houses, interpretation of the property is difficult as it may bear no relation to the lives of its visitors. The problem is compounded at Brodsworth because of the changes made to the house by its various owners, which are all preserved as a mish-mash, and the decay of the house and gardens. Expectations held by the visitors about English Heritage as an organisation are also challenged at Brodsworth, as some expect all English Heritage properties (usually ruins) to have plenty of space to run about in and clamber over – the regulations typical for a country house make such activities impossible. For much of the interpretation in the main show rooms, there is a reliance on the use of the volunteer room stewards – and accompanying need for training to give the volunteers the ability to provide customer care.

Weaknesses: Benefits (WB)

Brodsworth is one of three country houses in the area providing little variety of heritage attractions for an area, which has little tourism development. Some visitors come away interested but somewhat disappointed with Brodsworth as they were expecting to see how the conservation was undertaken, and thought it might be restored. Some were sad to see the house in decline. On being questioned whether a visit had increased the visitor's commitment to conservation there was a mixed response: there was no doubt that people were pleased that Brodsworth had been conserved and opened to view, but worries that the varying management agencies (not just English Heritage) ought to do a lot more, though this was in regards to heritage generally and not just Brodsworth. English Heritage as a managing organisation faces a difficult task with Brodsworth and may now give the impression that it will look after all country houses, in a similar expectation to that held about the National Trust. Possibly expecting 'typical' sanitised heritage (Hewison 1987), visitors' encounters with Brodsworth may challenge expectations as the house has not been renovated: this challenge may confuse some visitors and is not addressed in any detail at the site. Perceptions of the managing agency are confused frequently at the site, as many people expect that it is the National Trust that is looking after Brodsworth. English Heritage is not equated by most visitors with the preservation of country houses.

3. Opportunities

Opportunities: Activities (OA)

There is limited scope for enhancement of physical activities at the site, though there is potential for further development of the interpretative materials there. English Heritage as the managing agency has a programme of development for the site, which includes the conservation of the stable block, and inclusion of a further exhibition on the conservation of the house; further conservation within the house and opening of further bedrooms; restoration within the garden; and provision and development of education services at the site. For visitor enjoyment and appreciation, Brodsworth's local management are organising special events to be held at the hall as part of the annual English Heritage events programme. The 1997 visitor season saw celebration of Queen Victoria's anniversary, for example. In a similar fashion to the reactions to Uppark, visitors were keen to see more 'behind the scenes' work, concerning the conservation, and increased use of the site for school visits. Some visitors, accustomed to visits to country houses (categorised as the 'connoisseurs'), particularly wanted to see more detailed information available about the hall and estate, possibly in the form of a more detailed guidebook.

Opportunities: Settings (OS)

These are limited due to the nature of the site, and the separate ownership of the estate. The continued restoration of the garden will provide an enhanced environmental setting. The social setting for the hall may in time be improved through the use of a timed ticket system, which might alleviate crowding inside the hall. For English Heritage as a manager, with a signpost on the motorway, it would be able to attract more visitors and thus increase revenue and develop Brodsworth as a major attraction in the area. The success of the volunteering team at the site can also be built upon, both on-site and elsewhere in the organisation.

Opportunities: Experiences (OE)

There is opportunity for further educational and professional use of Brodsworth as a historical object and example of conservation practice. Treating Brodsworth as a unique property in English Heritage's portfolio of sites presents opportunities for both visitors and the organisation as a whole. There is opportunity for visitors to appreciate changes in society that resulted in the house falling into a decaying state, and within the organisation to develop methodologies for treating properties managed by both English Heritage and the owners of other properties assisted by its grant schemes. Interpretation of the site may thus be developed as a challenge for visitors and management of the site a continuing challenge for English Heritage. Continuing staff development and training at the site will further enhance the visitor experience and management experience of alternative methodologies for property management.

Opportunities: Benefits (OB)

The possible benefits that can be identified for both visitors and managers at the site are closely linked to the opportunities for experiences. There are benefits to be gained from expertise used in the conservation and management of the house through increased education about practical problems and solutions developing the discipline of country house conservation. For the visitors, there are opportunities to understand more about the site, the period of history, the practice of conservation, and English Heritage as an organisation that does more than just look after ruins. The site may also increase an overall commitment to conservation on the part of the visitor, and the staff and volunteers trained at the site. The increased diversity in the range of properties English Heritage manages brings further support from visitors, and particularly members, who may make an ongoing contribution to the organisation in financial terms.

4. Threats

Threats: Activities (TA)

Because of the long-term conservation project at the hall and its overall fragile nature, access may become limited due to visitor pressure or the need for further remedial conservation works. The site may reach its total visitor capacity, limiting the ability to visit. The admission price structure and site location may prevent certain people from visiting, especially if the local bus service is discontinued. Alternatively, English Heritage might not be able to attract any more visitors to the site, thereby limiting further investment in facilities. Special events held at the site may not be successful for a variety of reasons – the 1997 concerts held at the site were not as successful as hoped due to weather and poor attendance and the site had been left out of the concerts programme for 1998. Events policies since have seen greater emphasis on 'property relevance'.

Threats: Settings (TS)

There is already a limited amount of noise from the nearby motorway – increased traffic would detract from the visit.

Equally, increases in visitor numbers may detract from visitor pleasure and their ability to see around the house, as seen at Uppark. Weather limits activities outside and the house cannot cope with an influx of visitors from the grounds in inclement conditions. It seems unlikely that the current agricultural use on the estate would alter dramatically, but changes in use may affect the site detrimentally. As the managing agency is limited by government spending, English Heritage may at some future stage feel that it cannot invest any further money in the property due to more pressing needs elsewhere. In this respect the size of the conservation project at Brodsworth could forseeably become a far greater liability for its managers.

Threats: Experiences (TE)

Again, should the site reach its total capacity, the experiences to be gained from a visit to Brodsworth could be threatened. Gaps in interpretation or education on-site may also threaten understanding of the hall, as well as the conservation project. If other tourist attractions in the region developed interpretation of 'country houses' further, this would also threaten experiences to be gained at Brodsworth. On a professional level, changes in attitude to conservation practice may alter leaving the current treatment of Brodsworth, with its 'preserve as found' philosophy as out of step, or even wrong. The volunteer stewarding programme has to be effectively maintained to staff the property fully and present it to the public: furthermore the site has to continue to attract such support.

Threats: Benefits (TB)

If no further educational or interpretative development occurs at the site, then the future benefits for the visitor may become more limited as other conservation projects proceed, or other similar sites open or redevelop. Social attitudes could change further, at either a regional or national scale, which could turn Brodsworth into an anachronistic example of preservation and display. In turn, English Heritage would feel the effects of this as it strives to maintain standards as the national heritage management agency for England. The National Trust, with its limited resources as a charity, may in future take the attitude that English Heritage is able to take over its assumed role as the guardian of country houses and cease its work in this field, thus putting English Heritage as an organisation and country house preservation at greater risk as it has to shoulder greater responsibility. The tiny minority of visitors who thought that the conservation of Brodsworth was only 'half completed', as it had not been tidied up and repainted, may increase putting the site at risk of public or professional criticism.

Brief commentary on Grid analysis for Brodsworth

It can be seen that the analysis for Brodsworth is shorter than that undertaken for Uppark. This is because whilst issues are shared between the sites, the analysis of Brodsworth brought out quite different responses from visitors and professionals involved in the management of the site. The

most pertinent differences are further explored in the following sections, where the site is considered carefully in its unique managerial context, and the way in which the site has been conserved in its local and historical context. The variety in objectification of Brodsworth can also be seen.

'One National Trust member and one adult please.'

Brodsworth Hall is owned and managed by English Heritage. Site management is overseen by a Property Manager assisted by two permanent custodians, the head and deputy-head custodian. The hall is staffed, when open to the public, by a further complement of approximately ten seasonal staff, each with specific duties. A team of volunteer room stewards also come in during the afternoons to assist visitors in the hall. At an organisational level, Brodsworth is part of a regional organisational grouping, which has its own presentation and marketing budget. This region in turn forms a part of the Historic Properties Group, based at the headquarters of English Heritage in London, with its own national marketing, development and events section. English Heritage is responsible for over 400 properties, of which ruins comprise the majority. A curatorial group has been created to provide coherent responsibility for collections and contents of country houses in the care of the organisation. This section has regional curators, one of whom is based at Brodsworth Hall. Mindful of the overall mission of the organisation, considered in greater detail in a separate chapter (Chapter 4), Brodsworth is objectified within the organisational context of English Heritage in a number of ways and at different operational levels.

Within the Northern Region of English Heritage, Brodsworth is the only historic house with contents on view, open to the public. Within the national Historic Properties Group, it is one of only a handful of historic houses in the care of English Heritage, out of the total of approximately 400 properties. Therefore at once, Brodsworth's place in the organisation is that of a specialist concern. Though English Heritage has responsibilities to the whole of the built historic environment, spends a large amount of money on grants to owners of historic properties, and provides expertise in this area, the organisation is not perceived as a manager of historic houses because of their scarcity within the portfolio of properties. Brodsworth fills a gap in such a portfolio, and due to the hall's circumstances and lack of accompanying endowment could not have been preserved by the National Trust: English Heritage was thus fulfilling its statutory duties and acting as an owner 'of last resort' (English Heritage 1997a) by taking Brodsworth into its care. In doing so, however, apart from enriching the portfolio of attractions to visit, the organisation took on a major conservation project, and has altered public expectations about the organisation. Visitors to the site regularly approach the admissions desk at Brodsworth and use the expression, which this section is titled with. There is a certain degree of expectation that the property will be owned by the National Trust, because *that is what the Trust does* (Davies 1985). There is sometimes surprise and confusion expressed at the admission desk when it turns out that the site is managed by English Heritage and National Trust members cannot gain free entry. Visitors questioned later in their visit still do not necessarily understand the differences between the organisations, and may have become confused about English Heritage's aims. English Heritage Members are however pleased with the addition to a variety of sites which they can visit. This interesting point and the managing agency's response to it are considered further below.

Brodsworth as a conservation project has focused English Heritage's attention on major conservation projects, and in part prompted the setting up of the Major Projects Division to tackle such properties: this unit has also dealt with Danson House in Bexley, and the Albert Memorial in London, both of which needed major conservation projects. Brodsworth was thus objectified in its initial conservation as a 'major project'. Within the Conservation Division of English Heritage, Brodsworth's collections are

curated by the Museums Section, which has extended their remit through the assessment of collections for which the organisation is responsible. The site is thus also considered to be a 'museum collection'. English Heritage's internal 'audit of collections' (Carr-Whitworth 1995) has looked carefully at the implications of owning the collections at Brodsworth, and aims to have varying collections within the organisation registered with the Museum & Galleries Commission in their national accreditation scheme for museums.

Marketing for Brodsworth is mainly undertaken as part of the national campaigns organised in London (Figure 7.1 and 7.11). The property is recognised as having various 'unique selling points' and these are capitalised on through extensive use of photographs of the site in promotional material for itself, and other organisational activities, including conservation reports, membership, and advertising. The property has had a colour souvenir guide produced for it, along with a range of site-specific souvenirs sold in the shop.

Figure 7.11 *Brodsworth details produced for tour operators.*

GROUP VISITS GUIDE

BRODSWORTH
HALL & GARDENS

Opened to the public just two years ago, Brodsworth Hall and gardens offer groups a fascinating and unique journey though the intriguing passage of time. From the luxurious life of England's landed gentry more than a century ago right up to the late 1980s, Brodsworth proudly bears the marks of over a century's continuous occupation. Today, the house exists as a picture of faded Victorian grandeur, rich in social history.

In the long abandoned kitchen with its clutter of original equipment and utensils, discover how meals were really made in the age of Mrs Beeton.

Imagine the very different life upstairs as you wander through elegant hallways, view the rich interiors and full contents and gaze at the splendour of the reception rooms and a whole succession of marble sculptures and paintings. Outside, visitors can enjoy a leisurely stroll around the extensive newly restored gardens.

Take your group to Brodsworth Hall and be enchanted by a house with a very special atmosphere.

61

ENGLISH HERITAGE

Figure 7.12 *Brodsworth details produced for tour operators. (Cont'd)*

GROUP VISITS GUIDE

BRODSWORTH
HALL & GARDENS

Brodsworth
Doncaster
South Yorkshire
DN5 7XJ
Tel: 01302 722598
Fax: 01302 337165

Location
In Brodsworth, north west of Doncaster.
Junction 37 off A1(M), west of A1
between A635 and A638.

Parking Facilities
Free parking for coaches, 250 metres
from the site entrance.

Opening Hours
1 April-1 November: Tues-Sun & Bank
Holidays
House: 1pm-6pm, last admission 5pm.
Gardens: 12pm-6pm and tea rooms from
12pm.
Guided tours pre-booked from 10am.
7 November -28 March 1999: The house is
closed but the gardens, shop and tea
rooms are open weekends only 11am-
4pm. Closed 24-27 December.

Admission Prices
Hall & Gardens: £4.50, £3.40, £2.30.
Gardens only summer: £2.50, £1.90,
£1.00.
Gardens only winter: £1.50, £1.00, free
entry for children. **15% discount for
groups of 11 or more.**

Advance Booking
Please contact the Head Custodian on
01302 722598 (mornings only).

Guided Tours
Mornings only. Usually available if
booked. Tour lasts 1½ hours.

Wheelchair Access
Access is good and wheelchairs are
available. There are suitable toilets.

Catering
Brodsworth Hall Tearoom: counter service
facility located within the old servants'
accommodation. Seating is available for
up to 90 in four separate adjacent
rooms, with a further 30 seats outside.

A small range of hot dishes is available
as well as home baked cakes, cream teas
and sandwiches. Open from 12pm to
5.30pm whenever the house is open.

Shop
Good selection of Victorian souvenirs,
gifts and English Heritage guidebooks.

Average Length of Visit
3 hours.

Facilities for Hire
Tearooms can be booked. Please
telephone the site for details.

Nearby Attractions
Cusworth Hall Museum, *Doncaster.*

Local TIC
Doncaster: 01302 734309.

62

ENGLISH HERITAGE

Educational material developed by English Heritage as part of its statutory duties (to educate and inform), have also utilised Brodsworth, as a specific example in consideration of the Victorians (English Heritage 1997f), and even in its primary education development has named a talking puppet dog 'Brodsworth'.

Interpretation on the site is also seen as a unique development, where little at the site has been restored in the 'conserve as found' philosophy. Though noted as possibly confusing (Blockley 1997, 1), events and living history are used in the special events programme to help appreciate the site further. The utilisation of Brodsworth does not go as far as certain other properties (Robertshaw 1997), but it is seen that there is potential for future developments in the local education sector.

Within the organisational context of English Heritage, it can be seen that the conceptual heritage (the aims of the organisation and perceptions of visitors and managers) are objectified as the heritage object 'Brodsworth Hall' in a variety of ways. The site is a major conservation project; it is a 'new' property in the portfolio; it is themed in accordance with educational demand; it is marketed as representative of the wider organisation; and it is presented as a unique historic house. Brodsworth and English Heritage do not operate on their own, however, and I shall now proceed to consider Brodsworth Hall in the wider context of heritage, conservation and tourism.

Brodsworth in the heritage context

There is a great deal of money invested in Brodsworth, in terms of conservation expertise, visitor facilities, staffing and management. There is no doubt that the hall's preservation has contributed much to the local and national heritage. In this wider context however, the altruistic motives for safeguarding important sites is difficult to measure, whilst objectification of Brodsworth as an object or statistic allows it to be used in a number of ways (Johnson & Thomas 1995). The property has contributed significantly to the local economy as a tourist attraction. South Yorkshire is not perceived to be 'on the tourist trail', but utilisation of Brodsworth in targeted marketing or development campaigns will certainly help boost tourism revenue and visits to Doncaster and the surrounding region.

In terms of admission price and visitor numbers, Brodsworth has received approximately 3,000 visitors a week, and charges are typical for an historic house of this kind (the nearest being Nostell Priory and Cusworth Hall). Facilities are best compared to those of the Trust, and are roughly similar, with a shop, tearoom, gardens, car park, educational facilities and membership scheme for admission. It is worth noting that a direct comparison for Brodsworth can be seen on a larger scale at Calke Abbey, owned by the Trust, though on a larger scale both physically and in visitor numbers, receiving approximately 97,000 visitors per year (Willes 1996; National Trust 1997, 56). The details provided for tour operators have been seen previously in Figure 7.12.

The philosophy of 'preserve as found' is increasingly used, supported by professional opinion and the increasing interest of the visiting public, apart from the mitigating circumstances of the costs of conservation (Beaulieu 1967). Allied to this is the growing use of heritage sites in both formal and informal educational contexts (Light 1995; Prentice 1995), and the ability to provide 'low-impact' interpretation at the same time as increasing use of the site through the use of events and audience participation (Light 1996).

Brodsworth also sees itself objectified as a showcase example of English Heritage's professional expertise, and re-establishes the place of the organisation in the context of other professional bodies that have interests in the management of country houses. The most notable of these are the National Trust, Historic Houses Association and Treasure Houses of England consortium. Furthermore, the management of Brodsworth allows English Heritage to extend its input into the utilisation of management and personnel action at historic sites – an area of management that is being re-established as of importance. Thus, at Brodsworth the property managers are experimenting with the use of volunteers, to maintain and raise visitor satisfaction levels at the site, and work in accordance with the government's Investors in People scheme for training and development (Peter Gordon-Smith, pers. com.). Staff and 'customer' or visitor relations are therefore given great emphasis at the site, the study of which may ultimately be used elsewhere within the organisation in pursuit of its objectives. Interest in this area of staff development is further highlighted in the case study concerned with English Heritage's corporate planning.

Consumption of the Brodsworth Label

The presentation and interpretation of Brodsworth is underplayed, as with many other country houses. Interpretation of the hall and its history is limited to the guidebook (Jeffrey 1995) and small exhibitions, and the conservation project receives even less attention, though has been concentrated at a professional level (Babington & Hughes 1992; Berkouwer & Church 1993; Carr-Whitworth 1995). However, whilst visitors are made aware of and become interested in the social history of the house, many are also aware that they are being shown an example of conservation, as marketing strategy has emphasised this particular unique selling point (USP) However, this USP is not followed up during the visit in available interpretation. This perception may be combined with perception of those labelled parts of the site and staff; the themed merchandising at the site; events on-site; and the emphasis placed on membership and 'product' loyalty at the site, to produce an interesting result.

Brodsworth appears to be branded very clearly in a way that is different to similar country houses, including those managed by the National Trust. The experience of visiting Brodsworth Hall becomes an exercise in consumption, as explored by Urry (1990 & 1995). The visitor comes to see the English Heritage site primarily, and Brodsworth Hall secondly. The explanation for this can be explained in part as the managing agency's (English Heritage's) attempt to clearly differentiate this house (as a novelty in English Heritage's portfolio) from the expected management as the National Trust, as well as the general trend of promoting English Heritage as the country's leading conservation organisation. Brodsworth's own peculiar circumstances as a conservation project exacerbate this, resulting in the consumption of the branded object, the English Heritage property, Brodsworth Hall, which has to be examined far more closely by the visitor to establish what the property consists of. The transformation from concept to object here concerns itself with reconfiguration and representation of an entire organisation in one object, which is possibly confusing for the visitor.

The variety of transformation at Brodsworth

The range of 'objectified pasts' to be perceived at Brodsworth are similar in scope and content to those found in Uppark. The collections within the hall, and the physical surroundings of the building and gardens, are all tangible representations of both the object and an attached conceptual historic value. This can be emphasised at a basic educative level as the site encompasses many of the themes studied within the primary and secondary schools' national curriculum. Hence the following conceptual disciplines are represented through the collection and presentation (brought about by planned action or management) of specific objects. This is coupled with an accorded historic value given to those objects, thereby sustaining the heritage label. The subjects include: archaeology; history; architecture; social history; biography; genealogy; local history; arboriculture; engineering; geography; horticulture; physical and natural science; art; sculpture; and literature. Further themes portrayed by the physical existence of the hall and its collections include: social situation; lifestyles; 'the country house' – a phenomenon now studied in its own right (Leeds University 1998); conservation and restoration; museological skill; the class system; and the perception of 'time capsules'. In further comparison to Uppark, in the grouping of the subjects and themes above, Brodsworth, as it exists today as an historic site open to the public, represents an objectification of a particular style of education, conservation and presentation. This style reflects the motivations of the managing agency, which has the ability to emphasise any one of these areas through action at the site.

Halted decline and the suspension of time at Brodsworth Hall

Though the suspension of time occurs at the majority of historic sites, it is particularly obvious at Brodsworth. This suspension of time can occur in a variety of other circumstances, and is considered in a different context within this thesis in the analysis of the Monuments Protection Programme. The phenomenon is not generally emphasised by the managing agency, as it has less to do with the site itself, and more to do with the context in which the site exists. Whilst it is primarily a management consideration therefore, there is an impact on the visitors to historic sites, by virtue of the fact that the visitor has chosen to visit a *historic* site. The link between the objectified heritage 'product' (site) and the motivation of, or attraction for, the 'consumer' (as a visitor) is reinforced in the suspension of time. Management action (of objectification) creates the suspension, and this ultimately provides the major USP for the site. However, this process is rarely mentioned within standard or even specialised management studies (e.g. Middleton 1995; Davies, S. 1995), and furthermore, the USP of 'stepping back in time', as promoted within the publicity material for Brodsworth, is not followed up once the site has been entered.

The suspension of time occurs, as noted, almost as a 'by-product' of management practice at historic sites. It is achieved as soon as any kind of physical barrier or banner is erected at the edge of the site in question. The demarcation that is perceived as a result of this triggers subsequent perception of a mental barrier or challenge in the mind of the visitor, and recognition that the objects being encountered are not ordinary aspects of everyday life,

though continuing to physically exist within it. The effect is literally that of placing a ring-fence around the site – probably already undertaken for other management reasons, such as security. This 'ring-fence', both conceptual and real, objectifies the physical space within its bounds, containing the historic site. The site, having been demarcated in this way is therefore taken out of present time: time is suspended in terms of both management and presentation (management action) or the opposite, encounter (visitor action).

Labelling, in the form of signs, such as the 'Welcome to Brodsworth Hall', or even the placing of the English Heritage name and logo at the site, reinforces this suspension of time, and objectification of the past. Brodsworth Hall is transformed from being a country house in decline, to an identified historic resource, taken out of its circle of decline through intervention of a particular management regime. In this case, Brodsworth has been conserved and opened to the public: alternatives might be re-use and conversion of a building, or demolition thereby creating an archaeological site and archive. The suspension of time allows the identified objects within the ring-fence to carry other semiotic messages, which further management intervention enhances by presentation in a certain fashion. At Brodsworth, the 'conserve-as-found' philosophy is followed, and what is therefore presented is an interesting piece of social history, and important collection of objects.

As noted above, this suspension happens at other sites, including Uppark. I have concentrated upon this phenomenon within this case study, as its effects are more noticeable though no feature is made of such a suspension of time by English Heritage during a visit to the house. Brodsworth is further set apart from its surroundings as it has been fenced in and set apart from the rest of its original estate, which no longer exists in the form that 'matches' the house. An island containing the historic site has been created, whilst other connected parts of the contextual history of Brodsworth have continued to change, and the former parkland is now agricultural land. There is therefore an unstated tension between the site's context and both past and present time.

How UNIQUE is Brodsworth?

It has been discovered elsewhere that for the 'historic' sector of tourism, the 'amount of visits has been growing, rather than the amount of visitors' (Schouten 1995, 259). Visitors are therefore looking for the following UNIQUE experience, encompassing the following traits: 'Uncommon; Novelty; Informative; Quality; Understanding; and Emotions' (*ibid.* 260). There seems little doubt, considering the analysis undertaken above, that a visit to Brodsworth Hall includes all of these features, though the above analysis suggests that the 'Informative' and 'Understanding' areas have not been fully addressed in the interpretative scheme. Overall satisfaction on the part of the visitors is however borne out by the very successful recruitment of new English Heritage members by staff at the site, and in its initial operating period over three visitor seasons, the large number of repeat visits that the site receives (Peter Gordon-Smith, pers. com.). Brodsworth seems to therefore be moving quickly beyond the status of 'novelty', in the eyes of many of its visitors, particularly those that have come back to the site for a second visit.

The site however achieves its 'UNIQUEness' by virtue of what it physically is, rather than what the managing agency operates it as. The semiotic messages pertaining to social history are very clearly perceived by visitors at Brodsworth. This is coupled with the facilities available; staff-visitor interaction; perception of the 'conservation project'; and the managing agency not being the National Trust, to create the UNIQUE effect. In a management context, whilst the site (as with any other heritage site) has certain unique aspects, it is not aimed at being any more UNIQUE than any other property. The statutory commitments that English Heritage undertakes in its work, in part look as if a UNIQUE aim is being sought at Brodsworth through the compounding of various management problems and their solution. Brodsworth came under the care of English Heritage as a statutory owner of 'last resort'; the hall and contents are an important collection and valued, therefore requiring some form of preservation; the conservation project necessary at the hall required major financial investment; English Heritage has a statutory duty in education; and there is both necessary public accountability for the managing organisation, and public interest in the site.

It can be claimed therefore that Brodsworth is and is not both UNIQUE or unique. There is clear weakness in a unique experience when the site is compared to the claims made for it in the site publicity. As one of many heritage properties, in comparison with the work of the National Trust and other owners, Brodsworth Hall is far from unique and yet it is the actions of English Heritage as a managing agency that maintain Brodsworth as a UNIQUE historic property. And, as has been established, although not deliberate, the actions of the management agency are clearly discernible in any encounter with Brodsworth as a heritage object.

What does Brodsworth consist of?

It has been shown through comparison with Uppark and the National Trust, that at Brodsworth Hall English Heritage shares similar experiences and effects in managing a historic property. However, it can furthermore be seen how each site raises particular issues of interest in terms of management action, and in the variety of transformations or objectification that occurs at the site. Brodsworth has been objectified and set in context as a historic site, a tourist attraction, and conservation project, and a branded consumable. All of these themes involve the continual transformation and interaction between operational management and presentation, the change from concept to object and object to concept. It has also been shown how the suspension of time reinforces the site's physical existence as heritage; a further kind of transformation that will be looked at again.

Though visitors' perception is affected by this multitude of constant transformation at the site, individually the transformations do not necessarily impact in any substantive form on the public and a certain degree of analysis is necessary for visitors to identify what they are really encountering at the site. It should be noted that there should be no particular necessity for the visitors to undertake such analysis, as motivation to visit is usually derived from a demand for a leisure pursuit and not a demand for education. Brodsworth can be seen to affect the managing agency in a substantial way. The site is operated as a successful tourism venture, and must undertake certain activities to maintain this position. Furthermore, the site, as a major project for the organisation has had effects on central policy-making in the fields of curatorial care, disaster planning, scientific analysis, presentation and so on. The feedback loop sees staff action objectified in the carrying out of tasks and accomplishment of goals at the site. Comparison, in organisational terms, can therefore be made between the central organisation's managing agency (Historic Properties Group) and the headquarters managers, and the relation with the individual site (Brodsworth Hall) and the day-to-day jobs for site staff. Each has an equivalent effect on the other, as information moves through different layers of the organisation.

Whilst English Heritage continues to develop as an organisation (as seen in the analysis of corporate planning in Chapter 4), it can be seen how through the objectification of heritage as Brodsworth Hall, an individual aspect of that organisation can support and even force certain adaptations at the larger organisational scale. It should, of course, be noted that the situation is in fact more complex than this sounds – though the principle is applicable. The heritage property 'Brodsworth Hall' is therefore necessarily objectified as a heritage object through the actions of management, to allow the valuation and further recognition of the site as a specific part of the wider conceptual heritage. The action undertaken to bring about this transformation has the ability to alter perception of both the object and the way in which it is manipulated, and thus provides further support for the understanding of the ways in which management operates. This, in turn, provides the facility for encounter with a certain kind of public heritage by a variety of audiences.

Uppark & Brodsworth: the variety in transformation exposed

The two different approaches, taken to what seem at first to be similar heritage properties, emphasise the importance of understanding the transformations that take place in the process of objectification and the essential analysis of and balancing of 'arguments' between the contexts in which the heritage objects exist. The National Trust can be seen to concentrate its efforts on preservation and visitor reception, and no invitation is given such as that made by English Heritage for stepping back in time. The Trust presents the heritage object as just that – an object to be appreciated. English Heritage, on the other hand, emphasises the object within the context of a way of life, though as has been seen in the analysis, it is not completely successful at Brodsworth. Visitors enjoy the 'social interaction' with the site, although on questioning they have not necessarily understood it.

The two different approaches taken by the managing agencies further contrast well with the following analysis of two museums, the Museum of London and the Cambridge University Museum of Archaeology and Anthropology. Both the National Trust and English Heritage would vigorously deny that either Uppark and Brodsworth are museums, though it will be shown how similarities and differences between these two country houses and the two museums are due to the context in which the managing agency operates. Within the museums, the visitor can get just as close to the 'historic objects' as at the houses, though the context in which those objects are now preserved have created the divide in philosophy and management between 'heritage sites' and 'museums'. The museums case study will therefore shift its focus slightly, once again, and examine the context in which the management systems operate, and which dictates the actions which the museum as a corporate body can undertake – constantly reaffirming its own unique position as a museum and not something else.

8 Constructing the glass case: transformation within the Museum of London and Cambridge University Museum of Archaeology and Anthropology

The ideal and the real: the concept of the museum

In focusing attention on the more traditional concept of a museum, and applying the model of transformation as a way of exploring such institutions, the divergence in thought between 'heritage management' and 'museology' can be bridged. Though museums have clearly developed their own approach to professional development (Hooper-Greenhill 1992; Pearce 1995), they are facing similar challenges, contextual developments and even threats in a business-like enterprise environment, as other 'enterprises' or institutions that have been looked at within this thesis. Funding sources, expectations, contexts and so on, are ever more diverse and changeable, whilst government is grouping heritage as a broad category within a larger cultural sector and one which

is subject to market forces (DNH 1996c). I use the model here to look at the role of management in two organisations with the same function.

In the analysis below, exploration of the model with regard to the Cambridge University Museum of Archaeology & Anthropology (Figure 8.1) and the Museum of London (Figure 8.2), suggests that there are clear differences between administering a museum institution and managing a museum institution. Note should be made that the case study timeframe equates with the preceeding case studies, and does not reflect developments in either institution after 2000 (e.g. development of the Museum in Docklands, opening of LAARC, or involvement in new Government funding streams for museums). The time period at the

Figure 8.1 *CUMAA Anthropology Gallery.*

Figure 8.2 *Museum of London in 2000.*

end of the 1990s therefore highlights the cusp of change/difference in approach between administration and strategic management as noted above.

The corpus of literature on museums and museology as a discipline is vast, as is assessment of specific instances of museum management. This case study compares two museums, the Museum of London (MoL) and Cambridge University Museum of Archaeology and Anthropology (CUMAA), which are completely different in scope, scale and operation. Seemingly incomparable in terms of both their physical nature and the activities undertaken, both institutions may be perceived as the same both through the application of the label 'museum', and their ultimate museological aim, that of curation of objects and presentation to an audience. In looking beyond the aims of the museums, their collections and the ways in which the collections are presented, the model explores management within the museums as the maintenance of an institution with a particular museological remit, to collect and present its collections. Further similarities and shared experiences can be identified, as museums are themselves transformed into heritage objects. Again it is the first stage of the transformation that provides the 'ability' and impetus to operate through objectification and identification of particular heritage resources, the essential task within heritage management. The first step of the transformation also provokes the institutional arrangements that adapt to the environmental context, and yet maintain an individual identity.

The message and medium is concentrated upon in most museum studies (Bennett 1995; Edson & Dean 1994) but is therefore less important here than the ability to present any kind of message using any medium. However, the second stage of the transformation, providing just such presentation and interpretation, cannot be ignored. It forms a part of the integrated cycle of transformation as it forges the encounter between public heritage object (the museum and its collections) and the 'public'. The first encounter between the museum and its public relies on the presentation, yet that presentation does not necessarily have any bearing on the management of the institution. The tensions that are mediated by management therefore become more obvious, as the museum 'exists' by virtue of the first stage, but is usually only judged by the second stage with the first overlooked or used for measures of efficiency where the second stage cannot be measured (noted in the corporate organisation of English Heritage). Indeed, it is only the fact that a museum has a 'front door' and is open to the public that allows the model of transformation to operate here. Otherwise, the museum remains at pre-Stage 1, as a private collection.

A situation is therefore found where the seemingly incomparable and unique must be compared for their own good, just as Merriman pointed out (1991), when he peered beyond the glass case, external perceptions of museums may be discouraging. Unique identities are recognised at a professional museological level, but not always recognisable at a 'public' level or at the level of funding source (such as local or national government), where increasing diversity leads rather to homogeneity in approach, as museums can be seen to be 'a museum is a museum is a museum'. The model as providing a way of exploring the diversity within a broadly identified 'heritage sector' establishes the necessity of understanding how institutions exist and function before assessing what they do. In this way both internal and external tensions may be identified and if necessary solved.

The complexity of transformations at MoL and CUMAA

In the light of the above assessment of the model's relation to museums, and the concept of the museum itself, MoL and CUMAA are looked at in terms of the objectification of the institution. Exploration can then be made of how the processes of management effect that transformation. As noted already the second stage of the model, concerned with the image of both collections and the museums, has been mentioned in passing because, though relevant, it is better dealt with elsewhere, in both practical and theoretical terms (Hamilton 1995; Shanks & Tilley 1987).

The museum's essential nature must be considered primarily, taking into account the more general expectations and thought within the museum sector (Edson & Dean 1994). Three tensions applicable across the sector are worth noting. Both MoL and CUMAA exist as museums in both theme and object. Furthermore, they are both containers of knowledge as a theme and object through the curation of their collections. The museums exist thematically as 'museums' by virtue of their labelling (the sign above the door); the functions that the collection of objects and their manipulation by trained individuals fulfil are those recognised as a museum. Equally, though existing as dedicated institutions, they exist in an objectified state as museums, with their own building, collections and curators. Such distinctions must be clearly made at this point as museums, including both MoL and CUMAA, embrace new technologies and can reassess their objectified state.

A slight tension has already been subtly exposed here which is rarely articulated but becomes more important as computer technologies impact further on the museum's work. The objectified museum exists as two objects – the museum that is the collection and the museum that is the institutional container for the collection. Whilst at one stage it would have been almost impossible to differentiate between the two, this is no longer the case and both aspects can be seen in MoL and CUMAA Web-site development amongst other technological projects in the field (Museum of London 1998; CUMAA 1998). Such tension between the institution and its collections may increase in the future.

A further tension, which can be identified as a concern prevalent in all museums, is the division created between curation (and collection) and presentation (and representation). This is an unsolved dilemma within museums, and echoed within the 'collection' of monuments in MPP, as to whether objects speak for themselves or

whether particular interpretation is necessary. Again, however this falls to professional debate about the status of objects existing as knowledge and art (Walsh 1992; Pearce 1995; Barthes 1964), outwith the remit of this thesis, but a particular consideration for the systems of management seen at MoL and CUMAA because of their dedicated concerns as museums.

The final general tension for museums, applicable here, is the overall status of museums within society as addressed by Merriman (1991) and others such as MacDonald & Alsford (1995) in different ways. A question hangs over the purpose of such institutions: who do they exist for, and should they be operated as educational tools, or are they best placed within the ideology of a leisure pursuit with optional educational potential, where the overriding factor remains that of enjoyment of both the institution and its collection. Technology and, in this thesis' case, business planning once again has an important role to play in this, as the traditional form of the museum is challenged or re-positioned from an educational to a leisure pursuit. This tension is pertinent within this case study as CUMAA is a dedicated university museum, whilst MoL is publicly funded.

These tensions, briefly explored, represent transformations explicit in both internal and external perception of museums. This suggests where some of the misconceptions about the similarity of museums come from – equally internal and external to the institutions. The tensions continue as the transformations within the museums are not always completed or continual, resulting in a concept of the museum that does not match the object museum or vice-versa. These conflicts of generality and particularity have to be addressed by the management systems: and where they are not addressed in the university museum, further challenges are presented internally and externally to an institution within a larger institutional entity.

Museum environments: professional, legal, social, economic, political

The environmental context can be clearly distinguished for both MoL and CUMAA and the contrast shows clearly the common issues which management systems must face, without disregarding the museum's own unique purpose. As two museums are contrasted here, the analysis is undertaken in a truncated form in comparison to the previous analysis of English Heritage – not least because the aim is to present common features of the transformation achieved within management across the diversity of the heritage resource, rather than an individual corporate analysis of a particular museum. The key features of the museum's environmental contexts are individually considered below.

Legal context

The Museum of London was established in 1977 by an Act of Parliament through the amalgamation of the Guildhall Museum and the London Museum. The duties and powers vested in the Board of Directors for the museum

Figure 8.3 *Museum of London Act (1965) relevant sections.* (HMG 1965)

Museum of London Act 1965
An Act to establish a Board of Governors of the Museum of London; to transfer to them the collections of the London Museum and of the Guildhall Museum and the benefit of certain funds; to define the functions of that Board, and to provide for purposes connected with the matters aforesaid. [2nd June 1965]
(1965) 3. The board shall have the general management and control of their collections... have power to make rules for securing the due administration and preservation of their collections, to acquire, hold and manage land... etc.
(1986 revision) 3.-(1) ...it shall be the duty of the Board-
    (a) to care for, preserve and add to the objects in their collections;
    (b) to secure that those objects are exhibited to the public and made available to persons seeking to inspect them in connection with study or research; and
    (c) generally to promote understanding and appreciation of historic and contemporary London and of its society and culture, both by means of their collections and by such other means as they consider appropriate.
3.-(3) ..the Board may-
    (a) provide archaeological services and undertake archaeological investigations and research in connection with land in London, publish information concerning such investigations and research and promote the provision of such services and the undertaking of such investigations and research and the publishing of such information;
    (b) ...acquire or dispose of any estate or interest in land (**needs consent of Sec. of State. section (4))
3.-(5) In this section 'London' includes all Greater London and the surrounding region.
4.-(1) The Board shall.. acquire premises for the purpose of maintaining their collections therein and holding exhibitions of their collections, or so much of those collections as from time to time they think fit, being premises situate within the City of London and, so long as they are held by the Board, to be known as the Museum of London.
8. The Board may... (in return for payment or not) hold exhibitions and meetings, the showing of films and slides, the giving of musical performances and the holding of other events of an educational or cultural nature.
(1986 revision) 8.-(1) The Board may use premises known as the MoL for any educational or cultural purpose whether or not connected with the Board's functions under this Act.
8.-(2) The Board may allow any premises... to be used by other persons (for payment or otherwise) for purposes not connected with the Board's functions... if satisfied that to do so would not conflict with those functions.

Figure 8.4 *Extract from 'Statutes & Ordinances of the University of Cambridge'. (University of Cambridge 1998)*

Statute A: The Chancellor and the Government of the University.
Chapter VI: Powers of the University.
    1. The university shall have power for the encouragement of learning, the maintenance of good order and discipline, and the management of its affairs....
Statute C: The Faculties, Departments and Schools.
Chapter I: The Faculties.
    The term Faculty shall denote a body of persons associated in accordance with the Statutes for the purpose of furthering the study of a subject or subjects.

Figure 8.5 *Extract from the Ordinances of the University of Cambridge, establishing the Museum of Archaeology & Anthropology. (University of Cambridge 1998, 544-5).*

Faculty of Archaeology & Anthropology
Museum of Archaeology & Anthropology
4. There shall be the following University offices on the staff of the Museum of Archaeology and Anthropology:
    (a) an office of Curator, the hold of which shall also be entitled Director of the Museum;
    (b) such number of offices of Senior Assistant Curator or Assistant Curator as the General Board shall from time to time determine. ......
6. The duties of the Curator shall be defined by the Faculty Board of Archaeology and Anthropology and shall include the following:
    (a) to be responsible for the preservation, augmentation, labelling, and cataloguing of collections; to display and label specimens in exhibition case in such a manner as will be instructive to students and visitors, and to arrange that unexhibited specimens are readily available for research; and to assist those who desire to consult the collections;
    (b) to give not more than twenty-four hours' teaching in each academical year for the Faculty, that teaching to include discussions and demonstrations in the Museum;
    (c) to be the official Head of the Museum for all administrative purposes.
In the absence of the Curator the Faculty Board shall nominate a Senior Assistant Curator or Assistant Curator to undertake the Curator's responsibilities under sub-paragraph (c) of the above regulation.
7. For the due performance of his or her duties, the Curator shall be responsible to the Faculty Board of Archaeology & Anthropology. The Faculty Board may delegate the administration of the Museum to a Museum Committee appointed by them for that purpose. A University officer on the staff of the Museum shall act as Secretary to the Museum Committee. ....
9. The duties of a Senior Assistant Curator or an Assistant Curator shall be defined by the Faculty Board of Archaeology and Anthropology and shall include the following:
    (a) to assist the Curator in the duties specified in Regulation 6(a), and
    (b) to give not more than twenty-four hour's teaching in each academical year for the Faculty, this teaching to include discussions and demonstrations in the Museum. ......
11. The Faculty Board shall make an Annual Report on the Museum to the General Board.

are presented in Figure 8.3. The museum is overseen and financed in two half shares by the Corporation of London and the Department for Culture, Media and Sport, which also make appointments to a board of governors. Commercial archaeological activities are undertaken by the Museum of London Archaeology Service (MOLAS), a subsidiary division of the museum, and profits from its operation pass to the museum. The museum produces an annual report, and since 1997 negotiates an annual Funding Agreement with the Department for Culture, Media and Sport in line with government objectives for the cultural sector (as noted in the English Heritage case study). This clarified the purposes and aims of an institution rather than explicitly considering funding and spending detail.

The Cambridge University Museum of Archaeology and Anthropology is an institution within the University of Cambridge. It is governed by the Statutes and Ordinances of the University of Cambridge (University of Cambridge 1998). The university itself is governed by a separate Act of Parliament, which give its Statutes and Ordinances legal power within the university as a common law institution. Certain powers of the university are relevant to the Museum, forming part of a larger institution, and have been reproduced as Figure 8.4. The museum itself is directly established and governed by Ordinance within the Faculty of Archaeology & Anthropology, and this is reproduced as Figure 8.5. The museum is funded by the university, which receives specific Non-Formula Funding in respect of CUMAA and the Fitzwilliam Museum from the Higher Education Funding Council for England (HEFCE 1995). Further financial support is provided by central university funds.

Professional context

The Museum of London is a publicly-funded museum based at the Barbican in the City of London. Its collections, stretching from the Prehistoric period to the present-day emphasise the variety and development of the urban condition of London, and are presented chronothematically. The professional context for the museum largely echoes the legal context for the museum, which has remained unchanged as the corporate duties and aims of the museum since its foundation. These further form the core of the Funding Agreement between the Government and the museum (DNH 1997b). The MoL thus aims:

'To care for, and preserve and add to the objects in their collections.

'To secure that those objects are exhibited to the public...

and

'Generally to promote understanding and appreciation of historic and contemporary London and of its society and culture, both by means of their collections and by such other means as they consider appropriate.'

The MoL is registered with the Museums and Galleries Commission as meeting national museum standards, and designated by the Department for Culture, Media and Sport as 'a museum with an outstanding collection' in its national designation scheme (DNH 1997c). Direction and policy for the museum is overseen by the Board of Governors, appointed by the Government and the Corporation of London, and day-to-day management is undertaken by the Director and staff, numbering approximately 125 (Museum of London 1996) and comprising curators, interpretation, research, sales and support staff. An internal corporate Business Plan (*ibid.*) is produced annually, which includes a Business Statement, Programme Targets, Performance Indicators, and Mission Statement.

Cambridge University Museum of Archaeology & Anthropology was established in 1884, as a research and teaching collection within the Faculty of Archaeology & Anthropology. It is governed by the Faculty Board of Archaeology & Anthropology, which delegates its powers to an established Museum Committee. The organisation is managed on a day-to-day basis by a Director and three Curators, with six support staff and gallery attendants. Like MoL, CUMAA is registered with the Museums & Galleries Commission and has also been designated by DCMS. The collections within CUMAA have worldwide coverage of ethnography and prehistoric archaeology. The museum produces an annual report listing activities and research, but does not produce an annual corporate or business plan. It has, however, produced a one-off internal Development Plan for its managing board (CUMAA 1997a).

Political context

The Museum of London's duties and powers are clearly defined within its Act of Parliament, and the organisation is subject only to the overall aims and direction of its sponsoring bodies: the Corporation of London provides financial support only, and political aims are determined by government through the Department for Culture, Media and Sport through policy direction for the entire national museums sector. Though the institution considered here is a non-governmental organisation, its funding agreement makes it necessary to align museum activities with government aims and in justification of receipt of publicly accountable funds. This does not cause any problem for MoL: DCMS aims have been considered previously with regards to English Heritage (Chapter 4). The museum is however subject to general political influences, which apply across the cultural sector, and in recent years this has caused problems through lack of resources and overall guidance. MoL's own actions with regard to this have been accepted by government, and are noted in its Funding Agreement (DNH 1997b) as the museum, for example, aims to 'maintain at a minimum level the Archaeological Archive, while being unable to accept new material.' without investment for storage space

Cambridge University provides no specific direction for the nine museums for which it has responsibility, though experiences are shared by curators through an established Joint Museums Committee (University of Cambridge 1995). The University does however expect all of its sectors to begin to undertake 'Academic Planning' providing information for the University's overall Strategic Plan (University of Cambridge 1997). The museum thus provides a statement through its managing committee to the Faculty Board, though as noted it undertakes no established strategic planning exercise. In a wider political sense, the museum finds itself in a difficult financial position along with other universities' collections, though it does receive specific funding from HEFCE. Further problems lie in the status of collections generally within universities, noted by Hamilton (1995) as a 'fluctuation in value...between teaching and research', and the question of whether such university museum services as there are should be providing facilities for a non-university audience (i.e. general public). University museums are thus subject to general trends within universities rather than traditional political or governmental influence, though it may be argued that educational politics are considerably more problematic.

Social context

The Museum of London finds itself in a challenging position with regard to its social context. Whilst holding collections relating to London, the city's position as a capital and the museum's funding position provided by both a London authority and by government means that it cannot just cater for Londoners as a 'city museum' like other local museums. Its approach, enshrined within its Act, recognises this and the equivalent ethos present in all its research and work solves such a problem. Using a chronothematic approach, and considering the 'urban condition' in London, the museum can not only cater for the variety of London audiences, but can also present the city to 'external' audiences, charting the development of London and its communities within Britain on a world stage, illustrating both society and culture. During the period of study an example is seen in a special exhibition, looking at London as a centre for fashion, with displays centred on shoes in 'Sole City' (Museum of London 1998b). Individual communities within London can thus be included as makers and wearers of such footwear, as well as external audiences through presenting London as a fashion centre.

In terms of visitor numbers during the study period, the Museum of London received 276,157 visits in 1996/97, and the Interpretation Unit recorded 3485 group visits (Museum of London 1998b, 20). CUMAA received 21,189 visitors, and 130 pre-booked educational parties (CUMAA 1997 b, 10).

The social context for CUMAA is also diverse, though whilst MoL is a museum dedicated to a general 'public' audience, whether from London or elsewhere, CUMAA has two very distinct audiences, one within the university and another 'general public' audience. The museum until recently has been dedicated solely to providing a university service, allowing minimal public access: however, increasingly, along with other universities' museums, much greater public service provision is having to be made, as part of a recognised professional development within museology, and a necessity for increased public accountability and access on the part of the universities. CUMAA has curatorial posts only, and no dedicated education provision other than teaching packs, unlike MoL which has a dedicated Access and Learning Department. This is not simply a case of economics but the underlying ethos behind CUMAA's existence as a teaching collection rather that a public museum. Within the university audience there is dedicated teaching in archaeology, anthropology and museology using the museum and its collections as a resource, and the reserve collections are utilised for research rather than display development. Temporary exhibitions are of a scholarly nature, and the overall presentation scheme is illustrative of subject matter for research purposes, though in some respects it does follow a thematic scheme like

MoL. The collections cover all of the four areas identified by Hamilton (1995) as object categories in university museums; ceremonial university objects, commemorative objects, decorative objects and didactic objects. The collection thus represents general academic subject matter using Cambridge University's work in the subject area for provision of the objects in the collection.

Economic context

During the study period, the Museum of London receives approximately £8.6 million in grants from the Government and Corporation of London, and through charging for admission and trading, sees a total annual income of £15.9 million in 1997 (Museum of London 1998b, 22). The MoL therefore operates in a commercial economic sense, with full accounting mechanisms. Economic targets, in both visitor numbers, trading income and efficiency savings, are therefore set each year by the sponsoring government body (DCMS 1998), and overall direct grants year-on-year show gradual decline. The museum's overall 'professional' museological aims, whilst maintained as a professional necessity, are mitigated by economic concerns, the need to generate income, reduce costs and provide a public service which is value for money. Thus, the archaeological archive closed pending redevelopment into LAARC (Museum of London 1996), emphasis has been placed on enhanced interpretative schemes in the museum building, and a National Lottery application has been made to provide new facilities and technology developments (Museum of London 1998b).

A similar tightening of the business and economic situation can be seen at CUMAA, though the precise economics are hidden within the overall operation of the museum as a unit within the university. This has both advantages and disadvantages. It allows relatively free operation within university (or faculty) budgets but cannot draw on its own 'reserves' for information or justification for business planning. Accounting mechanisms in place determine overall budgets for the museum within the university and internal museum expenditure (Accounting Estimates 1997-98). The annual expenditure on the CUMAA is around £280,000 per annum, including a share of the money provided by the HEFCE for the Museum and the Fitzwilliam Museum jointly (amounting to £135,000 for CUMAA) (HEFCE 1995; CUMAA 1997a, 1). An endowment fund in the museum provides funds for support of research and development of the collections, and external funds are sought for particular educational projects undertaken by curatorial staff, such as the Virtual Teaching Collection (CUMAA 1996). An average figure of £120,000 per year external income has been produced by the museum (CUMAA 1997a, 1). The museum cannot charge for its services within the university on a cost basis as other units within the university do, nor does it charge admission fees for the public. Income revenue is limited to a small amount of trading activity in the museum, and through charges for professional photographic services. Donations are requested from visitors (though not from corporate sponsors in any systematic way), and grants have been made available by the city and county councils for extension of opening hours during summer months in the past (CUMAA 1997a, 4).

With a general move within Cambridge University towards a strategic approach to educational service provision, and other moves within the profession and the wider education sector, the museum is beginning to re-align itself and its aims. Thus developments in presentation, education provision for outside users, and use of new technologies are slowly moving the emphasis on the ways in which the collections are treated and used. CUMAA is thus having to slowly move from a university teaching collection to a general educational resource for archaeology, anthropology, and professional museum development, as the only way of maintaining and attracting future income and status within specialised 'management' groups within the university.

The above analysis of the environmental context reveals a great deal about the transformations that take place in both museums in the first instance of establishing the institution and its goals. Furthermore, as has already been said, the identified transformations show similarities for the process of operating the institutions, though differences between the museums in terms of 'administration' versus 'management'. Having identified various particular and general environmental factors for museums and these two institutions, attention can be focused on further expectations placed on the two museums and their staff, which are not explicitly articulated in any environmental analysis. The combination of environmental factors, along with internal and external expectations placed on the institution and its staff, ultimately dictate the actions that the staff can take in operating the museum, and therefore effecting the second of the transformations or objectification seen in museums, that of creating a museum collection and operating in a certain fashion with regard to that collection.

Expectations: internal and external

Environmental analysis identifies general themes with particular instances relevant to the museums in question. However, further expectations are placed on the museum and its work both by the staff within the institution and its 'customer' or audience. Many of the internal expectations derive from the organisational recipe (previously looked at within English Heritage) and the professional standards expected of museum staff within the museums sector, as well as expectations placed on the staff within the environmental context. External expectations derive from the particular needs of audiences within the environmental context of the museum's existence, as well as that from outside the museums' spheres of influence. Again, it can be seen that a tension is created between what the museum as a corporate entity wants and is able to do, as an institution and with regard to any collections it holds, and what others expect the museum to do by virtue of its perceived existence and value in other unidentified environmental contexts. MoL and CUMAA provide excellent examples of these expectations and tensions.

Internally, MoL staff have specific responsibilities for the museum's collections relating to London. However, curatorial skills and operations do not clearly produce identifiable cost benefits, other than the indirect (although central to the purpose of the institution) preservation and management of those collections. Therefore there remains a clear tension between the needs of maintaining the collections, and access to and display of those collections, which the government continues to press as a high priority. This tension is often cited in professional literature where arguments are made that the curatorial side of museum work is increasingly undervalued precisely because it apparently cannot be valued in economic terms as other museum work can be. The research for such presentation has to lie with the professional knowledge of the curatorial staff, and presentations are expected to change ever more frequently, yet a permanent 'skill base' is increasingly hard to support in financial terms when no direct financial benefits are forthcoming. The dilemma posed is that funding agencies take a shorter term view than the Museum itself, and there is a challenge in retaining and constantly developing the 'knowledge base' when curatorial time in collection development and management is limited (Max Hebditch, pers. com.). Therefore, environmental analysis is important in allowing curatorial skill and this tension to be placed in context and re-established as the vital corporate element of the museum on which economic functions are, in fact, based.

Other expectations relate directly to presentation of the collections, in both the permanent and temporary displays, and it is in this area that tensions between internal and external expectations meet. Museum display and use now tends to be geared around the National Curriculum, and subjects not directly covered by the curriculum may be difficult to develop in an increasingly market-led institution, such as MoL. Developments such as the re-display of the Prehistoric Gallery were thought unlikely to happen again within the late 1990s study period due to the (then) strategic and financial context, as the curriculum now begins with the Romans in historical coverage. The re-display therefore happened 'just in time', as the curatorial demands would have been outweighed by the expectations of the education sector had the project been planned any later, and the money and curatorial time for the re-display would have been 'more profitably' spent elsewhere in the presentation scheme (Jane Bywaters, pers. com.).

Commercial sponsorship is found frequently for the temporary displays, and the museum therefore has to invest much time in balancing the aspirations of the corporate sponsors and the professional expectations of the curatorial programme, as well as establishing a suitable skill and knowledge base to develop the exhibitions, which are planned years in advance. An example is the temporary exhibition related to the Rothschilds and the effects on the banking world: which must reflect sponsor expectations, educational needs, and museum aspirations in both individual presentation policy and museum aims.

External expectations for MoL often depend on the understanding of the museum, its collections and its remit. Thus, it is not a museum that sets out to display the entire history of London, nor does it collect from all parts of London. It cannot present certain aspects of London's history; either because it is unsuitable for the museum, the collections do not cover the subject matter, or simply that money is not available. The aim of thematically exhibiting the development of the urban condition therefore proves challenging for both the museum and possibly some of its potential audiences, though much effort is made, for example through the Outreach Programme, so that the museum's work is made relevant to as many people as possible.

At CUMAA the tensions and expectations are more acute, because the institution exists as a dedicated university teaching collection, has to be operated as a facility for both the university and the public (two very diverse audiences), and is staffed by curators who are expected to undertake academic activities in line with university aims and objectives. Therefore, unlike MoL, which treats its overall audience as a single entity, albeit with specialised concerns, CUMAA divides its audience very clearly and concentrates mainly on the academic sector. This, as noted already, causes both internal and external tensions as the museum sees its environment in flux in all the identified areas of economy, politics, professional nature and social terms.

Internal work and expectations concern themselves with the collections and their development, and though collections are displayed, there is little development in them, and they are dedicated to an educational theme for the subject area, as opposed to engaging audiences thematically. Temporary exhibitions, such as the Metals in Africa and Torres Strait Centenary presentations are self referential to the museum's collections and interests, and whilst they are undoubtedly of educational excellence and value within the university teaching and research programme, no heed is paid to external expectations from a public audience. Temporary exhibitions also relate to museological themes and development in professional practice. Internal professional expectations are dictated by the position the staff hold as university officers, and the tension between this position and professional expectations externally (within the museums sector) of what even a university museum should be for, is becoming more intense.

Other external expectations and tensions derive from the fact that Cambridge has an extremely limited museums service or provision within the city and wider county. In recognising that nine separate museums have been established within the university structure, the public authorities apparently unofficially delegate much museum provision within the city and county to the university, though at the university level, there is no recognition of such a dedicated responsibility, as the university's policy (with the exception of the Fitzwilliam Museum which is under the supervision of the General Board of the University of Cambridge) is to provide the museums as internal teaching resources. That does not

however undermine co-operation between the university museums and the outside world established at the 'local' level of the museum. For example, within CUMAA, a long-term relationship with the local Antiquarian Society has led by default to the museum being responsible for local archaeological collection management and curation, though this is not a core aim of the museum within the university structure. Furthermore, the demand for access to a 'public' archaeological and ethnological museum within Cambridge has to be provided by CUMAA, though public and educational facilities are extremely limited. For example, the museum is only open twelve hours per week to the public, in a city that receives 300-400,000 visitors per year, visitors identified as coming to the city for its 'heritage resources' (English Tourist Board 1996, 45).

It should be noted that even though the above examples of expectations placed on CUMAA and MoL still all reflect the first stage of the model, that is the ability of the institutions to operate as museums and hold collections: these tensions exist prior to demands and aims of particular presentational content and style, a concern of the second stage, not explored here. Also, it is clear that the overriding tension to be addressed is one of the financial valuation of museums against the social and professional value of museums in society. This is an area outside the scope of this thesis, though it should be recognised as an ongoing source of debate. The intention here has been to use the model of transformation to emphasise the use of placing the institutions in their wider environmental context, in turn allowing these other issues to be addressed more effectively.

Reaction and action

In the light of the above environmental constraints and expectations, the institutions 'manage' themselves (in operational terms) on a daily basis, and it is their actions which both objectify the museum and its collections. The MoL's management structure identifies the museum's environment through strategic management and business planning, using SWOT and other methods to establish how it should act in given situations. Curation and presentation have been primary concerns, but these are now shifting towards providing educational resources and increased audience participation in a leisure and tourism 'market', with accompanying economic concern reflecting changes outside the museum in wider society.

CUMAA, on the other hand, undertakes little planning, and reacts on an ad-hoc basis to perceived needs and expectations. Within the environment of traditional academic operations this has not proved a problem in the past, though the point is now being reached where dedicated planning as a 'management unit' is necessary in order to establish the museum's place in both the university, the professional museums sector, and the public sphere. Hence the 'cushion' provided for the unit operating within the university is slowly being removed, which will force the CUMAA to assess in detail its environmental context and the changing expectations internal and external to it. There is a clear shift in the educational sector from direct teacher-pupil learning to participatory educational skill development, and wider public access for educational opportunities, along with demands for the educational sector to identify clearer social and economic value for its work.

Effects of objectification

Much of the necessity for increased 'management' as a dedicated action, and the utility of this model for exploring institutional contexts, comes from an awareness that whilst public institutions (including CUMAA by virtue of its place in the education sector) apparently serve various audiences, not all of those audiences are the institutions' paymasters. Both of the museums here, whilst operating in different managerial environments, must face similar management problems, and act in an increasingly similar fashion. Furthermore 'management' as a concept cannot be used to answer financial and personnel issues alone – an integrated approach has to be followed. As I have shown in the other case studies, the homogeneity feared in the strategic management approach may actually preserve the diversity of action through its recognition of similar and distinct features of institutions such as MoL and CUMAA.

Even simplified management tools, as used in this case study for environmental analysis of the museums, show how cultural resources are objectified and then fitted back into the contexts in which they exist. Questioning the justification for institutions existing as they do is a major part of proper management, and there is recognised to be a balance between justification of the institutional status quo and either small-scale or large-scale change. Major decisions have been seen to be made at MoL through the closing of the archaeological archive (reopened in 2002), the support for the establishment of a museum housing the Docklands Collections (Museum in Docklands), and the development of the Access and Learning Department (Museum of London 1998b). CUMAA similarly is undergoing development through expectation within the university that the museum will increasingly 'think strategically', and already the possibility of developing an education service is being considered. Further effects of objectification are yet to be assessed within CUMAA however, and its management system will have to develop to deal with this.

Museums transformed: theoretically and practically

The case study has outlined the principles behind the nature of objectification at MoL and CUMAA. What has been illustrated is that, through application of the model of transformation and use of certain management science techniques, the museums can be considered dispassionately as objects within a variety of contexts: and to see how the subjective 'concepts' of the museums are played out and affect the reality of the museums' operations and aims.

The systems and processes therefore become clear as greater subjectivity and variety is analysed in as an objective fashion as possible. Tensions about the hows and whys of the museums' existence can be assessed from the gathering of information and knowledge about them. The conceptual museum can thus be seen existing in professional and public expectations, as can the objectified museum, physically existing in the Barbican or as a building on the university campus. The central nature of the objectification revolves around the collection, which literally 'makes' the museums, and this is the one usually concentrated on. However, the first stage of the model used in exploring the museums here shows that in the first instance the collection is irrelevant, as an institutional framework needs to be created for any kind of museum to exist and before any collection can be gathered.

The 'different' nature of museums promulgated within the profession becomes less clear using this model. This is advantageous in allowing a bridge to be built between the heritage 'managers' and the heritage. The centrality of the collections within museums cannot be used as an excuse for museums being less strategic in their thinking than other organisations explored in this thesis and elsewhere. The situation has developed where the generic term 'museum' has meant that many museum institutions have focused on their collections to prove their distinctiveness, rather than the institutions themselves, their operation, viability and development. This further created the divide between the 'profession' and 'management' needlessly. As noted with the consideration of market failure, this does not mean to say that all museums can 'stand on their own feet' without public support. The model applied to this case study advocates the understanding of the institution and its 'abilities' as both a corporate entity and a collection of professional staff. The heritage objects are treated in this way as assets, and not constraints, for management in practice. MoL has developed its management structure recognising this to some extent partly because of its hybrid nature through the amalgamation of two museums and concentration on thematic aspects of development, and it has been useful to consider CUMAA as it has yet to develop along such lines, though subject to similar pressures.

Comparison of the two museums in this case study clearly shows the difference in management approaches and their effects on the organisation's internal operation and external perception. The Museum of London is clearly 'managing' its collections and the 'past' of London through self-determination of objectives and imposition of goals from DCMS. CUMAA, however, is administering its collections under the title of curation. This is not the fault of CUMAA as a museum, but rather the fault of the university, as the managing institution, which has set no specific remit of goals for any of its museums. Furthermore, this lack of direction limits the sphere in which CUMAA can operate to that of an academic institution. Even though there are expectations (both internal and external) placed on CUMAA within the public sphere, as yet it cannot operate effectively here.

The picture elsewhere in the museums sector shows similar characteristics, and in management terms the 'difference' of museums is perhaps overstated, whilst difference in 'management' and effective operation may be understated and under explored. This is clear when comparing dedicated museum management works (Cossons 1994; Griffiths 1994; Middleton 1994) against more general management analysis, from business studies and tourism studies in analysis of English Heritage, Brodsworth and Uppark.

As with the other case studies, it has not been the place of the analysis to either suggest change or comment positively or negatively on particular management actions. The brief analysis has shown the applicability of the model in a different sector from the more traditional heritage management concern with the built environment. Furthermore I have analysed shared management concerns in different contexts, allowing the understanding of relationships in management within institutions and in external relations.

Museums as the collectors and recipients of heritage objects in the format of a collection or archive thus can be treated equally, as part of a strategic outlook for heritage to the advantage of all and allowing useful comparison. More detailed consideration of specific institutional arrangements, which I have undertaken in the previous chapters for English Heritage and the National Trust, can also assist in development of effective management solutions to problems faced in an environmental context, as the institution itself is better understood. The model therefore provides a broad band of management analysis to quickly identify institutions as heritage objects, and highlight the importance in understanding the variety of systems and processes in operation, the kinds of unique heritage that exist in institutional form, and the continuing variability in 'transformation'.

9 Conclusion: heritage transformed

Concluding comments are short, as the case studies have already brought out the key issues of the transformation in their individual conclusions. It has been the intention of the thesis to show the use of management analysis as a way of articulating the transformation of heritage from its intangible state to a tangible state encountered in our environment. In order to do this it has explored the notion of heritage and heritage objects from a management perspective. The analysis has shown that the idea of 'management' may be equated with the agency of change, in both physical and cognitive terms, where objects are identified within a specialist discipline, such as archaeology, as being of archaeological value, and also that those objects may be representative of a public heritage or past. Management can be seen to provide the practical tools for effecting the transformation from concept to object through use of its labelling and normalising mechanisms: a scientific and practical methodology for enabling and controlling change.

The case studies' explorations have shown that, within the field labelled solely as heritage, there are a variety of different aims and purposes, activities and outcomes, both intended and unintended. For example, English Heritage's intention behind the presentation of Brodsworth Hall as a piece of conservation is not always interpreted in such a way by visitors, and although the Museum of London and Cambridge University Museum of Archaeology and Anthropology ultimately share the function of conserving a collection of historic objects, the methods used in operating the institution affect production of heritage objects in very different ways.

It follows that different kinds of management also produce different kinds of heritage object – and the conceptual heritage may thus be objectified and encountered in different ways. This has become much clearer in recent years with a general shift in the public sector, from administration to strategic management, which places objects in an environmental context and clearly explores their utility value. That is not to say that if objects have no clear economic value they are discarded: as I have shown in my analysis of the corporate management of English Heritage, the notion of public heritage is closely explored by the organisation in order to give it effective protection as far as possible. Where markets for heritage can be created this is attempted, allowing heritage which is still subject to market failure to have greater attention focused on it. The work of the Monuments Protection Programme is an excellent example of this where archaeological sites are valued in accordance with a number of system-aided judgements finding wherever possible 'utility' for the site in question, including preservation of an archaeological resource which is not fully understood, but considered socially important. It is here that we see creation actually being undertaken unconstrained by earlier choice.

If the model proposed at the start of the thesis is accepted, then it gives rise to questions about the use of management policy and the manager's role in CRM institutions. I have shifted the focus away from the prevailing debate about the opposition of heritage objects and the concept of a national past, to a structural linkage of a national past relevant to a public, consisting of a variety of labelled objects. The variety of systems and processes of management, explored in the case studies in the previous chapters, gives a holistic perspective on how the heritage is created and used and how it exists within any given environment, sphere and scale. It can be seen therefore that the focus within heritage studies could be shifted from the second stage of the model of transformation – the interpretation of heritage objects within their environment – to the first stage of the model considered in this thesis, where exploration is made of how heritage objects are created within a particular public context.

The case studies I have used have considered heritage objects created by a range of public institutions, and the range of objects within the public heritage that have been mentioned suggest that institutional analysis is central to understanding the transformation. Organisational culture (in both aim and activity) must be relevant to the environments and markets in which it exists, and just as management has been explored as the way of bringing about change, so it must also change itself. The institution moulds itself and develops within its environmental context to ensure that it remains relevant, and so the objects it produces remain of use, i.e. the object labelled as public heritage is relevant to a public and representative of its heritage and a national past. The move from administration to management charted in the analysis of institutions in this thesis has seen a two-way process whereby the institution has reaffirmed its position by looking carefully at what it does. Goals are set internally and externally, and customers must be clearly identified and served. If institutional change, i.e. management, is continual so the model of transformation is thus continual – concept to object and vice-versa – both within the organisation and outside it.

The manager's role may then come to be seen as crucial in tasks other than just business and economic operation. The processes utilised by strategic management, for example, of which only a few have been considered in this thesis, are increasingly important in providing answers to questions which are provoked by institutional activity and position. English Heritage has been seen to ask who its customers are – and it has discovered that though its statutory purpose is to provide protection for the built heritage, its customers are, in fact, the communities in which the built heritage happens to physically exist. The Museum of London in adopting a strategic management outlook has reaffirmed the utility of presenting its collections in a variety of traditional and innovative ways as the best way of interpreting the history of London. CUMAA in having a management structure and outlook which cannot yet react to the changing environmental context of university collections and educational resources finds greater difficulty in establishing its role within a larger institution, which is itself questioning the way in which education is provided. The National Trust's management structure must carefully balance the aims of the charity and conservation needs of its property portfolio with an environment into which it has been manoeuvred as a key player in the tourism market.

The analysis of system and process, and an understanding of the institutions in which the transformation of heritage is taking place, can also be seen to be of importance to every individual with a concern in the past and particularly those organisations and groups of managers with specific responsibility as seen in Figure 4.1. The importance of question asking and goal-setting within the management process requires a large amount of specialist information to be available at any time. Thus the specialisms of archaeology, survey, information technology and so on are developed and enhanced professionally by a need to provide answers and actions – information and results that are useful in supporting not only the creation of heritage objects but also the interpretation of the conceptual heritage in which such activities exist.

I have shown in this study that greater understanding of management and use of institutional analysis provides pertinent information about the nature and use of the public heritage within the United Kingdom. It sheds light on questions frequently asked within society of why or how an object comes to be representative of the character or history of the country, and how any object may be valued. It has shown that the heritage is transformed from an intangible to a tangible existence, and considered that management acts as the agency of change. Furthermore, the exploration within the case studies has shown that institutional information gathering and analysis, which in some cases has been pigeonholed as a task for external consultancy, is possible, relatively simple and necessary to achieve internally. Most of all it is useful in establishing of what the phenomenon of heritage and a public heritage actually consists, and the implications of the transformation of heritage.

There remain two questions that may be asked of the model and the case studies considered in this thesis. Firstly, in the light of the exploration of the case studies, has the model or the understanding of the model changed in any way? In part such a question stems from other underlying queries about the responsibility for the way in which managers manage cultural resources within an institutional framework taken by individuals in those institutions and elsewhere. Nervousness about the concept of management and its power as the agency of change (as identified here) forced me to consider the necessity of a functional/processual understanding and adoption of certain management techniques from the 'toolbox' being applied to a phenomenon that is understood in a 'post-modern' sense. The model therefore recognises a certain inevitability in objectification, and the best way of exploring that may be found through the use of categorising and labelling the various processes in such a functional way.

The general essence of the objectification process and the dialectic undertaken has seen concept and object set up in a greater opposition than actually exists in the real world, due to the immediacy of the transformation process. Again it is the nervousness about the concept of responsibility for effecting change through management that necessitate this, with the eventual outcome showing that there is nothing to be scared of, and a 'Pandora's Box' of management has not been opened. The qualification to this is that the processes of management should not be allowed to become self-sustaining and driving the organisation contrary to the identified environmental framework, expectations in society, and institutional objective. It remains that people effect change and not management itself, which is nothing more than a label for categorisation. The model has therefore changed in the sense that there is a greater understanding of the questions that it raises and which are addressed in the case studies concerning the notion of encounter with a historic environment or objects labelled or categorised as having historic value.

The case studies explored here have quantified the transformation from a point of view situated within cultural resource management. The transformation can be applied outside this context, and may usefully point out how to answer the second of the concluding questions: how can the model be improved? If one considers natural species preservation, the production of literature, craft activities and so on, the transformation may be seen not only across a spectrum of 'public' institutional activities, but in other 'private' and 'public' contexts. This results from the understanding of encounter with an environment that has been implicitly considered in this thesis. The improvements to the model may therefore be focused on suggesting its initial use should be on the researcher using such a model, to establish the environment and point of view in encounter that he or she is undertaking through study, and making that process of encounter explicit. It may be useful to introduce further stages into the model having considered that throughout the case studies one factor became clear – information was being manipulated more than the physical object itself. The physical object seems to become a secondary consideration as the transformation is followed, and it may be useful to consider introducing intermediary stages before Stage 1 and 2, where there is clear production of 'physical' pieces of information and knowledge. Alternatively, it may be suggested that a second model of transformation can be added or intertwined with the one considered here. Information and knowledge as a resource, in a literal 'learning curve', is objectified and conceptualised in this second model. Application of these two models together may be best approached visually by imagining an intertwined coil, linking the two transformation models where the experience of encounter and the knowledge gained through categorisation and management passes both tangible and intangible facets between the two. Such a development of the model further breaks the closed circle which has been presented in this thesis, perhaps

unwittingly, which could be interpreted as self-serving with no opportunity for independent input, such as views from other disciplines, encounters and so on.

Certainly, the model used in the form suggested in this thesis, or if developed as suggested above, needs to be applied across a number of other case studies for comparative purposes outside England. The environmental analysis built into any use of the model serves to provide a great deal of information about manipulation of heritage (or other) resources, and also about the society/environment in which objectified resources exist and can be encountered. Much may therefore be learnt from application of the model as a way of understanding how resources are used, and how management operates in other countries. Across broader areas, such as comparison between Europe and America, institutions have been established that must 'cope' with far greater diversity than has been considered here, and the various strategies used with interaction between a number of similar agencies may provide useful lessons in comparison.

However, in conclusion, I must assert again that I believe the basic model as explored here works, and is useful in pointing the way towards a greater understanding of the agency of change, and its effects on the production of a physical resource and its subsequent encounter. Furthermore, it clearly shows that the role of the institution may still be poorly understood, and further investigation of the environment in which we all work can prove to be beneficial to all.

Bibliography

Adams, W M, 1996 *Future Nature, a vision for conservationm,* London.

Alexander, P, 1998 Onward with a stronger regional focus, in *Conservation Bulletin,* Jan 98, **33**, 1-2.

Alfrey, J, and Putnam, T, 1992 *The industrial heritage – managing resources and uses,* London.

Ambrose, T, and Runyard, S (eds), 1991 *Forward Planning,* London.

Andreski, S (ed), 1983 *Max Weber on capitalism, bureaucracy and religion, a selection of texts,* London.

Argenti, J, 1989 *Practical Corporate Planning,* London.

Augustine 400 *The Confessions of Saint Augustine,* (translated by Blaiklock, E M) 1983 London.

Babington, C, and Hughes, H, 1992 Conservation of the painted decoration at Brodsworth Hall, in *English Heritage Scientific and Technical Review* **1**, 3-6.

Barrow, C, Barrow, P, and Brown, R, 1993 *The Business Plan Workbook,* London.

Barthes, R, 1964 Rhetorique de l'image, in *Communications* **1**.

Beeho, A J, and Prentice, R C, 1995 Evaluating the Experiences and Benefits Gained by Tourists Visiting A Socio-Industrial Heritage Museum, An Application of ASEB Grid Analysis to Blists Hill Open-Air Museum, the Ironbridge Gorge Museum, UK, in *Museum Management and Curatorship,* **14 3**, 229-251.

Bennett, T, 1995 *The birth of the museum, history, theory, politics,* London.

Berkouwer, M, and Church, D, 1993 Textiles at Brodsworth Hall, in *Conservation Bulletin,* **19**, 12-14.

Berry, A Q, and Brown, I W (eds), 1995 *Managing Ancient Monuments, An Integrated Approach,* Mold, Clwyd County Council Archaeology Service.

Blockley, M, 1995 Archaeologists in the marketplace, in Cooper et al 1995, 101-117.

Blockley, M, 1997 Editorial, in *Interpretation (SIBH Journal)* July 1997, 1-4.

Boniface, P, and Fowler, P J, 1993 *Heritage and Tourism in the 'global village',* London.

Borley, L, 1994 Managing strategies and financial considerations, historic properties, in Harrison 1994, 21-33.

Breeze, D J, 1993 Ancient monuments legislation, in Hunter and Ralston 1993, 44-55.

Bruier, F L, and Mathers, C, 1996 *Trends and Patterns in Cultural Resource Significance, An Historical Perspective and Annotated Bibliography,* Vicksburg.

Cabinet Office, 1996a *The Civil Service Yearbook 1996,* London, HMSO.

Cabinet Office, 1996b *Cabinet Office Efficiency Unit, Objective Setting and Monitoring in Executive Non-Departmental Public Bodies,* London, Cabinet Office.

Cabinet Office, 1997 Government's 12 guiding principles for market testing and contracting out, *Press Release,* 114/97.

Cadogan, G, 1995 Buildings, in Newby 1995, 135-149.

Carman, R J, 1996 *Valuing Ancient Things Archaeology and Law,* Leicester.

Carman, J. (2002) *Archaeology & Heritage: an introduction.* London: Continuum.

Carr-Whitworth, C, 1995 Remembrance of things past, in *Conservation Bulletin* **27**, 3-4.

Carter, E, 1984 Alice in the consumer wonderland, in Gray and McGuigan 1993, 104-121.

Carver, M, 1996 On archaeological value, in *Antiquity* **70**, 45-56.

CBA, 1996a *British Archaeological Yearbook,* York, Council for British Archaeology.

CBA, 1996b *Defence Lines – newsletter of The Defence of Britain Project,* York, Council for British Archaeology.

Champion, T, 1996 Protecting the monuments, archaeological legislation from the 1882 Act to PPG16, in Hunter, M 1996, 38-56.

Chase, M, and Shaw, C, 1989 The dimensions of nostalgia, in Shaw and Chase 1989, 1-18.

Cherry, M, 1995 How to protect our industrial heritage? In *Conservation Bulletin* **26**, 3-4.

Chippindale, C, 1983 The making of the first Ancient Monuments Act 1882, in *Journal of the British Archaeological Association* **136**, 1-55.

Chippindale, C, 1997 Trusting the National Trust, in Archaeology, online features September 30, Web page (www archaeology org/online/features/britain/index html)

Chitty, G, 1995 *Monuments Protection Programme, Publication programme feasibility study,* London, English Heritage/LUAU.

Cleere, H (ed), 1984 *Approaches to the archaeological heritage,* Cambridge.

Cleere, H (ed), 1989 *Archaeological heritage management in the modern world,* (One World Archaeology 9) London.

Clubb, N, 1988 Computer mapping and the SAM record, in Rahtz 1988, 399-408.

Clubb, N, and Startin, B, 1995 Information systems strategies in national organisations and the identification, legal protection and management of the most important sites in England, in Wilcock and Lockyear 1995, 67-73.

Conservative Research Department, 1996 Serving the Nation – Our record since 1979, Our work since the 1992 election, in *Politics Today* **8**.

Cooper, M A, 1993 Archaeology and Management Perspectives, in *The Field Archaeologist* **18**, 346-350.

Cooper, M A, 1995 The Archaeological Manager Applying management models to archaeology, in Cooper et al 1995, 70-88.

Cooper, M A, Firth, A, Carman, J, and Wheatley, D (eds), 1995 *Managing Archaeology,* London.

Corner, J, and Harvey, S, (eds), 1991 *Enterprise and heritage,* London.

Corner, J, and Harvey, S, 1991 Mediating tradition and modernity, the heritage/enterprise couplet, in Corner and Harvey (eds), 45-75.

Cossons, N, 1994 Designing and implementing corporate plans, in Harrison 1994, 12-20.

Countryside Commission, 1994 *The New Map of England, a celebration of the south western landscape,* Cheltenham.

Countryside Commission, 1996 *A living countryside, our strategy for the next ten years,* Cheltenham.

CPRE (Council for the Protection of Rural England), 1994 *Leisure Landscapes Leisure, Culture and the English Countryside, challenges and conflicts,* Lancaster.

Creed, N, 1995a Out of the ashes, in *The National Trust Magazine* **74**, Spring, 54-60.

Creed, N, 1995b *A guide for children, Uppark,* London.

Cruikshank, D, 1990 Rebuilding Uppark, in *Country Life* **154**, 18 Jan, 56-57.

Culpin, C, 1995 *Learning from country houses,* London.

CUMAA (Cambridge University Museum of Archaeology and Anthropology), 1996 *Museum of Archaeology and Anthropology Annual Report for 1995-96,* Cambridge.

CUMAA (Cambridge University Museum of Archaeology and Anthropology), 1997a *University of Cambridge Museum of Archaeology and Anthropology Development Plan, June 1997,* Internal Faculty Board Document, FB97 30B.

CUMAA (Cambridge University Museum of Archaeology and Anthropology), 1997b *Museum of Archaeology and Anthropology Annual Report for 1996-97,* Cambridge.

CUMAA (Cambridge University Museum of Archaeology and Anthropology), 1998 *The Cambridge University Museum of Archaeology and Anthropology.*

Darvill, T, 1987 *Ancient Monuments in the Countryside An archaeological management review,* London, English Heritage.

Darvill, T, 1988 *Monuments Protection Programme, Monument Evaluation Manuals [Vols 1-5,]* London, English Heritage.

Darvill, T, 1993 *Valuing Britain's Archaeological Resource, Inaugural Lecture,* Bournemouth.

Darvill, T, and Wainwright, G, 1994a The Monuments at Risk Survey, an introduction, in *Antiquity* **68**, 820-24.

Darvill, T, and Wainwright, G, 1994b Mars measures monuments at risk, in *Conservation Bulletin* **23**, 29-30.

Darvill, T, Saunders, A, and Startin, B, 1987 A question of national importance, approaches to the evaluation of ancient monuments for the Monuments Protection Programme in England, in *Antiquity* **61** 393-408.

Davies, D R, 1985 The Management of Guardianship Monuments, in *ASCHB Trans* **10**, 49-53.

Davies, S, 1995 Attendance Records, in *Leisure Management,* **15.2**, 40-44.

DCMS (Department for Culture, Media and Sport), 1998 *Department for Culture Media and Sport Annual Report 1998,* London, The Stationery Office.

DCMS (2001) *The Historic Environment – a force for our future.* London: Department for Culture, Media and Sport.

DCMS (2004) *Review of Heritage Protection: The Way Forward.* London: Department for Culture, Media and Sport.

Difference Engine, 1994 *Members and non members perceptions and attitudes towards English Heritage,* Internal report, English Heritage.

Dillon, P J, and Jones, E L, 1996 Environmental Consumerism in the United Kingdom, Some Reflections on Managerial Responses and Educational Needs, in *European Journal of Agricultural Education Extension,* **3.2**, 107-118

DNH (Department of National Heritage) and Welsh Office, 1996 *Protecting Our Heritage A consultation document on the built heritage of England and Wales,* London, Department of National Heritage.

DNH (Department of National Heritage), 1996a *Annual Report 1996 The Government's expenditure plans 96/97-98/99,* London, HMSO.

DNH (Department of National Heritage), 1996b *Portable Antiquities – a discussion document,* London, Department of National Heritage.

DNH (Department of National Heritage), 1996c *Treasures in Trust, A Review of Museum Policy,* London, Department of National Heritage.

DNH (Department of National Heritage), 1996d *People Taking Part,* London, Department of National Heritage.

DNH (Department of National Heritage), 1997a *Success through partnership – a strategy for tourism Competing with the best,* London, Department of National Heritage.

DNH (Department of National Heritage), 1997b *Funding Agreement between the Department of National Heritage and the Museum of London 1 April 1997 – 31 March 1998,* London, Department of National Heritage.

DNH (Department of National Heritage), 1997c *First list of pre-eminent museum collections unveiled by Chris Smith, (DNH Press Release 148/97,)* London, Department of National Heritage.

DoE (Department of the Environment), 1981 *Organisation of Ancient Monuments and Historic Buildings in England – A Consultation Paper,* London, HMSO.

DoE (Department of the Environment), 1982 *Organisation of Ancient Monuments and Historic Buildings in England – The Way Forward,* London, HMSO.

DoE (Department of the Environment), 1983 *Criteria for the selection of Ancient Monuments* [Press Release 523], London, Department of Environment.

DoE (Department of the Environment), 1990a *Planning Policy Guidance Note 16, Archaeology and Planning* London, Department of Environment.

DoE (Department of the Environment), 1990b *This Common Inheritance,* London, HMSO.

Dryden, J, 1729 *Absalom and Achitophel, A Poem,* Dublin.

Edson, G, and Dean, D, 1994 *The Handbook for Museums,* London.

EFTEC 2005 *Valuation of the Historic Environment: The scope for using results of valuation studies in the appraisal and assessment of heritage-related projects and Programmes. Report for DCMS, DfT, HLF & English Heritage.* London: EFTEC.

English Heritage, Countryside Commission and English Nature, 1996 *Conservation issues in local plans,* London, English Heritage.

English Heritage, 1987 *Register of historic parks and gardens of special historic interest,* London, English Heritage.

English Heritage, 1989a *Corporate Plan 1989-1993,* London, English Heritage.

English Heritage, 1989b *Report and Accounts 1988/89,* London, English Heritage.

English Heritage, 1990a *Corporate Plan 1990-1994,* London, English Heritage.

English Heritage, 1990b *Report and Accounts 1989-1990,* London, English Heritage.

English Heritage, 1991a *Corporate Plan 1991-1995,* London, English Heritage.

English Heritage, 1991b *Exploring our past – Strategies for the archaeology of England,* London, English Heritage.

English Heritage, 1992a *Corporate Plan 1992-1996,* London, English Heritage.

English Heritage, 1992b *Monuments Protection Programme Monument Evaluation Manual – Part IV Urban Areas [2 vols],* London, English Heritage.

English Heritage, 1993a *Corporate Plan 1993-1997,* London, English Heritage.

English Heritage, 1993b *The investment performance of listed buildings,* London, English Heritage/RICS.

English Heritage, 1993c *Annual Report and Accounts 1992/93,* London, English Heritage.

English Heritage, 1993d *Archaeology Review 1992-93,* London, English Heritage.

English Heritage, 1993e *Scheduling procedures manual,* Internal document, English Heritage.

English Heritage ,1994 *Corporate Plan 1994-1998,* London, English Heritage.

English Heritage, 1995 *Corporate Plan 1995-1999,* London, English Heritage.

English Heritage, 1996a *Corporate Plan 1996-2000,* London, English Heritage.

English Heritage, 1996b *Statement of Values and Behaviours,* Internal Document, English Heritage.

English Heritage, 1996c *English Heritage Annual Report and Accounts 1994/95,* London, English Heritage.

English Heritage, 1996d *The Monuments Protection Programme 1986-96 in retrospect,* London, English Heritage.

English Heritage, 1996e *Programme delivery,* Internal Paper, English Heritage.

English Heritage, 1997a *English Heritage Annual Report and Accounts 1995/96,* London, English Heritage.

English Heritage, 1997b *Hadrian's Wall World Heritage Site Management Plan – July 1996,* London, English Heritage.

English Heritage, 1997c *Sustaining the historic environment, new perspectives on the future (Discussion document),* London, English Heritage.

English Heritage, 1997d *Archaeology Division Research Agenda,* London, English Heritage.

English Heritage, 1997e *Brodsworth Hall – A Victorian Delight in Yorkshire,* Marketing leaflet, English Heritage.

English Heritage, 1997f *Education Service Resources Catalogue,* London, English Heritage.

English Nature, 1992 *A statement of intent for the conservation of the natural and archaeological environment,* Peterborough, English Nature.

English Nature, 1993 *Natural areas – Setting nature conservation objectives, A consultation paper,* Peterborough, English Nature.

English Tourist Board, 1996 *English Heritage Monitor 1996,* London, BTA/ETB Research Services.

Fahy, A, and Sudbury, W (eds), 1995 *Information, The Hidden Resource, Museums and the Internet Proceedings of the 7th international conference of the MDA,* Cambridge, Museum Documentation Association.

Fairclough, G, 1996a *MPP 1986-1996,* Draft report for English Heritage.

Fairclough, G, 1996b English Heritage and landscape, in Fairclough et al 1996, 1-10.

Fairclough, G J, Lambrick, G, and McNab, A, 1996 *Yesterday's landscape, tomorrow's world, the English Heritage landscape project,* London, English Heritage.

Fayol, H, 1949 *General and industrial management,* London.

Fedden, R, 1968 *The National Trust, A Continuing purpose,* London.

Fedden, R, 1974 *The National Trust,* London, National Trust.

Fidler, F, and McCaig, I, 1992 Disaster mitigation for historic buildings, in *English Heritage Scientific and Technical Review* **1**, 8-10.

Fleming, D, and Paine, C, and Rhodes, J G (eds), 1993 *Social history in museums, a handbook for professionals,* London, HMSO.

Flynn, N, 1990 *Public Sector Management,* Hemel Hempstead.

Fowler, P, 1992 *The past in contemporary society, then, now,* London.

Garnham, N, 1983 *Concepts of Culture – public policy and the cultural industries,* Greater London Council internal discussion paper.

Gathercole, P, and Lowenthal, D (eds), 1990 *The Politics of the Past,* London.

Giddens, A, 1993 *Sociology* (second edition), Cambridge.

Gifford, D, 1990 *The Farther Shore, A Natural History of Perception*, London.

Gilchrist, R, 1989 *Monument class description, monasteries for men (post-Conquest)*, London, English Heritage.

Gillie, O, 1990 Memorial to a vanished age of opulence, in *The Independent* 28 April, 30.

Girouard, M, 1979 *The Victorian Country House*, New Haven.

Gordon, Rev. H D, 1877 *The history of Harting*, London.

Gosden, C, 1994 *Social being and time*, Oxford.

Gray, A, and McGuigan, J (eds), 1993 *Studying Culture, an introductory reader*, London.

Griffiths, B, 1994 Financial management, in Harrison 1994, 235-248.

Hamilton, J, 1995 The role of the university curator in the 1990s, in *Museum Management and Curatorship* **14, 1**, 73-79.

Handy, C B, 1985 *Understanding organizations* (third edition), Harmondsworth.

Hanna, M, 1995 Scoring a Century, the National Trust, in *Leisure Management* **15.4**, 24-27.

Hannan, M T, and Freeman, J, 1989 *Organizatonal ecology*, Harvard.

Harcourt-Smith, S, 1944 *The last of Uptake*, London.

Harland, J, Kinder, K, Hartley, K, and Wilkin, A, 1996 *Attitudes to participation in the arts, heritage, broadcasting and sport, A review of recent research*, London, NFER/DNH.

Harrison, R (ed), 1994 *Manual of Heritage Management*, London.

Haslam, R, 1995 Uppark, West Sussex, in *Country Life* May 25, 69-73.

HBMCE, 1985 *Historic Buildings and Monuments Commission for England Report and Accounts 1983-1985*, London, HBMCE.

HEFCE (Higher Education Funding Council for England), 1995 *Museums, Galleries and Collections, the Outcome of the Review of Non-Formula Funding (Circular 9/95)*, Bristol, HEFCE.

Hennessy, P, 1988 *Whitehall*, London.

HEREC & English Heritage (2005) *Heritage Counts 2004*. London: English Heritage.

Herbert, D T, 1995 Heritage as literary place, in Herbert 1995, 32-48.

Herbert, D T (ed), 1995 *Heritage, tourism and society*, London.

Herzberg, F, et al, 1959 *The motivation to work*, New York.

Hewison, R, 1987 *The heritage industry, Britain in a climate of decline*, London.

Historic Scotland, 1994 *Framework Document (October 1994)*, Edinburgh, HMSO.

Historic Scotland, 1996 *Corporate Plan 1996-1999*, Edinburgh, Historic Scotland.

HMG (Her Majesty's Government), 1965 *Museum of London Act 1965*, London, HMSO.

HMG (Her Majesty's Government), 1979 *Ancient Monuments and Archaeological Areas Act 1979 Chapter 46*, London, HMSO.

HMG (Her Majesty's Government), 1983 *National Heritage Act 1983 Chapter 47*, London, HMSO.

HMG (Her Majesty's Government), 1990 *Planning (Listed Buildings and Conservation Areas) Act 1990*, London, HMSO.

HMG (Her Majesty's Government), 1994 *National Heritage Committee (Session 1993-94) 3rd Report Our Heritage, Preserving It, Prospering from It*, London, HMSO.

HMG (Her Majesty's Government), 1996a *National Heritage Committee (Session 1995-96) 3rd Report The Structure and Remit of the Department of National Heritage*, London, HMSO.

HMG (Her Majesty's Government), 1996b *Railway Heritage Act 1996 Chapter 42*, London, HMSO.

HMG (Her Majesty's Government), 1997 *National Heritage Act 1997 Chapter 14*, London, HMSO.

Hoare, S, and Fennell, E, 1997 Applying private acumen to public service, in *The Times* January 28, 34.

Hodder, I, 1986 *Reading the past*, Cambridge.

Hodge, R, and D'Souza, W, 1994 The Museum as a Communicator, in Hooper-Greenhill 1994, 40-2.

Hooper-Greenhill, E, 1992 *Museums and the shaping of knowledge*, London.

Hooper-Greenhill, E (ed), 1994 *The Educational Role of Museums*, London.

Hughes, O E, 1994 *Public Management and Administration, An Introduction*, New York.

Hunter, J, and Ralston, I (eds), 1993 *Archaeological Resource Management in the UK, An Introduction*, Stroud.

Hunter, M (ed), 1996 *Preserving the past*, Stroud.

Hussey, C, 1941 Uppark I, II and III, in *Country Life* **89**, 520, 540 and 562.

Ingold, T, 1993 The Temporality of Landscape, in *World Archaeology* **25.2**, 162-172.

Jeffrey, K (ed), 1995 *Brodsworth Hall*, London, English Heritage.

Jencks, C, 1995 *Culture, key ideas*, London.

Jenkins, J, and James, P, 1994 *From Acorn to Oak Tree*, London.

Jensen, K B, 1995 *The social semiotics of mass communication*, London.

Johnson, G, and Scholes, K, 1989 *Exploring corporate strategy*, Hemel Hempstead.

Johnson, P, and Thomas, B, 1995 Heritage as business, in Herbert 1995, 170-190.

Jones, H, 1996 The death of planning, in *The Leisure Manager* **14.2**, 10-11.

Jordan, G, 1994 *The British Administrative System, principles versus practice*, London.

Kawashima, N, 1998 Planning ahead, in *Museums Journal* **98.3** March, 34-35.

Knowles, L, 1993 Conventional displays, in Fleming et al 1993, 370-373.

Kubler, G, 1962 *The shape of time, remarks on the history of things* New Haven.

Land Use Consultants, 1996 *Sustainability and the historic environment*, London, English Heritage/LUC and CAG.

Larsen, C V (ed), 1992 *Sites and monuments, national archaeological records*, Copenhagen.

Leavy, B, 1996 *Key processes in strategy, themes and theories*, London, ITP.

Leeds University, 1998 *Course Guide – Department of Fine Art, MA Country House Studies*, (Web page, www leeds ac uk/fine_art/DeptInfo/Pros/MA/MACHS/)

Lees, D, and Coyne, J, 1979 Can we afford our national heritage? In *Lloyds Bank Review* **131**, 35-46.

Lees-Milne J, 1975 *Ancestral voices*, London.

Lewis, P, 1992 Death and transfiguration, in *Conservation Bulletin* **18**, 12-15.

Liberal Democrats, 1996 *Arts, Liberal Democrats Consultation Paper* **26**, London, Liberal Democrat Publications.

Light, D, 1995 Heritage as informal education, in Herbert (1995,117-145.

Light, D, 1996 Characteristics of the audience for 'events' at a heritage site, in *Tourism Management* **17.3**, 183-190.

Lipe, W D, 1984 Value and meaning in cultural resources, in Cleere 1984, 1-11.

Littlejohn, D, 1997 *The fate of the English country house*, Oxford.

Lowenthal, D, 1985 *The past is a foreign country*, Cambridge.

Lowenthal, D, 1996 *The heritage crusade and the spoils of history*, New York.

Lowenthal, D, and Binney, M (eds), 1981 *Our past before us, why do we save it?*, London.

LUAU (Lancaster University Archaeological Unit), 1995 *MPP industrial monuments, specification*, Lancaster, LUAU.

Lummins, T, and Marsh, J, 1990 *The Woman's Domain, Women and the English Country House*, London.

MacDonald, G F, and Alsford, S, 1995 Museums and theme parks, worlds in collision?, in *Museum Management and Curatorship* **14.2**, 129-47.

Macinnes, L, and Ader, K, 1995 Integrated management plans, Historic Scotland's experience, in Berry and Brown 1995, 29-56.

Mandler, P, 1996 Nationalising the country house, in Hunter M 1996, 99-114.

Manning, R E, 1986 *Studies in Outdoor Recreation A Review and Synthesis of the Social Science Literature in Outdoor Recreation*, Corvallis, Oregon.

Maslow, A H, 1970 *Motivation and personality* (second edition), New York.

Mayo, E, 1949 *The social problems of an industrial civilisation*, London.

McGill, G, 1995 *Building on the past, A guide to archaeology and the development process*, London.

McKenzie, N (ed), 1958 *Convictions*, London.

McNab, A, and Lambrick, G, 1996 Results of the Historic Landscape Project (Chapters 13 and 14), in Fairclough et al 1996, 84-98.

Meade-Fetherstonhaugh, M, and Warner, O, 1964 *Uppark and its people*, London, National Trust.

Merriman, N, 1991 *Beyond the glass case, the past, heritage and the public in Britain*, Leicester.

Middleton, P, 1994 Measuring Performance and Contingency Planning, in Harrison 1994, 34-42.

Middleton, V, 1995 Vision, Strategy and Corporate Planning, An overview, in Harrison 1995, 3-11.

Milliken, M, 1989 Brodsworth Hall, in *English Heritage Magazine* 7.

Montagu of Beaulieu, 1967 *The Gilt and the Gingerbread or How to Live in a Stately Home and Make Money*, London.

Morgan, J, and Walton, P, 1994 The process of communication, in Hooper-Greenhill 1994, 27-36.

Murphy, G, 1987 *Founders of the National Trust*, London.

Museum of London, 1996 *Business statement 1996/97*, London, Museum of London.

Museum of London, 1998a *The Museum of London*, Web-page, www.museumoflondon.org.uk

Museum of London, 1998b *Museum of London Annual Report 1996-1997*, London, Museum of London.

NAO (National Audit Office), 1992 *Protecting and Managing England's Heritage Property, report b the comptroller and auditor general*, London, HMSO.

National Trust, 1995a *Places to visit in the south-east*, Publicity leaflet, National Trust.

National Trust, 1995b *Linking People and Place* Gloucester, National Trust.

National Trust, 1996 *1995/96 Annual Report and Accounts*, London, National Trust.

National Trust, 1997a *1996/97 Annual Report and Accounts*, London, National Trust.

National Trust, 1997b *Welcome to Uppark*, Orientation leaflet, National Trust.

National Trust, 1997c *Functions and conferences at National Trust properties*, Leaflet, National Trust.

National Trust, 1998 *The National Trust Handbook 1998*, London, National Trust.

Newby, H (ed), 1995 *The National Trust, The Next Hundred Years*, London, National Trust.

NHMF (National Heritage Memorial Fund), 1996 *Annual Report and accounts of the Heritage Lottery Fund and the National Heritage Memorial Fund 1995 – 1996*, London, NHMF.

Nicolson, A, 1990 *The Fire at Uppark*, London, National Trust.

Olivier, A, 1996 *Frameworks for our past A review of research frameworks, strategies and perceptions*, London, English Heritage.

Pearce, S M, 1995 *On collecting, an investigation into collecting in the European tradition*, London, Routledge.

Pearcey, O J, 1992 The dilemma of the industrial archaeologist, in *Conservation Bulletin* **17**, 6-8.

Pevsner, N, 1974 *Buildings of England, Yorkshire, The West Riding*, Harmondsworth.

Pevsner, N, and Nairn, I, 1965 *Buildings of England, Sussex*, Harmondsworth.

Pollitt, C, 1990 *Managerialism and the public services, the Anglo-American experience*, Oxford.

Power of Place Office/English Heritage (2000) *Power of place: the future of the historic environment*. London: English Heritage.

Prentice, R, 1993a Motivations of the heritage consumer in the leisure market, an application of the Manning-Haas Demand Hierarchy, in *Leisure Sciences* **15**, 273-90.

Prentice, R, 1993b *Tourism and heritage attractions*, London.

Prentice, R, 1995 Heritage as formal education, in Herbert 1995, 146-169.

Proctor, T, 1982 *Management, theory and principles*, Plymouth.

Rahtz, S (ed), 1988 *Computer applications and quantitative methods in archaeology 1988*, Oxford, British Archaeological Reports International Ser **446**.

Ravenscroft, N, 1994 Leisure Policy in the New Europe, the UK Department of National Heritage as a model of development and integration, in *European Urban and Regional Studies* **1(2)**, 131-142.

RCHME (Royal Commission on the Historical Monuments of England), 1994a *Strategic plan,* Swindon, RCHME.

RCHME (Royal Commission on the Historical Monuments of England), 1994b *Annual Report 1993/94,* Swindon, RCHME.

Robertshaw, A, 1997 "A dry shell of the past", Living history and the interpretation of historic houses, in *Interpretation (SIBH Journal)* July 1997.

Ross, M, 1991 *Planning and the heritage, policy and procedures,* London.

Rowell, C, 1995 *Uppark,* London, National Trust.

Rowell, C, and Robinson, J M, 1996 *Uppark Restored,* London, National Trust.

Rowlands, M, 1994 The Politics of Identity in Archaeology, in Gathercole and Lowenthal 1994, 129-43.

Runciman, W G (ed), 1978 *Max Weber, selections in translation* Cambridge.

Russell, J (ed), 1997 *Music on a summer evening 1997, Brodsworth Hall,* London, English Heritage

Saunders, A D, 1983 A century of ancient monuments legislation in *The Antiquaries Journal* 63, 11-29.

Schofield, J, and Lake, J, 1995 Defining our defence heritage, in *Conservation Bulletin* 27, 12-13.

Schouten, F, 1995 Improving visitor care in heritage attractions, in *Tourism Management* 16.4, 259-261.

SDCB (South Downs Conservation Board), 1993 *Who we are, what we do,* Storrington, SDCB.

Sekers, D, 1990 Uppark, *Non Omnis Moriar,* in *The National Trust Magazine* 59, Spring, 15-18.

Shanks, M, 1992 *Experiencing the Past, on the character of archaeology,* London.

Shanks, M, and Tilley, C, 1987 *Re-constructing Archaeology, theory and practice,* London.

Sharman, J, 1997 Working with the new Government, in *Conservation Bulletin* 32.3, July.

Shaw, C, and Chase, M (eds), 1989 *The imagined past, history and nostalgia,* Manchester.

Shoard, M, 1981 Why landscapes are harder to protect than buildings, in Lowenthal and Binney 1981, 84-88.

Sola, T, 1994 Museum Generalists – new professionals in the age of synthesis, in *Museum Management and Curatorship* 13, 61-65.

Stafford, W, 1989 "This once happy country", nostalgia for pre-modern society, in Shaw and Chase 1989, 33-47.

Startin, B, 1987 The Monuments Protection Programme, in *British Archaeological News* 2.3 May, 32.

Startin, B, 1991 Protecting the archaeology of our historic towns, in *Conservation Bulletin* 13, 14-15.

Startin, B, 1992 The Monuments Protection Programme, archaeological records, in Larsen 1992, 201-206.

Startin, B, 1993 Assessment of field remains, in Hunter and Ralston 1993, 184-96.

Stocker, D, 1995 Choosing industrial monuments, in *Conservation Bulletin* 27, 8-9.

Taliotis, X, 1995 Distant voices, still lives, in *Heritage Today* 30, 20-29.

Target, J, 1996 Conservation matters, in *Antique Collecting,* www Article.

Thackray, D, Jarman, R, and Burgon J, 1995 The National Trust's approach to integrated management, in Berry and Brown 1995, 37-47.

Thapar, B K, 1984 India, in Cleere 1984, 63-72.

Thomas, S, 1995 Media and the exhibition, a new vocabulary for documentation, in Fahy and Sudbury 1995, 71-77.

Thompson, M, 1979 *Rubbish Theory, The Creation and Destruction of Value,* Oxford.

Tilley, C, 1994 *A Phenomenology of Landscape (Places, Paths, Monuments),* Oxford.

Tinniswood, A, 1989 *A history of country house visiting,* Oxford.

UKIndex, 1998 *The National Trust Web-Site,* National Trust, Web page (www ukindex co uk)

Underwood, S, 1993 Period rooms, the house of fiction has many windows, in Fleming et al 1993, 378-382.

University of Cambridge, 1995 The University's Museums, Survey by the Joint Museums Committee, in *Cambridge University Reporter* 135.22.

University of Cambridge, 1997 *University of Cambridge Strategic Plan,* Internal planning document, Cambridge University.

University of Cambridge, 1998 *Statutes and Ordinances of the University of Cambridge,* Cambridge.

Urry, J, 1990 *The Tourist Gaze,* London.

Urry, J, 1995 *Consuming Places,* London.

Veal, A J, 1994 *Leisure Policy and Planning,* Harlow.

Victoria County History, 1973 *History of the County of Sussex (4 vols),* London.

Wainwright, G J, 1984 The pressure of the past, in *Proceedings of the Prehistoric Society* 50, 1-22.

Wainwright, G J, 1994 Archaeology, define first, dig later, in *Conservation Bulletin* 23, 10-11.

Walsh, K, 1992 *The representation of the past (Museums and heritage in the post-modern world),* London.

Waterson, M, 1994 *The National Trust, the first hundred years,* London.

Watkins, T, 1995 What kind of archaeology do we want?, in *Scottish Archaeological Review* 9/10, 171-3.

Webb, E, 1993 *The Peopling of London, 15,000 years of settlement from overseas,* London, Museum of London.

Weideger, P, 1994 *Gilding the acorn, behind the facade of the National Trust,* London.

Wells, H G, 1908 *Tono-Bungay,* London.

Wells, H G, 1934 *Experiment in Autobiography,*London.

Whitworth, C, 1995 *Brodsworth Hall,* London, English Heritage.

Wilcock, J, and Lockyear, K (eds), 1995 *Computer applications and quantitative methods in archaeology 1993,* Oxford, British Archaeological Reports International Ser 598.

Willes, M (ed), 1996 *Calke Abbey,* London, The National Trust.

Williams, R, 1958 Culture is Ordinary, in McKenzie, N 1958.

Wright, P, 1985 *On Living in an Old Country, The National Past in Contemporary Britain,* London.

Wright, P, 1993 *A journey through ruins, a keyhole portrait of British postwar life and culture,* London.